THE ETHICS OF AUTHORSHIP

Fordham University Press has no responsibility for the persistence or accuracy of URLs for external or third-party Internet websites referred to in this publication and does not guarantee that any content on such websites is, or will remain, accurate or appropriate.

Fordham University Press also publishes its books in a variety of electronic formats. Some content that appears in print may not be available in electronic books.

Library of Congress Cataloging-in-Publication Data

Berthold-Bond, Daniel, 1953–
    The ethics of authorship : communication, seduction, and death in Hegel and Kierkegaard / Daniel Berthold.—1st ed.
        p.   cm.
    Includes bibliographical references (p.   ) and index.
    ISBN 978-0-8232-3394-6 (cloth : alk. paper)
    ISBN 978-0-8232-3395-3 (pbk. : alk. paper)
    ISBN 978-0-8232-3396-0 (ebook)
    1. Kierkegaard, Søren, 1813–1855.   2. Hegel, Georg Wilhelm Friedrich, 1770–1831.   3. Authorship—Moral and ethical aspects. 4. Philosophy—Authorship—Moral and ethical aspects.   I. Title.
B4378.P74B47   2011
801—dc22

                                          2010033991

Printed in the United States of America

    13   12   11   5   4   3   2   1

First edition

To Melanie, to Lily, and to my students (teachers)
at Eastern Correctional Facility

CONTENTS

ABBREVIATIONS

ALL REFERENCES to the works of Hegel and Kierkegaard will be given parenthetically in the text using the listed abbreviations.

References to *Hegel's Logic (EL), Philosophy of Mind (PM), Philosophy of Nature (PN), and Philosophy of Right (PR)* are to sections (§), not pages. "A" designates Hegel's "remarks" (*Anmerkungen*), and "Z" designates "additions" (*Zusätze*) to the original texts compiled by various editors from Hegel's lecture manuscripts and the detailed notes of several students who attended these lectures. References to *Søren Kierkegaard's Journals and Papers (JP)* and *The Journals of Søren Kierkegaard (JSK)* are to entry numbers, not pages. References to *Søren Kierkegaards Papierer (P)* are to the standard citations of the original Danish edition of Kierkegaard's journals. For bibliographic details, see the Bibliography.

Hegel

A   *Aesthetics: Lectures on Fine Art*
D   *The Difference between Fichte's and Schelling's System of Philosophy*
EL   *Hegel's Logic* (or *"Encyclopedia" Logic*)
FK   *Faith and Knowledge*
HP   *Lectures on the History of Philosophy*
HW   *Hegels Werke*
JR   *Jenaer Realphilosophie: Die Vorlesungen von 1803–4, 1805–6*
L   *The Science of Logic*
Letters *Hegel: The Letters*
Love   *"Love"*

PH	Lectures on the Philosophy of History
PM	Philosophy of Mind
PN	Philosophy of Nature
PR	Philosophy of Right
PS	Phenomenology of Spirit
PSS	Hegel's Philosophy of Subjective Spirit
SC	The Spirit of Christianity and Its Fate
W	Werke

Kierkegaard

CD	The Concept of Dread
CI	The Concept of Irony
CUP	Concluding Unscientific Postscript
DSK	The Diary of Søren Kierkegaard
ED	Edifying Discourses
E/Or	Either/Or
FT	Fear and Trembling
JC	Johannes Climacus, or De Omnibus Dubitandum Est
JP	Søren Kierkegaard's Journals and Papers
JSK	The Journals of Søren Kierkegaard
LF	"The Lily in the Field and the Bird of the Air"
MAW	"My Activity as a Writer"
P	Søren Kierkegaards Papierer
PA	The Present Age
PF	Philosophical Fragments
PV	The Point of View for My Work as an Author: A Report to History
R	Repetition
SD	The Sickness unto Death
SLW	Stages on Life's Way
TA	The Two Ages
TC	Training in Christianity

ACKNOWLEDGMENTS

I HAVE LEARNED more about the ethics of authorship from my students at Eastern Correctional Facility, a maximum security prison in Napanoch, New York, than I have from any of the excellent books and articles I have read on the topic over the past several years. These men have inspired me to think in new ways about the possibilities of empowerment of the reader in his engagement with the author. These are men who have every reason to be without hope, whose lives are defined by surveillance, and who are disciplined in body and mind into a remorseless regimentation that aims to erase the last trace of their independence, individuality, and urge for self-creation.

Yet in the classroom they somehow manage to cast off these constraints and to display a remarkable hunger to engage texts whose ideas would probably have seemed utterly esoteric and pointless in their prior lives. And the stakes are high. It isn't a question of learning facts or of being initiated into the erudite vocabulary of learned discourse. It is a question, rather, of "What does this mean for my life?" as Alex DeJesus put it in the very first question I received from a student at the prison some seven years ago, in a course on existentialism. This is not a question I was accustomed to hearing from the sophisticated, privileged, twenty-year-old, prematurely world-weary students I was familiar with—although I hasten to add that I love these students as well and have been blessed to have spent many years learning with them.

An author is both a figure of great respect for the men in the college program at Eastern and someone who is "called out," who must prove his or her relevance to the life of the reader, the inmate, who has no need for an author who will only further discipline him into submission or even who will give only the gift of knowledge. What these men hunger for is a yet grander and inspiring gift, the gift of liberation, the opportunity for the reader to discover his own voice and thereby transform himself.

To my students at Eastern Correctional Facility, then, I express my deep gratitude for all you have given me.

I also thank my colleague Nancy Leonard for helping me become a better reader of Kierkegaard's works as works of literature. Thanks also to my father, Fred Berthold, for remaining after all this time an inspiration for what it means to be a scholar whose life is more than a world of ideas. Finally, thanks to my wonderful daughter, Lily, and my extraordinary friend and lover, Melanie, for making me a much happier person than I no doubt deserve to be.

Death and life are in the power of the tongue.

Introduction:
Rorschach Tests

So then the book is superfluous; let no one therefore take the pains to appeal to it as an authority; for he who thus appeals to it has *eo ipso* misunderstood it. To be an authority is far too burdensome an existence for a humorist.

JOHANNES CLIMACUS/"Søren Kierkegaard,"
Concluding Unscientific Postscript

[The author must] refuse to intrude into the immanent rhythm of the notion [by appealing to the] vanity of his own knowing.

G. W. F. HEGEL, *Philosophy of Spirit*

WHAT THE Greek comic playwright Aristophanes did for Socrates, the Danish Christian humorist (as he often called himself) Søren Kierkegaard did for Hegel. With delectably malicious wit, these master tormentors reduced their famous elders to the status of half-dangerous, half-ridiculous characters in a tragicomedy. Socrates, who was present at the performance of Aristophanes' *Clouds*—in which, among other things, he is described as a sophistical ("logic-chopping," "hair-splitting," "tongue-wrestling") windbag who seeks to replace the old gods ("Zeus is dead!") with the Clouds, whose ethereality and mistiness perfectly symbolize the philosopher's own vaporous thoughts[1]—is reported to have stood up in his place in the audience in order to be recognized.[2] Perhaps he stood in an act of defiance: "That's not me you see on the stage! I'm nothing like that! Here I am!" Or perhaps, and this is what I prefer to believe, he stood in order to show his fellow Athenians that he was laughing as hard as the next spectator. It is much more difficult to imagine Hegel, the dignified and staid Prussian, likewise convulsed in laughter at Kierkegaard's scorching polemics (remarkably similar to those of Aristophanes against Socrates).

Kierkegaard lovers and scholars no doubt look on with delight at the hilarious seriousness with which Hegel's defenders proclaim the master's innocence with respect to the unscrupulous simplifications and outright buffooneries Kierkegaard has subjected him to. That it is so easy to imagine Socrates laughing at the performance of the *Clouds* is to recognize his splendid sense of humor, a delight in the comical that was so much a part of his being that it ironically threatens to disarm much of the force of Aristophanes' caricature. Hegelians, though, with their deadly seriousness, betray themselves: They protest too much.

Even if Jon Stewart is right that for the most part, the "Hegel" of Kierkegaard's polemics is a stand-in or pseudonym for the Hegelianism that mesmerized Denmark beginning in the 1820s,[3] it is unlikely that Hegel would be amused, even if we could expect Kierkegaard's readers to recognize the invisible quotes around the name "Hegel" in his texts. "Socrates" may also have been a pseudonym for the cast of sophists who were the real targets of Aristophanes' disdain, but it was Socrates who was put to death for being found guilty of charges taken virtually verbatim from Aristophanes' comedy, and it has been Hegel rather than the all but forgotten Danish "Hegelians" whose reputation has suffered from Kierkegaard's deprecations.

Between the camps of partisans of Kierkegaard and Hegel, there have been a few scholars who have explored the possibility of a genuine dialogue between the two antipodes.[4] Kierkegaard adherents tend to see such mediators as betraying their Hegelian bias in the very project of their erstwhile rapprochement: In this debate, there is no compromise, no wishy-washy "unity of difference" or "identity of opposites" (to use the familiar terms of Hegel's logic) to be found—between Hegel and Kierkegaard there is an unsurpassable either/or. In contrast, Hegel supporters tend to resist any mediation that would place Kierkegaard on an equal footing with Hegel, since Kierkegaard's subjectivist and religious standpoint can be reconciled

with the Hegelian system only by being subsumed—and hence sur-
passed—within the preliminary stages of the system's all-encompass-
ing embrace.

Although I acknowledge the perils of such a mediation, I would
like nevertheless to venture a contribution to this dialogical project,
centering on the theme of Hegel's and Kierkegaard's ethics of authorship, a major preoccupation of Kierkegaard. A great deal has
been written on Kierkegaard's theory and practice of communication—his use of pseudonyms, his practice of "indirect communication," his prolific experimentation with styles of expression, and the
ethical commitment embodied in his maieutic method of writing.
And there has been a certain amount of commentary both on Hegel's
philosophy of language and (less thoroughly) on the topic of his philosophical style. But I am not aware of any sustained questioning of
Kierkegaard's central distinction between his own "indirect" style
of communication and the (purportedly) "direct" style of Hegel's
philosophy with respect to the question of the ethics of authorship.
In fact, this distinction has been largely ignored by Hegelians and
accepted as obvious by Kierkegaardians.

One might wonder why it is of any special interest to focus on a
mere question of style, when, after all, the pressing issues of conflict
between Hegel and Kierkegaard are issues of content: Kierkegaard
is a Christian author, while Hegel translates religion into the supposedly "higher" sphere of philosophic wisdom; Kierkegaard proclaims
that "truth is subjectivity," while Hegel absorbs the subjective into
the "objective spirit"; Kierkegaard embraces passion, while Hegel is
devoted to reason; Kierkegaard insists on the centrality of the individual, while Hegel's focus is on the universal; Kierkegaard is preoc-
cupied with questions of existence, Hegel with questions of logic;
Kierkegaard's dictum is "either/or!" while Hegel is absorbed with
the mediation of oppositions ("both/and"). What is crucial to see,
though, is that the issue of style does not displace these issues of
content but is intimately involved with them. In fact, both Kierkegaard and Hegel believed that the form of communication is absolutely central to the content of what is communicated: *What* one says
(or hears) and writes (or reads) is inextricably bound up with *how*

one speaks or writes, listens or reads. And this "how" is precisely a question of the ethics of authorship.

Thus in the preface to the *Phenomenology of Spirit,* Hegel sketches out his commitment to a fundamentally new approach to grammar in which the "form of the ordinary proposition" is to be replaced by a new form (the "philosophical" or "speculative" propositional form) that "compels our knowing to go back to the proposition and understand it in some other way" (*PS* 36–40).[5] This "some other way" radically displaces the ordinary way of reading and responding to a text and establishes a distinctively ethical relation to the reader. As for Kierkegaard, his pseudonym Johannes Climacus writes in the *Concluding Unscientific Postscript* that "the difference between subjective and objective thinking must express itself also in the *form* of communication suitable to each" (*CUP* 68),[6] an idea Kierkegaard develops at length in his journals (see *JP* 1:630–79). Kierkegaard's claim, with respect to Hegel, is that the Hegelian system necessarily employed a *direct* form of communication, the "direct assertion" of objective knowledge claims as opposed to the artistically elusive, oblique, and indirect style of his own pseudonymous authorship that alone is appropriate for expressing the inwardness and subjectivity of the ethical and religious (*CUP* 68n). As Kierkegaard puts it in a journal entry, Hegel communicates as though through a megaphone.

> If someone wanting to speak had a speaking-trumpet so strong that it could be heard throughout the whole country, he would soon create the impression that he was not a single person (but something much more—for example, the voice of the age, etc., an abstraction) and that he was not talking to an individual or to individual human beings but to the whole world (the race, etc., an abstraction). . . . Communication is as if through an enormous trumpet, *ergo*—yes, even if it is utterly unimportant, completely stupid, . . . the communicator becomes self-important and has a fantastic notion of who it is he is talking to. (*JP* 1:650)

Part of the aim of this book is to complicate this picture of Hegel so as to allow him to emerge, as from behind an eclipse, as an author deeply concerned with the ethics of authorship, one who, in fact, so far from favoring the martial music of the trumpet, speaks in a voice so muted that it trails off into silence. In this silence, Hegel achieves what Roland Barthes proposes as the aim of ethical authorship, that "a text's unity lies not in its origin [author] but in its destination [reader]."[7] It is in Hegel's dedication to his own self-disappearance that we encounter the possibility of a meaningful dialogue with Kierkegaard, who much more obviously than Hegel devoted his own authorship to the project of vanishing from sight (*JP* 1:657) and learning from the lilies of the field the practice of silence (LF 333).

Hegel and Kierkegaard were undeniably two of the more notoriously elusive authors writing in the first half of the nineteenth century—a century noteworthy on the European continent for producing more than its fair share of elusive authors. Their elusiveness is such that to read either of them is much like taking a Rorschach test: What we find tells us as much about ourselves as it does about Kierkegaard or Hegel. But to think through the relationship between the two is a yet more challenging task, perhaps like seeking to align the inkblotted lenses of a Rorschachian kaleidoscope. Some commentators have found no alignment of the lenses to produce anything resembling a meaningful picture and have concluded, as Niels Thulstrup puts it in *Kierkegaard's Relation to Hegel*, that "Hegel and Kierkegaard have in the main nothing in common."[8] With equal forthrightness, Richard Kroner suggests in "Kierkegaard's Understanding of Hegel" that "Hegel and Kierkegaard are separated from each other by an abyss that no agreement can ever succeed in bridging."[9]

Such a reading of the Kierkegaard-Hegel relation is in fact made tempting by Kierkegaard's construction of the relation as one of radical difference. Hegel is the archetypal Other, the perpetual foil whose philosophic values and whole way of thinking and writing Kierkegaard devotes his own authorship to perfectly inverting. If Kierkegaard's Hegel is the philosopher of the "objective spirit" and the champion of reason, more interested in the logical relations between concepts than in the actual reality of existing individuals, Kierkegaard presents himself as the adherent of subjectivity, of faith, of existence.

6 ‡ RORSCHACH TESTS

Notably, for someone whom Kierkegaard constructs as having nothing in common with his own aims, Hegel certainly graces Kierkegaard's pages with a constant presence. Although Hegel is often left unnamed, he is there nevertheless, referred to by a series of code phrases—"the systematic philosopher," "the objective thinker," "a philosopher of the recent past." Thus even when unidentified, he is omnipresent as a lurking éminence grise, or, like the character of Johannes the Seducer in Kierkegaard's first pseudonymous work, *Either/Or,* he is "invisibly visible" (*E/Or* 1:346). Kierkegaard's own explanation for his preoccupation with Hegel is that Hegelian philosophy had so corrupted the spirit of the age with its pretentious objectivism and dangerously alluring seduction away from the ethics of existence that it required an unrelenting confrontation. Thus Hegel must always be present—as the adversary. But his presence is an uncanny one. As the object of polemic, he has the shadowy presence of the negative space of Kierkegaard's authorship, the other who haunts his pages as an apparitional "not this." Paul Ricoeur writes that

> the opposition between Kierkegaard and Hegel cannot be contested. . . . The question is not to attenuate it but precisely to think it as a meaningful opposition. This opposition belongs to understanding Kierkegaard. It signifies that Kierkegaard decidedly cannot be understood apart from Hegel. It is not just a biographical trait or a fortuitous encounter but a constitutive structure of Kierkegaard's thought that it is not thinkable apart from Hegel.[10]

The question is, *which* Hegel is it that Kierkegaard cannot be understood apart from—Kierkegaard's own visualization of the inkblot "Hegel," Hegel the corrupter of the age, or some other Hegel? By realigning the kaleidoscopic images of Hegel and Kierkegaard, Hegel emerges as a much more subtle practitioner of style than in Kierkegaard's representation of him—indeed as a practitioner whose style is in the service of an ambitious reconceptualization of the ethics of authorship—and Kierkegaard emerges as someone whose "indirect" style raises a whole series of ethical questions about how the reader is imagined in her relation to the author. There *is* finally an either/or between Hegel and Kierkegaard, just not the one Kierkegaard proposes as between an author devoid of ethics and one who makes a true ethics of authorship possible. Rather, the either/or is between two competing conceptions of the ethics of authorship, one that is largely hidden beneath the daunting cadences of a highly technical style, the other that is delightful for its elegance and playfulness.

This is a book about the ethics of authorship. It explores different conceptualizations of the author's responsibilities to the reader. But it also engages the question of which styles of authorship allow for these responsibilities to be met. As Judith Butler argues, style is not ethically neutral; the practice of styles reflects assumptions about the meaning of self-identity and the presentation of the self to others. Each in his own way, Hegel and Kierkegaard explore styles that are, as Butler says of her style, "in the service of calling taken-for-granted truths into question," thus unsettling traditional rules that govern intelligibility.[11] But style is not simply a matter of ethics because of its capacity to challenge conventions; style implies an ethics of authorship as well, since it shapes how the I chooses to reveal itself to the reader who will encounter the text.

Of course, authorship can be conceived of as simply an allegiance to art for its own sake, where the only responsibility is to the craft of authorship. Style would then be entirely in the service of art, and the relation to the reader, to the extent that this is important at all, would be entirely aesthetic. Many have held this view, from Victor Cousin to Walter Pater and the English aesthetic movement, from Edgar Allan Poe to Oscar Wilde. William Faulkner gives my favorite expression of it: "The artist's only responsibility is his art," Faulkner says in a 1956 interview, and the artist "will be completely ruthless if he is a good one. . . . If a writer has to rob his mother, he will not hesitate: the 'Ode on a Grecian Urn' is worth any number of old ladies."[12] Faulkner disdains the more genteel and high-minded justifications of the philosophy of *l'art pour l'art* and recognizes (and embraces) its essential ruthlessness, its denial of any authorial responsibility to the reader other than the responsibility to art itself.

Or perhaps the only responsibility of the author is to himself: Authorship is a way of encountering the self, of self-discovery and self-confrontation. In a letter written at the age of twenty-two to the brother-in-law of his sister Petrea, the naturalist Peter Wilhelm Lund, Kierkegaard wrote that "the thing is to understand myself, . . . to find a truth which is true *for me.*"[13] Eight years later, in *Either/Or,* Kierkegaard's "A" prefaces his "Diapsalmata" with the dedication *"ad se ipsum"*—"to himself" (*E/Or* 1:17). And one of Kierkegaard's many other pseudonyms, Johannes Climacus, writes in the appendix to *Concluding Unscientific Postscript* that "the whole work has to do with me myself, solely and simply with me" (*CUP* 545). Similarly, Franz Kafka says that "writing is utter solitude, the descent into the cold abyss of oneself."[14] And Alfred Kazin reflects that "the writer writes in order to teach himself, to understand himself, to satisfy himself; the publishing of his ideas . . . is a curious anticlimax."[15]

Kierkegaard emphatically recognizes a responsibility to the reader beyond his responsibility to himself, but even in the case of the author who writes in utter solitude (if such a thing is possible), insofar as he publishes what he writes—even though as a curious anticlimax—he intentionally enters into a relationship with readers, so that presumably he believes others have something to learn from reading about his descent into the abyss of himself. For such authors the first responsibility is to themselves, to the private voyage of self-discovery, and many readers will likely find the author's subjective experience too hermetic and alien. But perhaps there are a few, even just one, that "single individual" (as Kierkegaard put it in the dedication he made to each of his "edifying discourses"),[16] who will be reached. Even "in the writings of a hermit," as Nietzsche describes his own works, where one hears "the echo of the desolate regions" and "the whispered tones . . . of solitude,"[17] there is an invitation to the exceptional reader. Nietzsche knows that his works will remain utterly "silent" for most, but what matter? "Let those who have ears hear!"[18]

I have chosen Hegel and Kierkegaard as the subjects for an exploration of the ethics of authorship because they invite us to confront particularly challenging questions about this topic. I argue that each in his own way explores styles of authorship that employ a variety of strategies of seduction in order to entice the reader into the narratives, strategies that at least on the surface appear to be fundamentally manipulative and unethical. Further, I suggest that both writers seek to enact their own deaths as authors, effectively disappearing as reliable guides for the reader, which might also seem to be ethically irresponsible, as an act of abandonment of the reader who has been seduced only to be deserted.

Kierkegaard, perhaps more than any other writer, made the question of the ethics of authorship a guiding theme of his lifelong experimentation with styles of writing, and he identified Hegel as the perfect example of an author without an ethics. Hegel purports to write a complete "system" of existence but is so "absentminded," Kierkegaard says, that "in sheer distraction of mind" he finishes "without having [remembered to include] an ethics" (*CUP* 110).[19] Thus, according to Kierkegaard, Hegel falls back on the age-old style of the philosopher, the broadcasting of his truths through a megaphone.

Although it is true in one sense that the Hegelian philosophy lacks an ethics, I argue that in a deeper sense Hegel is as concerned with the ethics of authorship as is Kierkegaard. True, there is no Hegelian ethics in the sense of an appeal to "an oracle within his breast" (*PS* 43) or as a revelation to the reader of the "law of his heart." Hegel leaves such appeals and revelations to those motivated by "the earnestness of a high purpose" who "seek . . . pleasure in displaying the excellence of [their] own nature[s]" (*PS* 222). The ethical for Hegel is socially constructed, and he confines himself to a phenomenology of the forms in which this construction is internalized by consciousness and a genealogy of the ways in which morality is constituted and unfolds in history. But in a profound sense, it is precisely Hegel's silence about the ethical (beyond his genealogy)—his scrupulous restraint from baring his chest—that reflects his own ethics of authorship: By refusing "edification" (*PS* 6),[20] Hegel declines to instate himself in the position of authority and opens a space for the voice of the reader.

Chapters 1 and 2 ("A Question of Style" and "Live or Tell") introduce some of the key elements of Hegel's and Kierkegaard's views of the function of language and the ethics of communication and authorship. Both held views of language that led them to develop styles of writing that sought a nonauthoritarian relation to the reader (Kierkegaard's depiction of Hegel as a quintessentially autocratic author notwithstanding), and the ethics of communication in each case circles around the problem of how to achieve this: how to author a text that does not reduce the reader to a mere pretext, or representation, or sign of the author's signification.

Further, both are concerned with the task of writing in such a way that points beyond the goal of a purely intellectual response from the reader, and both aspire to engender action, a way of living—although Kierkegaard sees this as another point of absolute difference between his own style and that of Hegel, who produces a "book world," a philosophy that exists "only on paper" (*JP* 1:649; *CUP* 375–76). The diarist of Jean-Paul Sartre's *Nausea,* Antoine Roquentin, is torn by what he perceives as an unavoidable ultimatum between acting and writing: "You have to choose: live or tell."[21] In their different ways, Hegel and Kierkegaard each experiment with forms of authorship that will solve this dilemma, so that their "telling" will be more than what Hegel calls "a mere matter of words" (*PS* 403).

Chapters 3 and 4 ("Kierkegaard's Seductions" and "Hegel's Seductions") present the case for seeing Hegel's and Kierkegaard's authorships as engaged in projects of seduction. With respect to Kierkegaard, I argue that the infamous "Diary of the Seducer" that closes the first volume of *Either/Or* can be read as a disguised commentary on Kierkegaard's own early experimentation with a style of "indirect communication" and the nature of seduction as a strategy of authorship. This reading allows us to come to terms with the emphasis Kierkegaard places on the necessity of deception in his authorship, what he calls his strategy "to deceive into the truth" (*JP* 1:653), and to distinguish (if possible) between the sort of deception the seducer of the "Diary" uses to lure the young Cordelia and the deception Kierkegaard proposes as the maieutic and ethical aim of his own attempted seduction of the reader.

With respect to Hegel, whom Kierkegaard portrays as the least seductive of all authors (the philosopher who intones his objective truths in an arcane language for the reader to simply accept as an act of discipleship), I argue that Hegel in fact employs his own version of seduction. In particular, I seek to show that seduction is embedded even at the level of Hegel's grammar, through his development of an alternative to "the ordinary grammar of the proposition." In Hegel's unconventional grammar, the reader is left without any assertions to hold on to and hence is not spoken *at* but invited in to the text to invest herself in the process of the discovery of meaning. Similarly, I show that Hegel's project of seduction is present in his adoption of the stance of "observer" or "spectator" of the narrative of his texts—a stance, I argue, that is not so different in purpose from that of Kierkegaard, who refers to himself as "only a reader" of his own work (*CUP* 551). Hegel's spectatorship reflects an ethic of listening rather than "intrud[ing] into the immanent rhythm" of his text by appealing to "the vanity of his own knowing" (*PS* 36).

For both Kierkegaard and Hegel, the question needs to be addressed of how an authorship that seeks to seduce its readers can be conceived as an ethical project at all, since seduction seems to aim at the entrapment of the other, creating an illusion of freedom that is really only the product of manipulation. Or, as Kierkegaard's Father Taciturnus suggests in *Stages on Life's Way,* "Is there not a . . . higher kind of seduction?" (*SLW* 311).

In Chapter 5 ("Talking Cures") I turn to a closer look at Hegel's and Kierkegaard's theories of communication, and show that both entail conceptions of the therapeutic power of language. I argue that whereas Hegel quite straightforwardly celebrates the emancipatory and curative power of language, Kierkegaard is more ambivalent, since on the one hand he dedicates his life to a maieutic authorship in service to the reader, but on the other, he believes that ultimately it is only faith in God that can cure us, and that faith requires silence. I use Lacan's psychoanalytic account of the role of language to explore Hegel's view that language constitutes the self as well as Kierkegaard's employment of an indirect form of communication that he hopes will enable him to fulfill each of his apparently conflicting goals, to write and yet to remain silent. Although both Hegel's and Kierkegaard's authorships are designed as forms of therapy, and as such imply a structural relation to the reader analogous to the relation between analyst and analysand, two quite different conceptions of the ethics of this relation emerge.

Finally, Chapters 6 and 7 ("A Penchant for Disguise: The Death [and Rebirth] of the Author in Kierkegaard and Nietzsche" and "Passing Over: The Death of the Author in Hegel") examine what has been implicit all along, that the ethics of Hegel's and Kierkegaard's authorships rest on their respective efforts to die as authors. Long before 1968, when Roland Barthes proclaimed the "death of the author,"[22] Hegel and Kierkegaard had pursued their own deaths in their authorships. I situate Kierkegaard's commitment to death in companionship with what I argue is a similar, if not identical, commitment on the part of Friedrich Nietzsche. Both conceptualize the relation between self and other as occurring across an abyss of difference that dissolves the authority of the author, and adhere to a philosophy of language in which the author's text becomes infinitely interpretable according to the position occupied by the reader. But notwithstanding the inventiveness with which Kierkegaard and Nietzsche practice the art of dying, I seek to show that we can discern a fundamental ambivalence: With every intention of dying, they have recurring second thoughts; at the entrance to the tomb they hesitate, giving in to a certain nostalgia for the privileged position of the author.

I argue that Hegel's death as an author is at once less obvious and yet in important ways more complete than Kierkegaard's. I supplement Kierkegaard's critique of the Hegelian philosophy as the paradigmatic expression of a philosophy whose author seeks immortality—*never* to die—with those of a variety of "postmodern" critiques, from critical theory and deconstruction to Lacanian psychoanalytic theory and Foucauldian "archaeology." A frequent criticism of these (mainly) French commentators is that Hegel's invocation of "absolute knowledge" establishes him in a position of authorial arrogance, of God-like authority, leaving the reader in a position of subservience to the sage's perfect wisdom. The argument of Chapter 7 is that this sort of criticism is profoundly ironic, since Hegel's construction of the role of the sage possessing absolute knowledge is in fact an elaborate mask covering over a radical project of disappearance of the author by which it becomes the reader who is left to author the text.

Michel Foucault writes that "we have to determine the extent to which our anti-Hegelianism is possibly one of [Hegel's] ruses directed against us, at the end of which he stands, motionless, waiting for us."[23] There is something ominous about this picture, the vision of a crafty seducer who maneuvers even the most critical reader into arriving at just the point he had intended for us, waiting to pronounce judgment and to explain away all our criticisms as mere transient moments of his own system. This is certainly the picture Kierkegaard paints of Hegel. And Hegel does wait for us, but not as the one Kierkegaard and Foucault fear. He waits, rather—as Kierkegaard himself waits—to hear what we have to say about our journey, how we will narrate our own story. He, along with Kierkegaard, waits as the therapist waits: As Lacan says, the therapist has little to say and must do his best to "keep quiet"; the point is "to get *her* [the patient, the reader] to speak."[24]

1. A Question of Style

Every profound thinker is more afraid of being
understood than of being misunderstood.

FRIEDRICH NIETZSCHE, *Beyond Good and Evil*

To be honest, I rarely understood [Hegel]. . . .
I believe he really did not want to be understood.

HEINRICH HEINE, *Geständnisse*

I give you advance notice that there will come moments . . . when I . . .
must set between ourselves the awakening of misunderstanding.

SØREN KIERKEGAARD, *Søren Kierkegaard's Journals and Papers*

KIERKEGAARD DEFINES his authorship in a negative space in relation to Hegel, the Great Philosopher, who serves as the ground
against which the figure of Kierkegaard emerges and takes on his
own identity. At the heart of this project of identity formation
through contrast is the distinction Kierkegaard draws between styles
of authorship. Hegel, we have seen, philosophizes with a megaphone—a "giant speaking trumpet"—perfecting the authoritarian
voice of the Father, laying down the Law of objective truth for all
to hear (and obey). Kierkegaard speaks in a whisper, with a voice so
soft that it disappears into silence, leaving the reader with no option
but to reconstruct the text for herself. Hegel's voice is direct: He
gives directions to the reader. Kierkegaard's voice is indirect: He
leaves the reader to find her own direction.

JOKES

At first glance, there is something rather funny here: Kierkegaard, such a beautiful, lucid writer, depicts his style as elusive and oblique; yet Hegel, so famously impenetrable and opaque, is portrayed as a "direct" communicator. But there is a deeper joke. Mere opaqueness does not make for "indirection" in Kierkegaard's sense; indirection requires art, subtlety, irony, and masquerade. The confusing and serpentine character of Hegel's texts is not due to art but to an abstruse scientization of existence. Hence the joke is on Hegel: He is *trying* to be direct, trying to compel his readers to accept the objective certainty of his logically derived truths, yet he is so poor a stylist that he botches it.

However funny this joke, there is something pathetic as well to be found in the picture of Hegel so ardently and humorlessly struggling to broadcast the Truths of his system, yet becoming famous among his students for the inchoate character of his lectures. One student speaks of Hegel's "lame, dragging lectures, interrupted by eternal repetitions and irrelevant filler words," and another records his impressions of Hegel's performance in this way:

> Exhausted, morose, he sat there as if collapsed into himself, his head bent down, and while speaking kept turning pages and searching in his long folio notebooks, forward and backward, high and low. His constant clearing of his throat and coughing interrupted any flow of speech. Every sentence stood alone and came out with effort, cut in pieces and jumbled.[1]

Even outside the lecture hall, Hegel was known to so bewilder his companions with his "oddly complicated grammatical forms" and "peculiarly employed philosophical formulas"—as Goethe's daughter-in-law reports of a luncheon at Goethe's house—that he would "reduce [his guests] to complete silence without [Hegel's] even noticing" (*Letters* 711).

As for Kierkegaard, we have the reverse situation, a brilliant speaker and writer whose eloquence is turned to the service of secrecy and hidden plans. His entire pseudonymous authorship is produced as an "enigmatic mystery," filled with *"double entente,"* "ambiguity," "riddle," and "duplicity" (*PV* 5, 8, 10). Everything is "so complicated," as Victor Eremita, the pseudonymous "editor" of *Either/Or,* admits, that one meaning is "enclosed in another, like the parts in a Chinese puzzle box" (*E/Or* 1:9). Thus whereas Hegel, the obscure author, nevertheless philosophizes with a megaphone, Kierkegaard, the dazzling author, philosophizes with, . . . well, we might say "silence"—with what remains unsaid in any explicit way—or with a mask or an ironic smile.

In what follows, I want to suggest that there is a yet deeper joke to be found here, a joke within a joke. However funny the picture of Hegel industriously striving to be direct but having his unintelligible style of speech get in his way, funnier still—and incomparably more interesting in terms of the opportunities for dialogue with Kierkegaard—is that Kierkegaard's project of distinguishing between his own form of communication and that of Hegel is largely a misdirected effort, since Hegel's philosophy itself is a consummate practice of the art of indirect communication. Although Hegel's practice does not employ the same styles of indirection as does Kierkegaard's, beneath the imposing and often ineloquent surface of his prose, there is a thoroughgoing commitment to foiling the reader's expectations for direction, and indeed there are as many silences and masks and ironic smiles as we encounter with Kierkegaard.

This chapter sketches out some significant similarities between Hegel and Kierkegaard on language and the ethics of communication and authorship. The extent of this shared ground requires us to think skeptically about Kierkegaard's depiction of the difference between his work and Hegel's as largely between competing styles of authorship. Not surprisingly, we will see that important differences do emerge, but they are differences that must now be rethought from within a shared set of commitments to indirect forms of communication.

LANGUAGE IS MORE HONEST THAN INTENTION

Before I turn to look at the theme of communication, it seems fitting to look at what Hegel and Kierkegaard say about language. Given

Kierkegaard's well-known affinity for the subjective (and hence the life of the interior) and his corresponding suspicion, even derision, of the objective (the "manifest" and external), one might expect him to be quite skeptical of Hegel's view of language as the act of expression by which the self loses its privacy and is transfigured into a "mediated" self, a self now inextricably constituted by its relation to others. Language is "at once the externalization and the vanishing of this particular I," Hegel writes. "The I that utters itself is heard, . . . [which] means that its real existence [as a private, particular I] dies away," becoming other to itself, immersed in the communal space of being-among-others (*PS* 308–9). Hegel's whole approach to language centers on his effort to expose the insufficiency, indeed the essentially inchoate character, of purely inner, subjective meaning. "Language," Hegel insists, "is more truthful" (or honest: *wahrhafter*) than the merely intended. The self that seeks to protect itself from the loss of private meanings through expression "is still dumb, shut up with itself within its inner life." Indeed, purely subjective meaning "*cannot be reached by language*" (*PS* 60, 296, 66), a situation that, far from idealizing the subjective, is for Hegel a sign of its utter poverty. Not to be able to say what one means is to expose one's meaning as "only something obscure, fermenting, something that gains clarity only when it is able to put itself into words" (*PM* §462Z).

Yet Kierkegaard substantially shares Hegel's characterization of the structure of language, if not his conclusions. In his early unpublished work *Johannes Climacus, or De Omnibus Dubitandum Est* (probably written in 1842, a few months before the publication of *Either/Or*),[2] Kierkegaard asks, "Cannot consciousness then remain in immediacy? This is a foolish question, for if it could, no consciousness would exist. . . . Man would be an animal, or in other words, he would be dumb. That which annuls immediacy, therefore, is language. If man could not speak, he would remain in immediacy" (*JC* 148). In other places one can even hear an uncanny echo of Hegel's famous argument about the contradiction of "sense-certainty" (a way of conceptualizing the act of perception that uncannily anticipates what in the early twentieth century came to be known as "sense data theory")—the impossibility of ever putting into language the immediacy of perceptual experience. The sheer particularity, the "this-here-now" character of sensation, is undermined by the very act of seeking to speak it, Hegel argues: In language, "we ourselves directly refute what we mean to say; . . . it is just not possible for us ever to say, or express in words, a sensuous being that we *mean*" (*PS* 60).[3] And now here is Kierkegaard, writing in *Johannes Climacus* without so much as a sideways nod to Hegel: "If . . . I want to express the actual world which I perceive with my senses, then opposition is present. For what I say is quite other than what I want to express" (*JC* 148).[4]

To cite just two more conspicuous examples of Kierkegaard's reliance on Hegel's philosophy of language, in a passage from *Either/Or* the anonymous aesthete ("A") directly recovers the Hegelian dictum that "language is more honest" than intention: "The immediate is really the indeterminate and therefore language cannot properly apprehend it; but the fact that it is indeterminate is not its perfection but an imperfection" (*E/Or* 1:69). And in an early journal entry, Kierkegaard, the master of concealment, surprises us with the following praise of Hegel:

> Whereas the philosophy of the recent past had almost exemplified the idea that language exists to conceal thought (since thought simply cannot express *das Ding an sich* at all), Hegel in any case deserves credit for showing that language has thought immanent in itself and that thought is developed language. The other thinking was a constant fumbling with the matter. (*JP* 2:1590)

One consequence of this shared view of language as the transformation of inner meanings into the public domain of signification will be important for my forthcoming discussion of the ethics of authorship. Since one cannot express purely inward intentions without directly saying something other than what one meant to say—that is, since language inherently reshapes the privacy of the inner into the "external" sphere of the social construction of meaning—the commonsense idea that the author has a privileged access to the meaning of his or her work becomes senseless. Hegel's *Phenomenology,* as a text, effectively obscures the boundaries between inner and outer and hence of author and reader. At every step of the way, meanings are turned inside-out, as each initial configuration of consciousness points beyond itself as it gropes for the language to express itself. Hegel thus shifts the site of meaning of the text from his own authorial declarations to the space in which the dramatis personae of his narrative—the various shapes of consciousness on its journey of self-exploration—express themselves, that is, in which *they* speak. Thus as the text obscures the relation of inner and outer, subjective intention and linguistic meaning, so too it obscures the place of the author: The author "merely looks on" (*PM* §379Z) as the reader is drawn into seeing herself in the personae of the text and hence is invited into her own speech.

Kierkegaard is well known for his explicit disavowal of any privileged relation to his own texts, insisting that he has "no opinion about these works except as a third person, no knowledge of their meaning except as a reader" (*CUP* 551; see also *PV* 15). He, too, merely looks on. What is interesting, though, is that this position follows directly from Kierkegaard's thoroughly Hegelian view of language.[5] The text, we might say, is more honest than the author's desire to maintain private ownership over its meaning: Meaning is linguistic and language is the externalization and therefore the alienation of private meaning. Hence the author, as Kierkegaard puts it, effectively "disappears," leaving the reader to his own resources (*JP* 1:657).

A critical point of difference must be noted before I trace out some consequences of Hegel and Kierkegaard's shared philosophy of language for their concepts of communication and the ethics of authorship. Although Hegel certainly acknowledges the sense of loss that accompanies the linguistic act (the pain of deserting the inner self), his predominant mood is one of celebration of the emancipatory nature of language as a deliverance from the limitations of self-enclosure. Kierkegaard, in contrast, accepts the necessity of language as constitutive of our humanity, but this acceptance is continually accompanied by a sense of lamentation over forsaking the interior.

For Hegel, what is truly lost in language is the position of the "I am I," the narcissistically enclosed self of sheer particularity, the self that desires to constitute itself on its own but that is finally empty and must reach out beyond its borders to the other in order to be recognized as (and hence to *be*) a self. "Human nature only really exists in an achieved community of minds," Hegel insists, and this is a community made possible by language: "Language is self-consciousness existing for others, . . . [where] the self separates itself [as purely private] from itself by expressing itself" (*PS* 43, 395). The "beautiful soul" that retreats into the safety of its own intentions and "hypocritically" wants these intentions "to be taken for an actual deed, . . . living in dread of besmirching the splendor of its inner being" by expression, "is still *dumb,*" and hence "impotent"—it is a sheer "yearning which . . . finds itself only as a lost soul: . . . its light dies away within it, and it vanishes like a shapeless vapor that dissolves into thin air" (*PS* 399–400, 403). Thus the sense of bereavement Hegel recognizes as accompanying the passage from (indeed the eerie vanishing of) self-enclosure into being-for-others when we speak is finally "the divine nature of language" (*PS* 66), the salvation of the beautiful but mute, and thus lost, soul. Even God, Hegel sometimes suggests, needed saving from his self-enclosure: The divinity of language is seen in God's need to express himself, to speak; thus the true origin of the divine was with the Word (see *HP* 2:75; *PN* §247Z).

If Hegel sees redemption in an emergence from the privacy of the interior, Kierkegaard is wary of the socially constructed self that results. The I that Hegel celebrates as "separating itself from itself" and as being made "objective" to itself through expression, is a public self, and Kierkegaard's distaste for "the public" is unremitting. The public is a "monstrous abstraction," a "devouring and demoralizing" space of "mathematical equality," "slavery," and "bloodless indolence," where we "aspire to be nothing at all" (*PA* 260–69). Kierkegaard's attachment is to "the single individual," to the aloneness of subjectivity. As a result, in every passage where Kierkegaard indicates his affiliation with a Hegelian view of the function of language there is a twist that expresses his sorrow over what is in danger of being lost. In the passage quoted from *Johannes Climacus* in which Kierkegaard writes that it is a "foolish question" to ask if consciousness could remain in immediacy, for then "man would be an animal," he adds: "This might be expressed by saying that immediacy is reality and speech is ideality. . . . Reality I cannot express in speech,

for to indicate it I use ideality, which is a contradiction, an untruth"
(*JC* 148). Thus the immediate, which Hegel refers to explicitly as
"the unutterable [that] is nothing else than the untrue" (*PS* 66), is for
Kierkegaard "reality," and language, which for Hegel is the truth
of spirit, is "ideality," and an untruth. "What then is immediacy?"
Kierkegaard asks; "It is reality. What is mediacy? It is the word.
How does Word annul reality? By talking about it" (*JC* 148).

MUSICAL INTERLUDE

Kierkegaard's sense of the tragic character of language—the inevitable forsaking of "reality" by the intervention of the word—is explored in a remarkable essay on three of Mozart's operas in the first
volume of *Either/Or* (*Figaro, The Magic Flute,* and—the main focus
of attention—*Don Giovanni*). The nearly hundred-page essay, "The
Immediate Stages of the Erotic, or the Musical Erotic," follows the
opening, much shorter, essay (or really, collection of diary entries),
the "Diapsalmata." David and Lillian Swenson, the translators, tell
us that "*diapsalmata*" is "the Greek plural of the Hebrew *selah,* a
word occurring frequently in the Psalms of David at the end of a
verse, . . . perhaps indicating a pause for the playing of a musical
interlude" (*E/Or* 1:443n4).

The "Diapsalmata" are brooding, melancholy, despairing confes-
sions of weariness and hopelessness. "Generally speaking," the aesthete writes in one entry, "I lack the patience to live. I cannot see the
grass grow, but since I cannot, I do not care to look at it at all. . . . [I
am] weary of everything, and yet I hunger." Yet interwoven in the
threnody of the text, at key moments (moments of hunger), the
theme of music appears. Music offers the despairing writer a moment of relief, or more, the seemingly impossible possibility of salvation. In the midst of passages speaking of unrelenting grief and
hollowness, the aesthete hears from out of his window a beggar playing "the deep choral tones of the immortal overture" from *Don
Giovanni.*

> Music finds its way where the rays of the sun cannot penetrate
> [into the tomblike enclosure of his garret]. My room is dark and

dismal. . . . What do I hear? The minuet from *Don Juan!* Carry
me away, . . . O tones so rich and powerful, to the company of the
maidens, to the pleasures of the dance. (*E/Or* 1:24–25, 29, 40)—

—to the possibility of redemption.

In "The Musical Erotic," music is presented as the possibility of
an elemental experience of "the real" uncontaminated by language.
Music is the medium of "sensuous genius," sheer "energy, storm, . . .
and passion," "the daemonic" that "demands expression in all its
immediacy." Language, however, is "mediacy" and "reflection," an
abstraction away from the pure sensuality of life that is "expressible
solely in music" (*E/Or* 1:55, 63). When the rapture experienced in
music is put into words, it is like waking from a dream and reflecting
on it.

> The soul becomes sad, . . . for it is as if you were bidding [the
> experience of the dream] farewell. . . . It seems as if you were false
> to it, faithless to your trust; you feel that you are no longer the
> same, neither so young nor so childlike; you fear for yourself, lest
> you lose what has made you . . . rich; you fear for the object of
> your love, [for it will] suffer in this transformation. (*E/Or* 1:59)

One might say, although the aesthete does not, that music represents the feminine and language the masculine. As we will see later
(in Chapter 3, "Kierkegaard's Seductions"), woman is for the aesthete "a natural force": "She is wholly subject to Nature," to the
realm of immediacy and passion. Man is her opposite, "spirit," whose
essence is mind, reflection, and speech (*E/Or* 1:424–27). In Lacanian
terms, the feminine is the prelinguistic register of the Real; the masculine is the Symbolic, the Law of the Father, the negation and repression of the real.

Here, in "The Musical Erotic," the aesthete yearns for music, for
the feminine, for an encounter with the energy and storm of life
unmediated by language. He is grateful to Mozart for "turning me
into a fool" and for "the loss of my reason" (*E/Or* 1:46, 47)—and yet
he retains his masculinity by subverting music, by *writing about it*. In
his "Insignificant Introduction," "A" writes that "I am convinced

that if ever Mozart became wholly comprehensible to me"—transformed from the rapturous dream of sensuous genius into the abstract idiom of thought—"he would then become fully incomprehensible to me." Only when "language ceases" can we "encounter the musical." Thus the aesthete must be careful to "eschew [a] linguistic orgy"; he must only listen. To give "a running commentary on [Mozart's] music" would be to rob it of its life, for "in language the sensuous as a medium is depressed to the level of a mere instrumentality and constantly negated" (E/Or 1:59, 68, 84, 85, 65). And yet "A"'s domain is the "kingdom of language," and he proceeds precisely to speak about music and to give just the running commentary on Mozart's operas he at the same time recognizes will negate their meaning.

The aesthete is "spirit," the masculine, and "not until the spiritual is posited is language invested with its rights; but when the spiritual is posited, all that which is not spirit"—nature, the sensuous, music, the feminine—"is thereby excluded" (E/Or 1:65). In the "Insignificant Postlude" that closes his examination of Mozart, "A" writes (tongue in cheek?) that "I, at least, feel myself indescribably happy in having even remotely understood Mozart" (E/Or 1:134)—this after admitting in the "Insignificant Introduction" that to comprehend Mozart would be to render his music incomprehensible.

The "Insignificant Introduction" and "Insignificant Postlude" are indeed insignificant in a significant sense: They negate themselves, speaking of what they proclaim cannot be spoken of. Thus they expose the impossibility of "A"'s project. He longs to abandon himself to music, to *become* music, to experience himself as a sheer force of nature (hence as "woman"), and yet his kingdom is that of language; he is "spirit," masculinity, and cannot help himself from wanting something more than the immediacy of passion. He needs to comprehend it, to put it into words, knowing at the same time that he is "bidding farewell" to rapture, becoming "false to it, faithless" and destined to "lose what has made [him] rich."

We saw Kierkegaard confess in *De Omnibus Dubitandum Est* that even if language "annuls immediacy" and indeed "the real"—for "immediacy is reality, . . . and reality I cannot express in speech"—nevertheless "consciousness cannot remain in immediacy," for then "man would be an animal." So too here, in "The Musical Erotic," the same ambivalence returns: on the one hand, the tragic sense of the cruelty of language—its inevitable destruction of the real—and on the other, the necessity of language for the human to exist as "spirit." The figure of Don Juan in Mozart's opera is an inhuman figure: He is no self at all, but "flesh incarnate," the sheer musical power of sensuous desire. "We do not hear Don Juan as a particular individual, nor his speech, but we hear a voice, the voice of sensuousness" itself (*E/Or* 1:87, 95). This is both Don Juan's allure and his inhumanity. The voice of sensuousness, although seductive, must become articulate, negating itself to make selfhood possible.

"A"—like Kierkegaard himself—thus seeks a form of speech that will itself be seductive, but without the direct, immediate forcefulness of the seductiveness of music. After warning himself to avoid a "linguistic orgy," but aware that his kingdom is that of language, "A" asks his readers to "listen! . . . I have tried to do the best of which [language] is capable," to "persistently tempt the musical forth"—to seduce the seducer, if you will. He then invokes the "friendly genii" to "fashion my soul into a harmonious instrument"—to achieve as much as possible a linguistic simulacrum of music. And he implores these "powerful spirits, you who know and understand the hearts of men," to "stand by me that I may catch the reader" (*E/Or* 1:84, 85). "A"'s voice, unlike the Hegelian megaphone, will be a harmonious instrument, seductive but aware of its own limits, pointing beyond itself to that which it cannot express, to music, to the feminine, to "the real" that it annuls but simultaneously invokes and beckons the reader to encounter beneath, or beyond, or in the gaps and silences of his words.

Hegel was well known for his advocacy of Philippe Pinel's "moral treatment" of the insane, which replaced physical remedies, and especially all physically coercive treatment, with a therapeutics based largely on a talking cure.[6] We might say that Hegel's own phenomenological method is a talking cure: The entire *Phenomenology* can be seen as presenting the struggle of consciousness to find the language suited to spirit, learning again and again that it cannot say what it means (when its meanings are intended to be private), that language is more honest, that it is through language that one comes to discover the truth of selfhood. Kierkegaard also sees language as necessary for selfhood—again, the purely musical Don Juan is no self at all. Yet for Kierkegaard language is a double-edged sword: Paradoxically, although there is no self without language, language is also what Sartre calls a "flight outside myself" (*fuite hors de moi*)[7] into the harsh region of the other's gaze.

Kierkegaard's authorship shows him to be a master of words, but still, his nostalgia for the interior space of what he terms "reality" leads him to the development of an indirect discourse whose words do not mean what they seem, whose meanings are concealed beneath disguises, and whose experimentalism explores the possibility of replacing a literal silence with an indirect silence. It is just this indirect discourse that Kierkegaard poses as a radical alternative to the "enormous speaking-trumpet" with which Hegel purportedly philosophizes with such grandiose pomposity and such obtrusive directness.

COMMUNICATION AND THE ETHICS OF AUTHORSHIP

For Kierkegaard, the ethics of authorship revolves around the question of the *form* of communication between author and reader. As we have noted, he is convinced that "the difference between subjective and objective thinking must express itself also in the form of communication suitable to each." Hegel also emphasizes the importance of form: In his search for a "new grammar" of communication, meaning will not be found "in" whatever propositions are stated, but in the form of the proposition, *"an der Form"* (W 3:59–61). What we must investigate here is the plausibility of Kierkegaard's claim that his own indirect communication is a form suited for ethics but that Hegel's direct communication precludes any such ethical relation to the reader.

Ironically, indirect communication requires the deployment of strategies generally not associated with ethics: disguise, concealment, and even deception. "I give you advance notice," Kierkegaard confides in his journal to his imagined reader, "that there will come moments . . . when I . . . must set between ourselves the awakening of misunderstanding." And lest there be any doubt about the method of this awakening, another journal entry puts it even more bluntly: "To deceive belongs essentially to [my method of] communication; . . . and the art consists in . . . remaining faithful to . . . the deception [throughout]" (*JP* 1:662, 653).

Of the many accounts Kierkegaard gives of his motives for indirection and deception, the one that occurs most often is that the ethics of communication obligates the author to remove himself from the position of teacher. "All direct communication" makes Kierkegaard "uncomfortable," since "what I have to say may not be taught." This is the most straightforward of Kierkegaard's reasons for adopting pseudonymity: By "never ventur[ing] to use quite directly my own I," he seeks to effect his own disappearance so that his reader is placed in the uncanny situation of encountering only fantastic, poetized "authors," that is, really, no one at all to rely on for answers (*JP* 1:646, 656).

The ethics of authorial indirection is a central concern of Kierkegaard's posthumously published *Point of View for My Work as an Author*—ironically so, since the *Point of View* frankly contravenes this ethics by adopting the basso profundo voice of direct protestation. The text begins: "In my career as an author, a point has now been reached where it is permissible to do what I feel a strong impulse to do . . . namely, to explain once for all, as directly and frankly as possible, what is what: what I as an author declare myself to be." The entire authorship, Kierkegaard admits, has been devoted to "ambiguity," "duplicity," and "deception." But he assures us that this has been an ethically guided project of deception, not a "mystification for its own sake," but rather "in the service of a serious purpose" (*PV* 5–6, 10–11, 16). His indirect communication has used duplicity precisely so as to reach the reader who is capable of genuine reading, a reading that provokes self-authorship. This is above all the ethical framework of indirect communication, that a "reduplication" occurs in which the reader frees herself from reliance on the author and finds herself "stand[ing] alone," claiming the text as her own, in her own way. As Anti-Climacus puts it in *Training in Christianity,* "To reduplicate is to 'exist' in what one understands" (*TC* 133).

There are many further complexities to Kierkegaard's practice of indirect communication, and perhaps first among them is the peculiarity that what the author is seeking to communicate cannot truly

be communicated. In his *Concluding Unscientific Postscript,* the pseudonym Johannes Climacus proclaims that "existential reality is incommunicable" (*CUP* 320)—and this in a text largely devoted precisely
to the exploration of existential reality, a reality starkly opposed to
the Hegelian "reality" of "pure thought." Possibly even more tanta-
lizing is the puzzle of the pseudonym Johannes de Silentio and his
text *Fear and Trembling.* Johannes, true to his name, is finally silent
about that which he speaks about. He talks of faith, and the arche-
type of faith, Abraham, who himself remained silent (to his wife, to
his son) about the test set to him by God, to sacrifice his son, Isaac.
Like Abraham, Johannes is silent, but their silences are not the same.
Abraham cannot speak since faith places him beyond the possibility
of language (*FT* 91–129). Johannes, however, is not a knight of faith
but a poet, and so must speak, but in such a way that he remains in
some sense silent: The true reader sees that Johannes's words are
spoken so as to be revoked, leaving a text to be reauthored by the
reader herself.

The labyrinthine ethics of Kierkegaard's indirect communication,
which involves an abandonment of the reader through the vanishing
of the author, should be understood in terms of his lifelong struggle
with the concept of "the ethical" itself. This concept goes through
many experimental transformations in Kierkegaard's authorship, but
with respect to that aspect of the ethical that has to do with the
relation between the self and the other, Kierkegaard remained forever haunted by the sense of the impossibility of ever truly reaching
the other. Every other, as Derrida puts it in his commentary on *Fear
and Trembling*, is absolutely other (*tout autre est tout autre*).[8] The
other always escapes us in her irreducible alterity. As Johannes Climacus says in his *Postscript,* we can "apprehend the ethical reality of
an other only by thinking it, and hence as a possibility." Each individual is "isolated and compelled to exist for himself," so that "to be
concerned ethically about another's reality is . . . a misunderstanding"
(*CUP* 286, 287). Thus the ethics of indirect communication has its
origins in the troubling thought of the impossibility of any direct
encounter with the other, yet seeks a circuitous path to the other by
the desperate move of self-withdrawal: The author provokes the

reader, but abandons her in an act of disappearance (and hence silence) so that the reader retains her autonomy and must fend for
herself.

The ethics of silence brings us back to Kierkegaard's more general
sense of disillusionment with the limitations of language. In a journal
entry titled "Silence," Kierkegaard writes that "speech is in fact an
abstraction and always presents the abstract rather than the concrete.
. . . And now the ethical approach! How easily a person is led to
think of man (an abstraction) instead of himself, this tremendous
concretion. Herein lies the truth in the Pythagorean instruction to
begin with silence. This was a way of gaining consciousness of the
concrete" (*JP* 5:2324). Kierkegaardian indirect communication is
thus a performance of silence by which an intricate series of ethical
sacrifices is attempted: The author (Kierkegaard) behind the author
(pseudonym) sacrifices himself, and thus retains his unapprehended
inwardness by remaining hidden, and the author's authors (pseudonyms) in turn sacrifice themselves by taking on the character of
abstractions through speaking, so that the reader is summoned to her
own concretion (selfhood) by sacrificing her reliance on the author
as the pseudonyms reveal themselves to be unreliable guides and
vanish from sight as trustworthy authorities.

Like Kierkegaard, Martin Heidegger experimented with an alternative theory and practice of discourse that might respond to what
he called "the widely and rapidly spreading devastation of language." For Heidegger, the "downfall of language" is a consequence
of our surrendering of it "to our mere willing and trafficking as an
instrument of domination over things."[9] We use language to "en-
frame" things, to reduce them to easily understandable entities ready
for use. Things become a sort of "standing reserve" (*Bestand*), on
hand to serve as mere objects of consumption.[10] "We encounter beings in a calculative business-like way," he writes in his "Letter on
Humanism," "but also scientifically and by way of philosophy, with
explanations and proofs."[11]

So too, for Kierkegaard, the "direct" discourse of Hegelian philosophy objectifies existence, making it transparently understandable.
More, it objectifies the reader, who is enframed as the entirely passive

object of the author's desire. Hegel, we might say, consumes his readers, by demanding their obedience to his declaration of Truth. As Johannes Climacus says in the *Postscript,* "objective thought is indifferent" to the agency and subjectivity of the other (*CUP* 67). For Heidegger, as for Kierkegaard, *how* we speak is a fundamentally ethical issue: The devastation of language "undermines . . . moral responsibility, . . . [and] it arises from a threat to the essence of humanity."[12] Heidegger, like Kierkegaard, is constantly *"unterwegs zur Sprache"*—on the way toward a new form of speech that might release the other into its own being-for-self. We must speak in such a way that, as Heidegger puts it in "Building Dwelling Thinking," "We leave [the other] in its own essence," thereby "freeing it" and "safeguarding" it for its own way of being.[13] As an author, then, the aim is to use language in such a way as to free the reader from dependency.

Also like Kierkegaard, Heidegger recognizes the need for a certain sort of silence on the part of the speaker: "If man is to find his way again into the nearness of Being, he must first learn to exist in the nameless."[14] Although Heidegger's notion of "Being" has no simple or obvious correlate in Kierkegaard, the point he is making is at least analogous to the one Kierkegaard makes about "the real," the nature of being as it is apart from and prior to its being named or represented or enframed (and hence "annulled") by words. Heidegger concludes his discussion of the devastation of language by saying that "before he speaks man must first let himself be claimed again by Being, taking the risk that under this claim he will seldom have much to say,"[15] just as Kierkegaard recommends the Pythagoreans' practice of silence as a way of reencountering "the concrete," and just as the aesthete of "The Musical Erotic" wishes to avoid a "linguistic orgy" in which the truth of music—the elemental "real"— will become only a "weak echo" of itself.

As I turn now to Hegel, it is interesting to note that he too praises the Pythagorean brotherhood's custom of requiring their novices to remain silent for five years. Yet he gives a completely different reason for his praise than does Kierkegaard. In 1810, Hegel gave a speech to the students of the Nürnberg Gymnasium where he was rector, in which he spoke of the Pythagorean practice of silence.

In a sense, this duty of silence is the essential condition of all culture and learning. We must begin with being able to apprehend
the thoughts of others, and this implies a disregarding of our own
ideas. . . . By silence . . . we gain the consciousness that subjective
opinions . . . are good for nothing, so that we cease at last even to
have them. (*W* 4:332)[16]

Kierkegaard would have had a field day with this passage had
he known of it. If the virtue of the Pythagorean rule of silence for
Kierkegaard is that it disciplines us in the turn inward to the true
ethical domain of the subjective, in Hegel's inverse reading of it,
silence turns us outward, toward others, and appears to entail a discipline in self-erasure. Correspondingly, if Kierkegaardian indirect
communication beckons the reader to her own interiority, Hegelian
direct communication seems to relegate the reader/acolyte to an obe-
dient silence in which he must "disregard his own ideas" as "good
for nothing" and attend deferentially to "the thoughts of others,"
namely, of the author/authority.

Both Kierkegaard and Hegel adopt the position of authorial impersonality. For Kierkegaard, the whole art of indirect communication "consists in reducing oneself, the communicator, to nobody" (*TC*
132), and this is meant to be a gift of mercy to the reader. The
impersonality Kierkegaard ascribes to Hegel, however, is quite different. Hegel's impersonality is for Kierkegaard a species of "the
fantastic": The author disappears in Hegel's texts because he is a
pure chimera, a mythological objective spectator of the experiences
of an equally generalized, abstract human consciousness. As Hegel
says, "We [Hegelian philosophers] merely look on, as it were, at the
object's own development, not altering it by importing into it our
own subjective ideas and fancies" (*PN* §397Z), and "philosophy has,
as it were, only to watch" (*PM* §381Z). Kierkegaard's impersonality,
although enigmatic, is not fantastic, but maieutic, an imitation of
Socrates' intention to "repel" his listeners from himself so that each
individual "would be compelled to understand that he had essentially
to do with himself" (*CUP* 222).[17] The reader is left with only the
pseudonyms, mere phantoms of the imagination, dramatis personae
rather than true persons—which is to say, the reader is left with only

herself, abandoned but autonomous. If Kierkegaard conceives of his own style of indirect communication as a gift of mercy to the reader, he regards Hegel's reader as being at the author's mercy. Hegel writes a merciless text, where the reader's autonomy is sacrificed to the author's voice, the megaphonic voice of objective knowledge.

Heidegger liked to speak of the way in which every act of "bringing into presence" leaves as much concealed as it reveals: Every revealing (*Entbergung*) is a concealing (*Verbergung*).[18] Whatever Kierkegaard's rhetoric of opposites—his mantra-like invocation of absolute difference between the merciful ethics of deception and the merciless language of direct discourse—may reveal about his relation to Hegel, I am convinced that we have stepped into darkness. For the fact is that Hegel's style of authorship is as committed to a radical experimentation with alternatives to direct communication as is Kierkegaard's. It is true that Hegel as author withdraws to a position of spectatorship—just as it must be said that Kierkegaard does as well: Kierkegaard observes his pseudonyms with a detached interest (he "has no opinion about them"), and all his pseudonyms situate themselves as observers as well. The Seducer in *Either/Or* spies on the object of his seduction, Cordelia; Constantin Constantius observes the young man of *Repetition* with clinical interest; Johannes de Silentio intently watches Abraham; Johannes Climacus (*Philosophical Fragments, Concluding Unscientific Postscript*) surveils the spectacle of Christendom; and Anti-Climacus (*Sickness unto Death, Training in Christianity*) observes the despair of those without faith. But Hegel's authorial withdrawal is no more motivated by a desire to stake out a position of authority from which to proclaim the Truth to his reader than is Kierkegaard's own authorial self-removal. If Hegel's text is merciless, it is merciless in its opposition to the language of proclamation and assertion. "One bare assurance is worth just as much as another," and indeed all direct assertions are bare and barren. The author must "refuse to intrude into the immanent rhythm" of the text by appealing to the "vanity of [his] own knowing" (*PS* 49, 36).

Joseph Flay speaks of Hegel's "virtually inaugurat[ing] a completely new theory of language as essentially performative in all of its modes."[19] Indeed, Hegel describes "the power of speech" as being "that which performs what has to be performed [*welche das ausführt, was auszuführen ist*]." It is in language that the self enacts itself as a self that is *there* in the world: "In speech, self-consciousness, qua independent separate individuality, comes as such into existence, so that it exists for others. Otherwise the I, this pure I, is non-existent, is not *there*" (*PS* 308). This is not just a theory of language as performative but an undertaking to be carried out in the manner of writing: Hegel's texts themselves are performative—they *do* rather than proclaim. The various shapes of experience that appear in Hegel's *Phenomenology,* for example, are not so much the objects of Hegel's philosophic commentary as the active subjects of the text; they enact themselves.

In an advertisement placed by the publishers of the *Phenomenology* in a Jena cultural journal, Hegel describes the aim of his phenomenological method to be the replacement of "abstract discussions" of the experience of consciousness with a presentation of "the wealth of appearances [*Reichtum der Erscheinungen*] in which spirit *presents itself*" (*W* 3:593).[20] Thus it is not Hegel, the author, who states the meaning of the master or slave consciousness, or of stoicism or skepticism or of the unhappy consciousness—indeed, he is skeptical of all approaches that "state" rather than "carry out" or perform (*PS* 2)— but the master and the slave, the stoic and the skeptic, and the despairing soul themselves. The reader has no directives from the author, who "merely looks on," and so she must enter into the world of the master, the slave, and the whole wealth of dramatis personae that populate the text, and experience them from within.

The world the reader enters into is not one where truth will be found "like a minted coin that can be pocketed ready-made." Notwithstanding Kierkegaard's polemics to the contrary, there is no such truth for Hegel. Truth, rather, is a "Bacchanalian revel in which no member is not drunk" (*PS* 22, 27). The world of Hegel's texts is dizzying, intoxicating, disorienting. And here we can see a close affinity with Kierkegaard's ethics of authorship. Kierkegaard's pseudonyms have as their "task to create difficulties everywhere" (*CUP* 166), an act of disorientation by which, as Paul Armstrong puts it, Kierkegaard seeks to "shak[e] [the reader] loose from his customary bearings; . . . he attempts to educate his audience through the very activity of reading."[21] "It is thus left to the reader himself to put two and two together, if he so desires," Johannes Climacus remarks, "but nothing is done to minister to [the] reader" (*CUP* 264–65). In a journal entry, Kierkegaard says that his purpose is "not so much [to] move, mollify, reassure, persuade, as [to] awaken and provoke men." To do so, the author "must first fetch them up out of the cellar, call to them, turn their comfortable way of thinking topsy-turvy with the dialectic" (*JP* 1:641).

So too Hegel sees his task as provoking the reader to learn to think in a new way, "to become acquainted with [things] in a new way, quite opposite to that in which we know them already." This new way of thinking "denie[s] [us] the use of [our] familiar ideas," so that we "feel the ground where [we] once stood firm and at home taken away from beneath [us], and . . . cannot tell where in the world" we are (*EL* §§19, 3). Hegel's phenomenological method places the reader on a path of "loss" and "doubt," "or more precisely [a] way of despair" (*PS* 49), a sort of via dolorosa in which our familiar, commonsense assumptions about ourselves and our world successively collapse and point beyond themselves.

The disorienting and uncanny character of Hegel's texts is in part achieved by a strategy of irony.[22] In the *Phenomenology,* each configuration of consciousness says what it means—expresses its worldview—and gradually discovers that what is said is something other than what is meant, that language is more honest than mere intention. The worldview that is held in thought, once expressed, is too partial and limited to correspond to one's actual experience of the world. Note that the irony here is effected from within the experience of the particular shape of consciousness itself, not by the author instructing us from on high: "Consciousness suffers this violence at its own hands" (*PS* 51). But Hegel's strategy of irony rests on a much deeper foundation, namely, his new approach to grammar, and it is here, in his linguistics, that one can best locate his own ethics of indirect communication.

The main goal of Hegel's new grammar is to develop an alternative to the grammar of the assertion (*Aussage*), in which the predicates of a proposition are understood to be "fixed" by the sentence's subject. His own use of propositions will be marked by the fluidity or "plasticity," rather than a fixity, of form: Meaning will be found not *in* the assertion but beyond it, since the proposition must be read as pointing past the confines of its own utterance to what is not explicitly (directly) said, to the "restless," dialectical, dynamic movement of meaning in time. Hegel's experimentation with the speculative proposition is notoriously complex and difficult,[23] but what is important to see is that *it is inherently a practice of indirect communication*. As Judith Butler puts it, Hegel's text "does not address his reader directly; . . . the narrative strategy of the *Phenomenology* is to implicate the reader indirectly. . . . We ourselves are invited on stage, . . . [so that] at the close of the *Phenomenology,* the philosopher is no longer 'Other' to ourselves, for that distinction would announce an 'outside,'" which is precisely what Hegel seeks to preclude by his style of authorship.[24] Direct communication, the language of the assertion, is always in its very nature a dissemblance of reality for Hegel. The new grammar of the speculative proposition radically complicates the relation of subject and predicate, replacing or "destroying" the logic of "containment" of the predicates in the subject with a semantics that requires the reader to "go back to the proposition and understand it in some other way" (*PS* 36–40).

In a diary entry titled "Speaking in Tongues," Kierkegaard speaks of Christianity's having "its own language," "different from all human language": It "uses the same words we men use, but its use of them is qualitatively different from our use of them" (*JP* 3:2333). To apprehend the language of the Bible authentically thus requires us to suspend our usual way of reading. Hegel has a very similar view of the challenge of reading the "speculative proposition." Since, after all, "it *is* a proposition"—it doesn't look any different from ordinary propositions—we are led "to believe that the usual subject-predicate relation obtains." On learning by the experience of (careful) reading that the proposition "meant something other than we meant [it] to mean"—that the text, we might say, is speaking in tongues—the reader may well complain that "so much has to be read over and over before it can be understood, a complaint whose burden is presumed to be quite outrageous, and, if justified, to admit of no defense" (*PS* 39). Some ten years earlier, in the *Spirit of Christianity* (1798), Hegel remarked that we cannot read such sentences as those found at the opening of the Gospel of John ("In the beginning was the Logos," "the Logos was with God," . . .) according to an ordinary grammar. For it is impossible "to assimilate passively" the meaning of such propositions, and "language hence attains sense and weight only in the spirit of the reader," who attends beyond the deceptively ordinary form of the propositions (*SC* 246).[25] Thus for Hegel, like Kierkegaard, Christianity has its own language, an indirect communication, and Hegel no less than Kierkegaard modeled his own style of authorship on the ethics of indirection implied by what it means to read scripture: Their texts will abandon the authority of assertion for a "plasticity" of form in which meaning appears only when the reader abandons her passivity and makes it her own.

HOMECOMING

Both Hegel and Kierkegaard clearly place a considerable burden on their readers. In each case, the intention is to confound the paternalistic role of the author as "ministering" to the reader, to problematize any "passive assimilation" of the meaning of the text, and to provoke the reader to self-reliance. And both pursue this task by exploring new forms of communication that employ indirection to disorient the reader's common habits of understanding.

But there remains a significant difference, a difference grounded in Hegel's and Kierkegaard's opposed sentiments about language. Hegel's celebratory response to language's function of expression (externalization) leads to an ethics of authorship that never relinquishes the idea of shared meanings. This is the import of Hegel's praise of the Pythagorean practice of silence—not, as Kierkegaard would see it, that Hegel is seeking to discipline the self to obedience. Silence allows us to see that purely "subjective opinions" are worth "nothing" *insofar* as they are entirely private. The right sort of practice of silence, not one that closes the self in on itself but one that cultivates the virtue of listening, directs us toward the other and hence toward the possibility of shared experience. Kierkegaard's lamentation over language's abandonment of subjectivity—its stranding of the single individual in the wretched ordinariness of the public world ("the crowd")—leads to an ethics that seeks to navigate a voyage back to the interior and the domain of private meanings.

Hegel believes that the commonsense hypothesis of an external world that is entirely "other" from the internal world of consciousness is an attitude that ultimately cuts us off from others and condemns human consciousness to a state of homelessness. "The aim of knowledge," Hegel claims, "is to divest the objective [external] world that stands opposed to us of its strangeness, and, as the phrase is, to find ourselves at home in it" (*EL* §194Z). And it is language that brings us home. However great the burden Hegel places on his reader by demanding a fundamentally new relation to language—one that both "destroys" the fixity of meanings of ordinary language and authorizes the reader's self-authorship of the text—he is convinced that language brings us to a shared space of meaning. "The I that utters itself is heard," and thus has "passed into unity with those for whom it is now *there* [*für welche es* da *ist*]" (*PS* 309/*W* 3:376). This unity is hardly the caricature of an "objective truth" that Kierkegaard's straw man of Hegel portrays. There is no such thing as One Truth for Hegel; truth is always in motion, always historical, and always negotiated through social struggle. Moreover, crucially, truth embraces difference. But difference for Hegel is not private, as it is for Kierkegaard. Hegel in fact explores the attitude of privacy in many places (for example, in his accounts of the "I am I," of the stoic, the skeptic, the law of the heart, and the beautiful soul), and seeks to show that such an attitude cannot say what it means, or better, that the stance of "privacy" is itself a linguistically and therefore socially constructed phenomenon.

For Kierkegaard, however, language exiles us from our true home, the space of sheer interiority. "The real *is* inwardness," Johannes Climacus writes (*CUP* 289), and we have seen that it is precisely language, "the word," that "annuls" this reality for Kierkegaard. Language makes us homeless, and Kierkegaard longs for a way to protect his "private personality," which is his true home, his "inner sanctum," "just as the entrance to a house is barred by stationing two soldiers with crossed bayonets" (*TA* 99). Thus if Hegel's home is the shared dwelling made possible by language, Kierkegaard's home bars entry to others so as to protect what we might say is his private property. Fences make the best neighbors, or, to cite Victor Eremita in his introduction to *Either/Or,* it is crucial always to have a screen between the speaker and the reader, just as the "priest is separated from the penitent by a screen," so that neither can see the other (*E/ Or* 1:3–4). The very possibility of an authorship, let alone an ethical authorship, thus becomes a much greater challenge for Kierkegaard than for Hegel. Indeed, since Kierkegaard is passionately convinced that "the only question of reality that is ethically pertinent is the question of one's own reality" (*CUP* 287), there is a final darkness, a permanent eclipse between I and Thou that no authorship could dissipate. However successful Kierkegaard may be, then, in provoking the reader to explore her own private interior through his methods of indirect communication, both he himself and the reader can only always vanish into the darkness that separates them from each other.

We have seen that Kierkegaard views the Hegelian author as "a fantastic creature who moves in the pure being of abstract thought." From Hegel's perspective, though, it is precisely the Kierkegaardian author who fantastically "vanishes like a shapeless vapor that dissolves into thin air," as he writes of the inwardly trapped beautiful soul (*PS* 403). In one of his darker moments of self-reflection, Kierkegaard seems to have posed this possibility to himself.

> For many years my melancholy has had the effect of preventing me from saying "Thou" to myself, from being on intimate terms with myself in the deepest sense. Between my melancholy and my intimate "Thou" there lay a whole world of fantasy. This world it is that I have partly exhausted in my pseudonyms. Just like a person who hasn't a happy home spends as much time away from it as possible and would prefer to be rid of it, so my melancholy has kept me away from my own self while I, making discoveries and poetical experiences, traveled through a world of fantasy. (*JSK* 641)

It is possible, of course, that both Hegel and Kierkegaard are fantastic authors, in different ways. Perhaps their dizzying experimentation with new forms of communication leads only to dizziness. It is, as Kierkegaard says, "left to the reader himself to put two and two together, if he so desires"—or if he can. But one thing I hope has been made clear, that the debate between these two experimentalists will be made more meaningful just to the extent that we reject Kierkegaard's framing of the relationship in terms of a stark opposition between an indirect (and therefore ethical) authorship and a direct (and therefore nonethical) authorship. This would entail the challenging task of reencountering Hegel's texts as readers who no longer hear his voice as booming to us through a megaphone and attuning our ears to the more muted and ambiguous tones that are produced by a style of indirection. Even after such a reencounter, there would remain plenty of areas of difference between the two authors—the contests over the meaning of the religious, the value of inwardness, and the significance of the Other would hardly be effaced, but they would be displaced and made more complex when we see them as occurring within a shared commitment to an ethics of authorship that is devoted to indirection.

2. Live or Tell

But you have to choose: live or tell.

JEAN-PAUL SARTRE, *Nausea*

KIERKEGAARD MOST OFTEN represents his difference from Hegel in terms of the contrast between action and thinking about action, existing and contemplating existence, living and philosophizing about living. "In the objective sense," Kierkegaard's pseudonym Johannes Climacus writes, "thought is understood as being pure thought, . . . [which] has no relation to the existing subject; and while [it is difficult to know] how the existing subject slips into this . . . pure abstraction, . . . it is certain that the existing subjectivity tends more and more to evaporate" (*CUP* 112).

Crucial to Kierkegaard's depiction of this contrast between action and thinking is his conception of the nature of language. Kierkegaard portrays himself as speaking (writing) in order to act: "To be an author is to act" (*JP* 1:637). Hegel, however, is presented as writing so as to merely speak about acting; hence Hegel is a "mere scribbler" and his philosophy occurs "only on paper" (*CUP* 176, 375–76). One of the ways Kierkegaard understands his contest with Hegel anticipates the ultimatum of Roquentin, the tormented diarist of Jean-Paul Sartre's novella *Nausea,* who says, "You have to choose: live or tell."[1] Roquentin is doubly cursed, first by a need to write so as to escape his sense of the nausea of existence by distancing himself from the cloying taste of reality; but second, by a recognition that his writing removes him from the possibility of truly existing. His ultimatum, "live or tell," is the constant reminder he carries with him of his inability to reconcile his fear of existence and his self-disgust at his escapism.

The contrast between action and thinking entails a fundamental question about the ethics of authorship: How is one to use words, to write, in such a way as to act—and to elicit action from one's reader? I suggest that a readjustment of the alignment of the kaleidoscope lenses that display the image of Kierkegaard's relation to Hegel allows for a more rewarding dialogue between the two. In the altered image, there is as much telling as living in Kierkegaard as in Hegel (indeed, as we will see, in some respects more), and as much a choice for living in Hegel as in Kierkegaard. Perhaps most important, this reorientation invites us to see the either/or construction of "living or telling" as a false dilemma. As Roquentin (perhaps!) discovers as *Nausea* reaches its enigmatic denouement, it is worth committing oneself to the idea that there is a way of writing in which existence becomes meaningful.

Although Hegel falls far short of the almost obsessive project of meta-authorial reflection that Kierkegaard engages in, there are indications to be found in Hegel's style of authorship that he too writes not in order to lure others to become like Hamlet, of whom Hegel writes that he "persists in the inactivity of a beautiful inner soul which cannot make itself actual or engage in the relationships of his present world" (*A* 1:584, and see *A* 2:1225–26), but, on the contrary, in order to bring the reader to a transformation of the self by which existence is made more than "a mere matter of words" (*PS* 403).

The Aerial Simulacra of Things, or the Police Frisk

Hegel haunts Kierkegaard's authorship like a phantom, at once comical, like Aristophanes' philosopher who hovers in cloudlike and misty imperturbability above reality, and as a figure of danger, a specter haunting the age. The conceit of the Hegelian philosophy, according to Kierkegaard's narrative, is that it discovers the long sought after elixir of objective truth. Objective truth is a magical truth that transcends the chaos of merely subjective perspectives and the endless multiplicity (what Hegel dismisses as the "bad infinite") of individual human circumstance. Difference—uniqueness, particularity, subjectivity—is thus overcome, *aufgehoben,* by sameness, by universality, totality, and objectivity. The alchemy Hegel uses to achieve this standpoint is a method of abstraction from the "merely" particular, and hence false, aspect of individual existence, so that a space is opened from which existence may be observed sub specie aeternitatis, without the distracting inconvenience of subjective standpoints (*CUP* 270–74).

All this is a bold and ingenious project, Kierkegaard admits tongue in cheek, and Hegel nearly carries it off with brilliance: "If Hegel had written his whole [philosophy] and written in the preface that it was only a thought experiment, in which at many points he still steered clear of some things, he undoubtedly would have been the greatest thinker who has ever lived. As it is he is comic" (*JP* 2:1605; and see *CD* 12n). Whether brilliant or comical (or both), Hegel strikes a devil's bargain: He seeks to purchase objective truth and Absolute Knowledge at the expense of existence. Actual human beings are not abstractions but are nailed to their own particularity and consigned to subjectivity. Hegel "proudly deserts existence, leaving the rest of us to face the worst" (*CUP* 267). There is thus a sort of extraterrestrialism to the Hegelian system, which promises an "emancipat[ion] from telluric conditions, a privilege reserved for winged creatures, and perhaps also shared by the inhabitants of the moon—and there perhaps the System will first find its true readers" (*CUP* 113).

However amusing the picture of Hegel soaring in outer space, giddily unencumbered by the gravitational force of the earth, there are serious ethical consequences to his lunar philosophy. Hegel's promise of absolute knowledge is irresistibly seductive in an age already weary of itself and longing for anything that might make the burden of existence easier to bear (*CUP* 216, 228–29). His philosophy assures us that we need not go to the trouble of actually living in such a way as to bring truth about but must only think in the appropriately abstract way. For Kierkegaard, though, truth is not in fact a property of thought at all, since for finite human beings objective truth always founders in the gap of separation between consciousness and its world, between the inevitably subjective character of thought and the reality it seeks to know but that is always out there, beyond us, unreachable (*CUP* 169ff.). As Vigilius Haufniensis, the pseudony-mous author of the *Concept of Dread,* puts it, "Truth exists for the individual only as produced in action" (*CD* 123). Whatever our per-sonal understanding of reality may be in a given situation—and un-derstanding is always personal and situational for Kierkegaard—for this understanding to become a truth we must live it, not merely think it or tell it: "If a man does not become what he understands, then he does not understand it either" (*JP* 4:4540).

One of Kierkegaard's favorite scriptures is from the apostle James, who implores us:

> Be doers of the word, and not hearers only, deceiving yourselves. For if any one is a hearer of the word and not a doer, he is like a man who observes his natural face in a mirror; for he observes himself and goes away and at once forgets what he was like. (James 1:22–25; see Kierkegaard, *ED* 2:84–85)

The contrast between thinking and living, or understanding and doing, is equally, as the apostle James suggests, a contrast between words and action. Kierkegaard sees Hegelianism as inextricably bound up with words, with speaking about what for Kierkegaard must be lived. "One thing continually escapes Hegel—what it is to live: he knows only how to make a facsimile of life" (*JP* 2:1611). The point is not, of course, that Hegel's strategy of abstracting his way to objective truth is enacted through his writing—Kierkegaard too is an author, after all—but that truth becomes a property of *propositions* rather than existence. As Stephen Crites puts it, "The point of [Kierkegaard's] much-misunderstood slogan [that] 'truth is subjec-tivity' . . . is simply that an existential truth has a conscious human temporality for its medium and not propositions."[2]

In his autobiographical novel *Les Mots* (*The Words*), Sartre speaks of how "I began my life as I shall no doubt end it: amidst books." He relates how he "found the human heart . . . insipid and hollow, except in books," and how he would take his books to the roof of his grandfather's apartment, "the roof of the world, the sixth floor, . . . [where] the Universe would rise in tiers at my feet and all things would humbly beg for a name; to name the thing was both to create and take it." Words became "the quintessence of things," so that "in Platonic fashion, I went from knowledge to its subject. I found more reality in the idea than in the thing . . . [and] it was in books that I encountered the universe." Finally, language became the substitute for existence, and life was a matter of words: "I wanted to live in the ether among the aerial simulacra of things."[3]

The image Sartre presents of his youth is precisely the lens of the kaleidoscope through which Kierkegaard views Hegelian philosophy. Hegel's extraterrestrialism, his flight through the zero-gravity atmosphere of abstraction, is made possible through the displacement of the weight of existence by the ethereality of pure thought and the lightness of words. Reality is exchanged for its simulacrum, propositions about reality, which weigh no more than the gossamer sheets of paper they are written on. "Nowadays existence is even produced on paper," Kierkegaard's Johannes Climacus laments, and the Hegelian philosophy is nothing but a well-oiled "paragraph machine" (CUP 376, 224). The great deception of the Hegelian philosophy, Kierkegaard writes in a journal entry, is that "the powers of the human world have been fantastically extracted and a book world has been produced" (JP 1:649). In another journal entry, Kierkegaard fantasizes about a strip search of Hegel.

> The police thoroughly frisk suspicious persons. If the mobs of speakers, teachers, professors etc. were to be thoroughly frisked in the same way, it would no doubt become a complicated criminal affair. To give them a thorough frisking—yes, to strip them of the clothing, the changes of clothing, and the disguises of language, to frisk them by ordering them to be silent, saying: "Shut up, and let us see what your life expresses, for once let this [your life] be the speaker who says who you are." (JP 3:2334)

Kierkegaard's authorship is just such a police frisk of Hegel, a disrobing of his disguise of words and an exposure of the guilt of his philosophy, that once all the grand talk of "existence" and "truth" and "knowledge" is unclothed, the reader is left with no sense of how to actually exist, for the truths of the System are unlivable fantasies.

TURNING THE KALEIDOSCOPE

We have now seen the kaleidoscopic image of the Hegel-Kierke-
gaard relation as it looks when the inkblot of Kierkegaard's Hegel
is inserted into the lens and aligned with Kierkegaard's presentation
of his own likeness. It is now time to explore a quite different
response to the Rorschach test of the two inkblots of Hegel and
Kierkegaard and to turn the kaleidoscope to view an image that
problematizes the simple dichotomy we have seen so far of "live or
tell."

It is child's play to find as many passages in Hegel's texts as we
could possibly wish for that seem to support Kierkegaard's reading
of him, and there are too many very smart commentators to cite who
share at least much of Kierkegaard's suspicions about the Hegelian
philosophy's tendency toward abstraction, objectivism, and apparent
abandonment of the uniqueness of individual human beings (we will
encounter several of these commentators in Chapter 7). Yet the evidence brought in support of such suspicions should be considered in
the context of an alternative reading of Hegel that is supported by a
very considerable body of counterevidence. What's more, as the
shape of Hegel changes according to this alternative reading, so too
does the shape of Kierkegaard, at the very least because Kierkegaard's identity as a writer is so enmeshed with his relation to Hegel,
his other.

Odd though it may seem, the first step toward this counterreading
of Hegel is to admit that there is an undeniable sense in which
Kierkegaard's portrayal of him as sacrificing the particular individual is entirely correct. The very first shape (*Gestalt*) of self-consciousness Hegel considers in his *Phenomenology* is precisely that of the
particular individual, the inwardly absorbed "I am I" (*PS* 104–5).
Here indeed, "truth is subjectivity," in the sense that the self has
despaired of finding truth outside itself, or more precisely, in any
correspondence between its sensations, perceptions, or understanding
of the world and the external world itself.[4] Its response is to withdraw into itself and to seek truth in its own subjectivity: "The existence of the world becomes for self-consciousness its own truth" (*PS*
140). Hegel seeks to demonstrate, however, that this stance is forever

doomed to collapse: The self can never be its own foundation, can never supply a content for itself without the mediation of an other. The inwardly turned self, we might say, is turned inside out, and Hegel names the agency of this transformation *desire*. "Self-consciousness *is* desire," which is a sign of our own lack and need for an other (*PS* 109).

So yes, the solitary, unique, particular self is indeed forsaken by Hegel, or rather is shown to be forced to forsake itself, since it is destabilized by its desire. And this forsakenness is a recurring movement throughout the *Phenomenology*. The enormous difficulty of satisfying the desire for unity with others continually tempts the self to retreat back into itself in a nostalgic effort to regain its mythic position of self-sufficiency—much, perhaps, as Freud sees ego development to consist of an initial break from the individual's "primary narcissism," the primal scene of inwardly directed libido, and a subsequent lifelong "vigorous attempt to recover that state."[5] Hegel speaks of the infant's scream as the first primordial expression of a recurring human paradox: On the one hand, the demand for the satisfaction of desire that is essentially narcissistic—"the independence of the outer world is non-existent" for the child—and yet on the other hand, the essential dependence of the self on the other that is revealed by this demand (*PM* §396Z). The primordial scream is the recognition of the self's fundamental insufficiency: The self *is* lack.

Hegel seeks to show that each strategy of withdrawal into the self is destined to disintegrate. The nostalgic and regressive desire for perfect self-reliance is continually unsettled by the hollowness of the solitary self and a counterdesire for the other.[6] Hence, to cite just one example, the stance of the stoic, who retreats from the world in which he feels forsaken and not-at-home, who seeks a wholly inward peace and freedom—"I am not in an other but remain simply and solely in communion with myself" (*PS* 120)—points beyond itself precisely because its self-communion, a thought-thinking-itself, is impotent. "What count[s] for [the stoic is] merely the form of thought as such" (*PS* 321), but freedom in "thought alone" is a "truth lacking the fullness of life" (*PS* 122).

Here we see that the dichotomy Kierkegaard uses to reveal his basic difference from Hegel is radically complicated, indeed inverted: Live or tell; act or merely think about action. For Hegel, thought without action, without "the fullness of life," is utterly empty, an inchoate language, and results from a sort of desperate nostalgia for self-sufficiency—a nostalgia that, it seems worth noting, calls to mind Kierkegaard's devotion to "the passion of inwardness" (e.g., *CUP* 177–82). Prior to action, thought is a mere intention, a private meaning, an interior lacking any exterior, and is what Hegel sometimes calls the self's "innocence." But the ontology of innocence is not a human ontology, for we must act in order to become human: "Innocence, therefore, is merely non-action, like the mere being of a stone, not even that of a child." Action is our guilt: "By the deed, . . . [the self] becomes guilt" (*PS* 282). Note well: Hegel does not say that the self becomes *guilty,* but that it becomes *guilt* (*Es wird durch die Tat zur* Schuld) (*W* 3:346). As creatures who act, we *are* guilt in our very being, responsible and culpable for bringing the merely inner and private nature of our thought into the world, where what we say and do inevitably comes into conflict with the intentions and values of others (*PS* 282).

Hegel's ontologizing of guilt—his insistence that guilt constitutes us in our very being—anticipates Heidegger's account of guilt in *Being and Time.* Human being, or *Dasein,* to use Heidegger's terminology, is "guilty in the very basis of [its] being."[7] Guilt is thus prior to any particular "guilty act." In fact, for Heidegger (as for Hegel), guilt must be "detached from relationship to any law or 'ought' such that by failing to comply with it one loads himself with guilt." The guilt that *Dasein* is has nothing to do with "having debts," with "owing something to an Other," or with a "breach of moral requirement." It does not fall within an economy of exchange: We must not "thrust [guilt] aside into the domain of . . . reckoning up claims and balancing them off."[8]

But there is an important difference of emphasis between Hegel and Heidegger on the nature of guilt. We *are* guilt for Heidegger because in our being we are "the basis of a nullity" (or nothingness: *nichtigkeit*). That is, *Dasein* "never has power over [its] ownmost being" because it is a transcendence, a projection of itself toward its future, which it is not: "*Dasein* constantly lags behind its possibilities."[9] Hegel, in contrast, although fully agreeing that *Dasein* is a transcendence, locates the specific nature of guilt in the *abandonment of interiority* that is the inevitable consequence of our being agents. By acting, we come out of ourselves, as it were; we lose the purity of simply coinciding with the self. But since we *are* the sum of our actions, we are always already outside of ourselves, and such purity is only a yearning; we are inherently "impure," guilty.

For Hegel, action is intrinsically tragic: The deed "calls forth" its "opposite"—the equally heartfelt "pathos" of an other who holds a different value or ideal—"calls it forth as violated" (*PS* 283). What is intended in action, the expression of the individual's own "pathos," reveals its one-sidedness and the justice of its opposite. Thus Sophocles' Hyllus explains his mother Deianira's crime to his skeptical father Heracles: "In all that she did wrong she had intended good" (*Women of Trachis* l. 1136). And the chorus of Euripides' *Orestes* expresses its bewilderment at the double meaning of the characters' deeds, and the inverted world they beget: "Just the act, crime unjust./ Right and wrong confounded/in a single act. . . . And what had seemed so right,/as soon as done, became /evil, monstrous, wrong" (*Orestes* ll. 193, 818). Agamemnon's act calls forth the furies of his slain daughter; Clytaemestra's justice evokes the justice of her son; Orestes' honor is converted into shame by "the Furies arising from his deed" (*A* 1:278); Creon and Antigone are equally one-sided, and their deeds elicit the mutual destruction of each other; and Oedipus' insistence on his own lucidity can only temporarily conceal the power of the opposite, the darkness of the unconscious, which, when revealed, unhinges him.

And we are all Agamemnon and Clytaemestra, Creon and Antigone, Oedipus and Deianira. To act is to be guilty because we do not live in the world alone; we are among others, and thus we are beings whose actions will be a violation of others. Although Heidegger, like Hegel, sees *Dasein*'s guilt as situated in our being-in-the-world-with-others, what is distinctive for Heidegger is that our guilt, if authentically encountered, brings us to ourselves as individuals *cut off from others*. Guilt "is more authentic the more *non-relationally Dasein* understands" it, and the more *Dasein* becomes radically "individualized."[10] Indeed, for Heidegger, "*Dasein* can be authentically itself only if . . . it [recognizes] that all . . . being-with-others will fail us when our ownmost potentiality-for-being is the issue," for this authentic self "must be taken over by *Dasein* alone."[11]

True, *Dasein* is never actually alone for Heidegger. Although authentic *Dasein* is disclosed as *"solus ipse"*—being alone—

> this existential "solipsism" is so far from the displacement of putting an isolated subject-Thing into the emptiness of a worldless occurring, that in an extreme sense what it does is precisely to bring *Dasein* face to face with its world as world, and thus bring it face to face with itself as being-in-the-world.[12]

Yet the world authentic *Dasein* is brought face to face with is for Heidegger "for the most part" a world of "inconspicuous domination" by "the They," of subjection to "publicness," of the "leveling down of everyone to the same averageness," where *Dasein* is "disburdened" of responsibility and "everyone is the other, and no one is himself"[13]—a world identical to the one Kierkegaard describes in *The Present Age* in speaking of "the individual" and "the public." Thus although *Dasein* is in its very essence "thrown" and "fallen" into a world-with-others, it is a world that "noiselessly suppresses . . . all possibilities" of authentic being,[14] which explains Heidegger's (and Kierkegaard's) turn to "non-relationality" as the necessary passageway to genuine selfhood.

Heidegger's account of guilt is thus framed within a conception of authenticity that is strongly reminiscent of Kierkegaard's valorizing of aloneness and the "passion of inwardness." And it is just Hegel's alternative emphasis on guilt as intrinsically *inter*subjective that makes his theory of action important for our consideration of his relation to Kierkegaard. For Hegel, we are guilty not because we "lag behind our possibilities," the self's projection of its "ownmost" being, as Heidegger puts it, but because our "ownmost" possibilities become real only through an abandonment of interiority in action, where we are constituted in part by others.

So Kierkegaard is correct: The very nature of action for Hegel entails the loss of the pure inwardness of the self—a negation of particularity—by bringing the self into relation with others, and hence into the space of a public domain of meaning. But to call this an abstraction away from "the self" is to beg the question. For Hegel, the self is not in its essence a particularity, and it is precisely the inwardly absorbed particular self, the "I am I," or the radically "individualized" self of Heidegger, which is abstract, because hollow, without the substance of experience that emerges only through the encounter with others. The desire for the other that unsettles the solipsistically enclosed I moves Hegelian philosophy into its exploration of a social construction of the self, where meaning ceases to be private but is rather contested and negotiated in the interaction between selves.

Kierkegaard's maxim that "truth is subjectivity" appears to decline all such negotiation. Indeed, "with respect to every reality external to myself," Johannes Climacus informs his reader (who is, ironically, presumably a reality external to himself), "I can get hold of it only through [imagining] it. In order to get hold of it really, I would have to make myself into the other . . . and make the foreign reality my own, which is impossible" (*CUP* 285). Hegel's alternative to the motto that "truth is subjectivity"—his allegiance to "objective truth," which Kierkegaard finds so fantastic—is emphatically not a claim about truth being a transcendent, timeless abstraction. One of the great heresies of Hegel's philosophy is that all truth is temporal, historical, a "movement," and a "restlessness" (see, e.g., *HP* 1:9, 25, 27, 33; *HP* 2:49; *PS* 27). In a profound sense, Hegel's belief in the "objectivity" of truth is first of all simply a commitment to the inherently interrelational and social—and in this sense, nonsubjective—character of truth.

In his own recognition of the difficulty of reaching the "foreign reality" of the other, Kierkegaard tends to let go of the other as an essential component of self-identity. The sacrifice of his relation to his fiancée, Regine Olsen, is only the most glaring biographical sign of this performance of renunciation, but it is inscribed thoroughly in the exposition of his ethics, whose principles include these:

"There is only one kind of ethical contemplation, namely, self-contemplation. Ethics closes immediately about the individual."

"The ethical is concerned with particular human beings, and with
   each and every one of them by himself."

"One human being cannot judge another ethically, because he cannot understand him except as a possibility."

"Each individual is isolated and compelled to exist for himself."

"It is unethical even to ask at all about another person's ethical
   inwardness."

"To be concerned ethically about another's reality is . . . a
   misunderstanding."

"The ethical reality of the individual is the only reality." (*CUP* 284,
   286, 287, 291)

It is true that Kierkegaard still retains a place for the other, but
as Emmanuel Levinas suggests, he tends to short-circuit his need for
the human other by displacing it onto a desire for God.[15] "I perfectly
understand myself in being a lonely man," Kierkegaard confides in
his journals, "without relation to anything, . . . with only one consolation, God who is love" (*JSK* 738). The journals are filled with the
ideal of "dying to the world, in order to be able to love God" (*JP*
1:538, 1006; and see *TC* 152).

Hegel sees (at least at times)[16] the redirection of the object of desire
onto God as the mark of the "unhappy consciousness" (*unglückliches
Bewußtsein*) that despairs of ever achieving unity with the other in
the social sphere of human intersubjectivity and that projects its desire onto a Beyond (*PS* 126–38). If for Kierkegaard "to love God is
the only happy love" (*JP* 2:1353), the love of God for Hegel—insofar
as it is a yearning for unity with a Being who is conceived to be
always beyond the horizon of our earthly lives—is the deepest despair, the "grief and longing of the unhappy consciousness" (*PS* 436).
For Hegel, the displacement of desire onto the relation to a Beyond
does not eradicate the desire for the human other, but only represses
and therefore intensifies it by further deepening our introversion and
thus our feeling of estrangement from the human community, which
for Hegel is the space in which we are destined to discover our
humanity. From a Hegelian perspective, it is not at all surprising
that Kierkegaard lists as reasons for his own "great need" of
faith—in addition to his sufferings and his sins—"my terrible introversion" (*JSK* 1056).

Hegel explores a gesture of sacrifice different from the one Kierkegaard explores, not the sacrifice of the relation to the other—of Isaac, one might say, keeping in mind Johannes de Silentio's reading of Abraham's sacrifice of Isaac as a "teleological suspension" of the ethical relation to the other (*FT* 64–77)—but the sacrifice of our particularity, our solipsism. Hegel's whole philosophy is centered on the need to move from the standpoint of "I" to that of "we," which requires a submission of the I to sacrifice, renunciation, and surrender (*Aufopferung, Verzicht, Aufgabe*) (*PS* 136–39, 212–13/*W* 3:175–78, 265). There is nothing blithe about Hegel's account of this sacrifice, which commits the self to a *via dolorosa,* precisely because there is no idyllic union with the other, no crystalline relation of I to Thou, no utopian achievement of community, and no tranquil state of meditation on "objective truth." Yet it is just in the pain of recognizing the incompleteness and insufficiency of our particularity, the pain given voice in our first act, our scream, that we first encounter our humanity.

To be human is to be incomplete, and to seek our selves in our being-with-others, like the creatures depicted by Aristophanes who are a mythological original unity with an other but cut in two by a jealous god, destined to a lifelong search for selfhood in a reunion with the other. The alternative, the position of subjectivity, is for Hegel a life cut in half, where we appeal "to an oracle within [our] breast," thus "trampl[ing] underfoot the roots of humanity, for . . . human nature only really exists in an achieved community." The implications of an ethics based on an oracle within the breast for the project of an authorship are equally troubling, if we accept Hegel's logic. Such an ethics entails that we are "finished and done with anyone who does not agree" with our subjective truth: We "only have to explain that [we] [have] nothing more to say to anyone who does not find and feel the same in himself" (*PS* 43).

But surely something is awry with this logic, for it hardly seems plausible so easily to dismiss Kierkegaard's prodigious authorship as having "nothing to say" to anyone who does not already agree. Moreover, Kierkegaard's authorship is not *l'art pour l'art,* meant for the sake of self-amusement or of dazzling and charming his readers—even if Kierkegaard suspected that this was precisely the effect it had on many of his fellow citizens of Copenhagen, who, if they read his works at all, never got much beyond a feeling of titillation at the sheer eccentricity of his pseudonymous authors. Rather, it is meant to be exactly what Hegel seems to think is excluded by the position of subjectivity, an authorship dedicated to "the art of helping others" (*PV* 27), a maieutic authorship.

GETTING BACK TO THE RUE LE GOFF

If Kierkegaard's Hegel tells without living, by producing a "book world" in which existence becomes a sheer fantasy, then Hegel's philosophy would seem to consign Kierkegaard to the situation of one who lives without telling—one who exists in his private sanctuary of subjectivity, communing with the oracle within his breast, without having anything to say to others, who are unreachable in their own sanctuaries. But both images are suspect. The refocused lens we have just used to reconsider Hegel suggests that his "objectivism" does not negate existence but calls us to action. As for Kierkegaard, the critique of his "subjectivism" that has emerged in the last few pages seems to run afoul of the fact that the most distinctive act of Kierkegaard's life was without doubt his telling, his authorship: "This work of mine as an author was the prompting of an irresistible inward impulse, a melancholy man's only possibility," he writes in his *Point of View for My Work as an Author* (*PV* 7). More bluntly, he acknowledges in a journal entry that "to produce was my life" (*P* X2 A 442).[17]

Thus we need yet another angle of vision from which to recalibrate the kaleidoscopic images of Hegel and Kierkegaard. And it is especially the image of Kierkegaard that needs refocusing. Our reconsideration of Hegel has afforded us a way of seeing him that might, should we choose, free us from being bound to the comical image he inhabits in Kierkegaard's texts. But Kierkegaard still presents us with a significant problem. One way to pose this problem is in terms of an apparent hypocrisy. Hegel, Kierkegaard says, produces only a book world and forgets what it means to exist, whereas Kierkegaard himself "remains silent and acts" (*JP* 1:646). Yet as Stephen Crites points out, Kierkegaard "spent most of the hours and days of [his life] applying ink to paper, . . . liv[ing] in his thoughts, thus exemplifying in highest degree the 'age of reflection,' " the age of telling, we might say, that he attacked.[18] For our purposes, though, the problem is really this: How is Kierkegaard's authorship possible at all, given the apparently impassable gulf of separation between the author and the reader, two subjectivities "assigned to themselves"? This is hardly an idle question, given that Kierkegaard himself asserts that "existential reality is incommunicable" (*CUP* 320). Whether or not we are persuaded by Hegel's call for the sacrifice of particularity (the position of "I am I") as the necessary condition for community, at the very least we can see how his philosophy embraces an intersubjectivity that makes such community possible, and thus also makes the relation between an author and a reader possible. It is still not at all clear, however, how to understand the ethics of Kierkegaard's own authorship, given his stance that ethically the other is not reachable.

At the risk of complicating the kaleidoscopic experiments yet further, I propose to introduce one more inkblot for examination, that of Jean-Paul Sartre, who has already appeared tangentially in my consideration of Kierkegaard's depiction of Hegel's purported abstractionism. We saw that Sartre's account of his youth, where words became "the quintessence of things" and he "wanted to live in the ether among the aerial simulacra of things," uncannily mirrored Kierkegaard's representation of Hegel's supposed extraterrestrialism. Sartre is in fact a particularly interesting figure to dwell on, since his inkblot turns out to be such a shifting and ambiguous image. The Sartre of *Les Mots,* and, as we shall see, of *Nausea,* appears to resemble very closely the inkblot of Kierkegaard's Hegel. Both the young Sartre of *Les Mots* and Roquentin, the diarist of *Nausea,* are seduced by words at the expense of living, and Sartre's implicit critique of this seduction, both as autobiographer of his youth (*Les Mots*) and as author behind the author of *Nausea,* echoes Kierkegaard's critique of Hegel's seduction by the phantasms of abstraction. But with a shift of focus, the images of the young Sartre and Roquentin begin to look more like Kierkegaard himself, the man whose life, like Roquentin's, is devoted to putting ink on paper.

Antoine Roquentin, the diarist of *Nausea,* has been taken over by a strange illness. Everything he perceives—stones, people's faces, tables, trees, his own hand—seems disturbingly altered, more opaque, alien, threatening, repulsive, grotesque. Stranger still, he is not sure whether the illness resides in himself or in the objects he perceives. He determines to seek a cure by "writing down events from day to day," to "keep a diary to see clearly—to let none of the nuances or small happenings escape."[19] The diary is to be his writing-cure. By allowing him to see more clearly than through direct experience itself, he will come to know his illness and thus be in a position to master it. But from the start, Roquentin is confused about whether his written record of events is helping. Maybe all these words are creating a false reality, and his sought-after cure is only a story he is telling himself: "This is what I thought: . . . a man is always a teller of tales, he lives surrounded by his stories . . . , he sees everything that happens to him through them; and he tries to live his own life as if he were telling a story."[20]

Immediately following this thought—so reminiscent of Kierkegaard's description of how the Hegelian philosophy tempts us away from life to the mere simulacra of life "on paper"—comes the "live or tell" diary entry. Roquentin is recalling a time in Hamburg, with a girl named Erna.

But you have to choose: live or tell. For example, when I was in Hamburg, . . . one evening, in a little café in San Pauli, [Erna] left me to go to the ladies' room. I stayed alone, there was a phonograph playing "Blue Skies." I began to tell myself what had happened since I landed. I told myself, "The third evening, as I was going into a dance hall called *La Grotte Bleue,* I noticed a large woman, half seas over. And that woman is the one I am waiting for now, listening to 'Blue Skies,' the woman who is going to come back and sit down at my right and put her arms around my neck." Then I felt violently that I was having an adventure. But Erna came back and sat down beside me, she wound her arms around my neck and I hated her without knowing why. I understand now: one had to begin living again and the adventure was fading out.[21]

The sense of adventure was fading out for Roquentin: Life had intruded upon the words of the story whose telling had transformed a desultory episode of life into something worth experiencing in the imagination. But notice that Sartre complicates Roquentin's diary entry of his episode at the San Pauli café by suggesting a certain tone of regret, or remorse, or self-admonition. It is as though Roquentin finds himself caught out: He had been surrounding himself merely with stories, and he had to begin living again. Erna's return, her arms around Roquentin's neck, were like the police frisk Kierkegaard would like to subject Hegel to, stripping him of his words and commanding, "Shut up! and let us see what your life expresses." In a self-recriminating entry from the day before the "live or tell" passage, Roquentin had written that "nothing is left but words: I could still tell stories, tell them too well, . . . but it isn't I [who appears in my stories], I have nothing in common with him. . . . My words are dreams, that is all."[22] Similarly, there are signs of self-accusation on Sartre's part in *Les Mots* about his self-entrapment in a world of words: "I was afraid of falling head first into a fabulous universe and of wandering about in it . . . without hope of getting back [home] to the Rue le Goff."[23]

This admonishment exactly mirrors Kierkegaard's chastisement of Hegel for creating a fantasy world of abstraction from existence. The reader of Kierkegaard's Hegel, too, has no hope of getting back to the rue le Goff. Ironically, though, one may find places in Kierkegaard's work where he laments his tendency toward fantasy, as in the journal entry cited in Chapter 1 where he speaks of how his pseudonymous authorship has been a journey through the world of fantasy that has "kept me away from my own self" (*JSK* 641).

The melancholy Kierkegaard admits to in his journal, like the fear Sartre expresses about his fall into a fabulous universe where he wanders about without hope of returning home, is tied up with his ambivalence about words, his being caught up in the tension between living and telling. In a haunting passage from *Nausea,* Roquentin tells of his experience in a park, observing the roots of a chestnut tree, a "black, knotty mass, entirely beastly." He comes to understand the source of his nausea, that "it is no longer an illness or a passing fit: it is I," since he intuits in a "horrible ecstasy" that his own existence is as unjustifiable and superfluous as that of the chestnut tree: "to exist is simply *to be there;* . . . I *was* the root of the chestnut tree, . . . born without reason, prolong[ed] out of weakness and [destined] to die by chance."[24] The key point, for our purposes, is not Roquentin's horrible vision itself, but the diary entry that records it. As Roquentin writes down his vision, he notices that "the word 'absurdity' is coming to life under my pen" but then recalls that "a little while ago, in the garden, I couldn't find it [the word], but neither was I looking for it, I didn't need it: I thought without words, *on* things, *with* things. . . . Absurdity: another word; I struggle against words; down there I touched the thing."[25] And yet, after standing against the gate of the garden seeking but failing to understand what he had encountered, "I left; I went back to the hotel and I wrote."[26]

Kierkegaard too struggles against words. He wishes to exist beyond the telling of stories about existence, to "remain silent and act." And yet he writes. Indeed writing, for all the danger of its seduction into fantasy, became for both Sartre and Kierkegaard what it was for Roquentin, an attempted cure: "I lived only in order to write," Sartre told Beauvoir,[27] and for his part, Kierkegaard confesses in his journal that "only when I write do I feel well" (*DSK* 64).

RESOLUTIONS: LANGUAGE AS SEDUCTION, LANGUAGE AS PERFORMANCE

In his study of Jean Genet, Sartre speaks of how language destroys the reality of things in order to reproduce them.[28] Late in life, in an interview with the *New York Times Magazine,* Sartre declared that "commitment is an act, not a word."[29] Kierkegaard's own philosophy of language expresses a similar idea. As we have seen, he believes that "the Word annuls reality by talking about it" (*JC* 148). And yet both Sartre and Kierkegaard know that language cannot be avoided. Thus although *Nausea* is in part a scathing critique of the naive faith in the power of words to cure us, it is also a critique of Roquentin's attempt in the garden to "think without words." As for Kierkegaard, we have noted that on the very same page of *Johannes Climacus, or De Omnibus Dubitandus Est* where he speaks of language annulling reality, he asks, "Cannot consciousness then remain in immediacy? This is a foolish question, for if it could, . . . man would be an animal, or in other words, he would be dumb" (*JC* 148). Meaning emerges only through language. Thus in the garden, Roquentin notices that "the words had vanished, and with them the significance of things."[30]

Hegel's whole philosophy can be understood as a philosophy of language—and in this sense Kierkegaard is right that Hegel is a philosopher of words. Like Kierkegaard, Hegel understands language as involving a certain "annulment of reality," or a "destruction of reality," as Sartre put it to Beauvoir. In particular, language entails the negation of the private reality of the speaker, for, as Hegel says, language is "at once the externalization and the vanishing of this particular I," and this I "dies away" as it is reborn into the communal space of being-with-others (*PS* 308–9).

Although Kierkegaard never disputes Hegel's view of language as being-for-others, he laments just what Hegel celebrates. If for Hegel the "divine nature of language" (*PS* 66) is precisely its redemption of the purely subjective I by its emergence into community, it is just this loss of privacy that troubles Kierkegaard, not only because of his well-known aversion to "the public," but more fundamentally because for him truth is subjectivity. Kierkegaard's task as an author, then, will be to experiment with a style of writing that undertakes a precarious balancing act. His authorship must initiate a relationship to the other, the reader, and yet simultaneously maintain the privacy and subjectivity of both the author and reader. This style is, of course, Kierkegaard's practice of "indirect communication," his alternative to the obtrusively "direct communication" of Hegel, which blares out its Absolute Truths for all to marvel at as though through a megaphone or "speaking-trumpet" (*JP* 1:650).

Sartre's analysis of language in *Being and Nothingness* provides a particularly intriguing frame for understanding just how challenging Kierkegaard's project of indirect communication is. The context of Sartre's discussion of language is "the problem of others," namely, how one is to relate to others in such a way as to grant them their freedom (their "being-for-self") while retaining one's own freedom. Sartre calls such a relation of mutual freedom "the ideal of love," but concludes that this is "an impossible ideal," "an illusion," "a game of mirrors" and a "contradictory effort."[31] Insofar as I acknowledge the freedom of the other, I myself become a being-for-the-other, and hence an object, and to the extent that I seek to recover my being-for-self in face of the other, the other is reduced to an object for me.[32] More particularly, the ideal of love, of unity with the other in reciprocal freedom, is doomed to failure for the same reason Kierkegaard feels that "each individual is isolated and compelled to exist for himself" (*CUP* 287)—the other, as a subjectivity, is unreachable by any other subjectivity. As Sartre puts it, "All consciousnesses are separated by an insurmountable nothingness."[33]

Language for Sartre is the symptom of our predicament. Although the nature of consciousness is being-for-self (Kierkegaard's subjectivity, Hegel's pure I), we are incomplete without the other: "The other holds the secret of who I am."[34] This entails, however, that once I speak, "I can only guess at the meaning of what I express—that is, the meaning of what I am," since "the other is always there . . . as the one who gives to language its meaning." In this sense, language is a "flight outside myself" (*fuite hors de moi*) and a "stealing of thought" (*vol de pensée*) by the other.[35]

Thus Sartre shares Kierkegaard's sense of pain over the price to be paid by our being linguistic creatures. And here is the frame Sartre provides for understanding the challenge posed by Kierkegaard's authorial project of indirect communication. For Sartre, the tragic character of language, that it aims at love (a unity with the other) and yet inevitably ends in conflict (the struggle against the danger posed by the other's freedom to "steal" the meaning of what I say), lures the speaking self into the project of *seduction* as a desperate attempt to achieve some facsimile of love. Seduction is a kind of playacting in which I mask my subjectivity, presenting myself as an object for the other's freedom, seeking to "fascinate" and to "captivate" the other and thereby "capture" what I need from her, her freedom (since only a free other can affirm me). "In seduction, language does not aim at giving to be known" but at "concealing" my subjectivity from the other. The aim is thus to entice the other's freedom by pretending to forfeit one's own while actually retaining it behind the disguise of my seduction and thus at the same time making the other into an object of my desire.[36]

For Sartre, seduction, like love itself, is a doomed project. Although the seduced other may believe he is a free subjectivity, since I appear to him as an object of his desire, in fact I am no object at all, but only playing at it. Beneath the disguises of my fascinating language, I am the subject, laying my plans for the other "to will its own captivity . . . as in madness, as in a dream."[37] It is on the stage of this theater of seduction that Kierkegaard acts out his own experimental performance of indirect communication. But Kierkegaard believes he can carry off what Sartre says is an impossibility, to seduce in such a way as to truly love, to speak in such a way as to give himself to a free other while retaining his own freedom.

The theme of seduction in Kierkegaard's authorship is the focus of the next chapter, but for now the central issue is the significance of the project of indirect communication. The mechanics, or stage work, of Kierkegaard's methods of indirect communication—his use of irony, the strategies of "double reflection" and "reduplication," the role of the pseudonyms—are complex and fascinating, but here it is sufficient to sketch out some key features of the ethical framework within which he practices this style of communication. As the name implies, in "indirect communication" the author never speaks directly of her meanings but conceals them behind the masks she wears to conceal her true intents. "All indirect communication is different from direct communication in that indirect communication first of all involves a deception" (*JP* 1:649). The author conceals himself in such a way that the more we look for him, the more he vanishes behind yet another layer of disguises. Locating the author is thus "as baffling as trying to depict an elf wearing a hat that makes him invisible," as Kierkegaard says in another context in *The Concept of Irony* (*CI* 50).

Thus far, Kierkegaard's indirect communication fits the picture Sartre draws of the language of seduction very neatly. And let there be no mistake, Kierkegaard's authorial style is aimed at seduction, at what he calls the "beguilement" of the reader (*MAW* 144)—the "prospective captive" (*PV* 25)—into the text through the methods of deception and self-concealment. Yet Kierkegaard's use of seduction is grounded in an ethics of authorship that seeks to establish a radically different relation to the reader from the ultimately self-serving motivations of Sartre's seducer. Kierkegaard is no Johannes the Seducer, whose diary of his seduction of the sixteen-year-old Cordelia in *Either/Or* perfectly fits Sartre's account. Johannes "weaves [Cordelia] into [his] plan," shaping her into his own image of "woman" as the "handiwork" of male desire (*E/Or* 1:420, 439). Like Sartre's seducer, Johannes seeks to present himself as though he were the object of Cordelia's free desire: "[I must] so arrange it that [the] girl's only desire is to give herself freely, . . . when she almost begs to make this free submission, then for the first time is true enjoyment, but this always requires . . . influence" (*E/Or* 1:337).

Kierkegaard's seductive authorship, on the contrary, is meant to use the influence of deception so as to awaken the reader's independence. Kierkegaard learned from Socrates that to awaken the other through proclamation, declaration, or lecturing—the didacticism of direct communication—is both tactically futile and, more important, ethically problematic. The ethical power of Socrates' maieutic method is that the other, the interlocutor, becomes the *subject* of the dialogue, and Socrates the learner. In a journal entry where Kierkegaard speaks of the ethics of indirect communication, he writes that the author "must always [recall] that he himself is not a master teacher but an apprentice, . . . because ethically the task [of indirect communication] is precisely this, that every man comes to stand alone" (*JP* 1:649). Thus it is that Socrates "abandons" the other (*CI* 203)—confesses his own ignorance, admits to his failure to resolve anything—just as Kierkegaard's pseudonymous authors all vanish. Each of the authors is utterly fantastic. As Stephen Crites says, "They are sheer personae, masks without actors underneath, [mere] voices,"[38] or, in Josiah Thompson's words, they are all "characters whose very essence is to lack flesh; . . . disembodied to a marked degree, they are all hermits in life, without parents or home, wife or job, appetite or fear."[39] The art of indirect communication, as Anti-Climacus puts it, consists in the author's becoming "an absentee" (*TC* 133).

All that is left behind of Socrates, or of the Kierkegaardian author, is a question mark. The interlocutor or reader is left to seek answers on her own. Although the reader may be lured into the text by the author's attempt at producing fascination, the disappearance of the author is the ethical act of indirect communication by which the reader comes face to face with her own freedom and responsibility for constructing a meaning of her own—and ultimately, for living it. Indirect communication is Kierkegaard's way of telling that points to the necessity of living.

Sartre is right that language is a flight outside oneself, but for Kierkegaard this is what makes the ethics of gift-giving possible and what underlies his conception of his authorship as a "service" (*PV* 8, 16). Moreover, Sartre is right that in language "I can only guess at the meaning of what I express" since "the other is always there." This is why Kierkegaard is so committed to the idea that he himself is "only a reader" of his own works, having "no knowledge of their meaning except as a reader" (*CUP* 551). He is careful not to fall into the conceit that "an author [is] . . . the best interpreter of his own words, as if it could help a reader [to know] that an author had intended this or that" (*CUP* 225).

But the author's revocation of authority over her texts not only supports the reader's liberty, it also protects the freedom of the author. The ironic foundation of indirect communication, that what is meant is not said, safeguards the author from what Sartre calls the "danger" of the other and the fate of the speaker to have his meanings "stolen." As Thompson puts it, "The ironist is the man absent from his words."[40] Kierkegaard explains it this way: "The ironic figure of speech conceals itself," in that the meaning is hidden; thus, "If what is said is not my meaning, . . . then *I am free . . . in relation to others*" (*CI* 265, emphasis added). Notice that the ethics of Kierkegaard's authorship is thus based on a practice of seduction that resolves what for Sartre was the "impossible ideal" of love, *not* by fulfilling any actual "unity" with the other. For Kierkegaard as much as for Sartre, I am always separated from the other by "an insurmountable nothingness." Rather, what we might call the structural requirement of love, the relation between two free subjectivities, is provided for by Kierkegaard's indirect communication through, on the one hand, an act of authorial abandonment by which the reader comes to stand on her own and, on the other, a preservation of the free subjectivity of the author. The reader's freedom is a private freedom, and so too is the author's: The author needs his "inner sanctum," guarded by a practice of self-concealment that serves as a "barrier that prevents all access" (*TA* 99).

As for Hegel's authorship, Hegel does not face the same question that Kierkegaard must, namely how his (Kierkegaard's) authorship is possible at all given his commitment to the radical aloneness of every individual subject. Since Hegel's ontology sees the self as an inherently intersubjective being, the relation between author and reader is in principle simply one instance of this intersubjectivity. No, the question for Hegel is about the ethics of his authorship, given Kierkegaard's characterization of his style as the direct declaration of objective truths. By this view, Hegel's philosophy is inherently authoritarian and leaves the reader at the author's mercy. Yet however notoriously imposing and intimidating Hegel's style of writing no doubt is, it is a style whose effectiveness depends not, as Kierkegaard would have it, on the sheer authority of Hegel's godlike wisdom, but on the contrary precisely on the decentering of that authority.

We saw in Chapter 1 that Hegel's style of communication is grounded in a philosophy of language in which "language is more truthful" than mere intention (*PS* 60). That is, the self's intentions become effectively meaningful only when expressed and appropriated by others (*PS* 60, 66, 296). This directly implies that it is impossible for the author to hold a privileged position of authority. Indeed, quite the contrary, the site of meaning is shifted onto the reader's response. We also saw that Hegel's view of language as performative dislocates the voice of the author, who "merely looks on," onto the different shapes of experience enacted in the text: *They* speak, and the reader must make these experiences her own if she is to truly engage the text. Hegel's telling, like Kierkegaard's, is a telling that locates the meaning of the text in the way the reader lives what she reads.

TELL, LIVE

In some ways, Hegel and Kierkegaard are quite unlikely subjects for an exploration of Roquentin's injunction to "live or tell."

Kierkegaard essentially lived as a hermit, going out onto the streets of Copenhagen only to sit on a bench in Deer Park and smoke a cigar, letting his fellow citizens observe his meticulously designed disguise as an eccentric and silly man who would then return to his rooms and live his true life as a brilliant writer everyone ignored. He was, as we have seen, tormented by the thought that he had become so lost in the "world of fantasy" of his pseudonyms that he was no longer able to say "Thou" to himself. Although Hegel certainly lived a more obviously public life than Kierkegaard, he too suffered periodically from a malaise he called, in a letter to the philosopher Karl Windischmann, his "nocturnal" side in which he suffered from an "inability to come out of myself" (*Letters* 561). In a review of several biographies of Hegel in the *London Review of Books* titled "Baffled Traveller," Jonathan Rée remarks on Hegel's "compulsion to wander off in his imagination and take refuge elsewhere. His sense of self was diffuse and distracted, and he would identify with almost anything except his own immediate situation, . . . seeing things from points of view other than his own."[41] This portrayal of Hegel is uncannily close to Kierkegaard's self-description as one who voyaged through a world of fantasy and whose pseudonymity is precisely an excursion through a multiplicity of points of view.

But the interest of Hegel and Kierkegaard is not whether they themselves became so absorbed in their telling that they forgot, at times, to live—like Thales, who was always tripping over the bucket his wife placed in front of him in frustration at his voyages into philosophic reverie—but the significance of their authorships for their readers. Notwithstanding Hegel's excruciatingly technical style and Kierkegaard's subjective isolationism, both develop methods of writing that, in their different ways, experiment with modes of telling where meaning emerges only to the extent that the reader re-creates and lives it.

3. Kierkegaard's Seductions

The beloved can not will to love. Therefore the lover must seduce the beloved, and his love can in no way be distinguished from the enterprise of seduction.

JEAN-PAUL SARTRE, *Being and Nothingness*

A man who cannot seduce men cannot save them either.

SØREN KIERKEGAARD, journal entry, cited in
A Kierkegaard Anthology, edited by Robert Bretall

IN 1843, at the age of twenty-nine, Søren Kierkegaard published *Either/Or,* a nearly eight-hundred-page book (the first of six published in 1843) written largely during a several-month visit to Berlin where he had ensconced himself to escape the complications of an impossible love affair. The work was published pseudonymously, "edited" by Victor Eremita, and consists of two volumes of papers discovered accidentally by Victor in the secret drawer of a desk he had bought at auction, the first volume by an aesthete ("A"), the second by an ethicist ("B," Judge William). The last and longest of the eight entries of volume 1 is the transcription of the diary of a "Seducer." But the account of the exploits of Johannes the Seducer is in part only the pretext of the text of *Either/Or,* for the diary is as much a disguised commentary on Kierkegaard's early experimentation with the nature of seduction as a strategy of authorship as it is about the strange, troubling, and fascinating diary of a master eroticist.

FAITHFUL TO DECEPTION

If, as Nietzsche claims in *Beyond Good and Evil,* "Every profound thinker is more afraid of being understood than of being misunderstood,"[1] then surely Søren Kierkegaard was a truly profound thinker. For a fundamental commitment of Kierkegaard's authorship was to develop an experimental art of communication whereby the relation to the reader is mediated by misdirection, evasion, and deceit. Since "what I have to say may not be taught," he writes in such a way as to disinstall himself from authority; he remains "silent" and writes "as if I would keep the truth to myself" (*JP* 1:646). By being scrupulous never to use "my own I" and rather producing a whole world of "poetic I's" (*JP* 1:650, 656) and "poetized personalities"—his many pseudonyms (chronologically, Victor Eremita, Constantin Constantius, Johannes de Silentio, Johannes Climacus, Vigilius Haufniensis, Nicolaus Notabene, Hilarius Bookbinder, Inter et Inter, H.H., and Anti-Climacus), along with the entire cast of imaginary characters the pseudonyms create—he denies the reader the comfort of locating an author who will take responsibility for their education.

Like Socrates, who serves as the model for Kierkegaard's maieutic authorship, and who constantly effects his own disappearance as an authority just when his interlocutors look to him for conclusions, so too Kierkegaard vanishes from sight, leaving the reader in the hands of the merely "poetic," mythological, whimsical pseudonyms. "Only when I write do I feel well," Kierkegaard confessed in his journal (*DSK* 64), and yet when he writes pseudonymously, he goes into hiding and cannot be found. In the pseudonymous works, "the communicator disappears, as it were" (*JP* 1:657), and the whole "art consists in reducing oneself, the communicator, to nobody" (*TC* 132).

Kierkegaard's first pseudonymous work, *Either/Or,* is an exuberant experimentation with the art of authorial disguise. Kierkegaard is not content to hide himself behind the "editor" of the massive work, Victor Eremita, but revels in the creation of mystery and obscurity surrounding the "authors" themselves. The work is composed of the scattered writings of an anonymous aesthetic author ("A")—and perhaps an additional aesthete, the "Seducer," who may or may not be the same as "A" ("A" denies it; Victor suggests it)—and by an ethical author, "B" (or Judge William), who may or may not himself be the same as "A" (Victor deviously hints that he may have "allowed myself a liberty, a deception," in suggesting through his choice of a title, *Either/Or,* that the work was produced by two separate authors). Finally, Victor ends his preface by concluding that there is so much uncertainty about the authorship of the papers that "when the book is read, then A and B are forgotten; only their views confront one another, and await no finite decision in particular personalities [authors]" (E/Or 1:13, 14).

But the puzzle and mystery Kierkegaard seeks to create in his pseudonymous authorship is much deeper than a desire to effect his own disappearance as authority. "Indirect communication" is not only indirect in that there is no "particular personality" or author who can be appealed to as arbiter of textual meaning, but more paradoxically, it is indirect in that (frequently) what is being spoken of cannot truly be *spoken* of. We mentioned in Chapter 1 the riddle surrounding Kierkegaard's second pseudonym, Johannes de Silentio—Johannes the silent one; Johannes, who in writing his book, *Fear and Trembling,* finally must be perceived as having been silent throughout. Johannes is the "poet" of Abraham (FT 24, 30–31), the poet of the one whose faith did not allow him to speak of his astonishing and horrifying test before the Lord, who was asked to sacrifice his only son, and who went up to the place of sacrifice on Mount Moriah in silence.[2] We noted that Johannes too is silent, but unlike Abraham must first speak. The deep paradox of the pseudonymous authorship is epitomized by the fact that it is *at the very same time as Johannes speaks* that he must be understood as being silent, from the beginning to the end of his text. As Louis Mackey says, Kierkegaard's practice of indirect communication "negates not only the said but also the saying."[3]

QUESTIONS OF ETHICS

The paradoxical character of Kierkegaard's indirect communication—a communication that remains in some sense silent—reflects a fundamental ethical quandary that haunts Kierkegaard throughout his authorship. Although "the ethical" is an unstable concept in the different voices of Kierkegaard's authorship, these voices are all involved in different ways with engaging a common construction of the ethical: The ideal of an encounter in which the other is not merely an object of my own representation of her, and the longing for the experience of a merging of the two in one. Yet Kierkegaard is generally tormented by a sense of the hopelessness of such an encounter, for, as we have seen, each of us is "isolated and compelled to exist for himself," so that "to be concerned ethically about another's reality is . . . a misunderstanding" (*CUP* 286, 287).

It is this intuition of the radical alterity of the other, and hence the impossibility of ever truly experiencing her, which in large part explains the typology of Kierkegaard's "three spheres of existence," the aesthetic, the ethical, and the religious. The aesthete will seek either a sensuous-erotic encounter with the other (see "A"'s lengthy discussion of Don Juan, *E/Or* 1:83–134) or a highly aestheticized and intellectualized but intentionally and exuberantly nonethical encounter (for example, that of Johannes the Seducer with Cordelia). The authentically religious individual will renounce "earthly love" as an impossible project and seek through faith an Absolute Other who has the power of grace to redeem us and, by virtue of the absurd, make the impossible possible. The ethicist, however, is caught in between, unwilling to sacrifice the other either by eroticism or manipulation or renunciation, and trapped in a dilemma: how ethically to encounter the other, whose interiority always eludes us.

Kierkegaard's experimentation with indirect communication, which he conceives as an intrinsically ethical enterprise (e.g., *JP* 1:649, 650), involves on the one hand an acknowledgment of the impossibility of any direct ethical encounter with the other (hence it is predicated on the withdrawal of the I of the author behind disguises and masks) and on the other a desire that this act of self-disappearance be the authentication of the other's independence. Indirect communication thus employs deception to achieve a sort of silence, in order to free the other from the imposition of the speaker's authority, that is, from being reduced to a being-for-another, a being signified by the author's speech.[4] As we turn now to consider Johannes the Seducer and the diary of his affair with a young girl, the questions surrounding this ethics of deception will become particularly acute.

THE SEDUCER: IN PURSUIT OF THE
INVISIBLY PRESENT AUTHOR

The long (some 130 pages in Swenson's translation) "Diary of the Seducer" is the last entry in the first volume of *Either/Or.* The aesthete, "A," who is allegedly responsible for the seven previous entries, has finished his work of exploring the landscape of the aesthetic life and has only to introduce the diary he says he has surreptitiously "secure[d] only in the greatest haste and with much disquietude" from the unlocked desk drawer of his acquaintance, Johannes. "The Diary" contains an account of Johannes's seduction of the sixteen-year-old Cordelia Wahl, and so troubles "A" by the "conscious madness" of the seducer's "scheming mind" and the "calculated carelessness" with which the seduction victimizes Cordelia, that he is quick to express his "revulsion" and "dread" at what he has found (*E/Or* 1:299–306, "A"'s preface).

Ironically, then, the aesthete expresses an *ethical* aversion to the Seducer. The aesthete himself acknowledges that the aesthetic taken to its extreme is horror, and we might therefore think that the culmination of *Either,* the life view of the aesthete, is framed so as to point beyond itself to *Or,* the essays of the ethicist "B" (or Judge William). Yet—and should we really be surprised?—there is a further complication, for we have seen that Victor, the editor of the two volumes, is quite sure that "A" is the Seducer himself: His disavowal is only "an old trick of the novelist," and the whole tenor of the other essays of *Either* "betrays" "A" as the author of the Diary (1:9). Thus "A"'s invocation of ethical judgment on the Seducer may be just another instance of indirection and deceit, a mock performance of being scandalized. Beneath the performance, perhaps, is an amusement at the hollowness of all ethical judgment. For the Seducer, at any rate, there is no attempt to justify himself ethically. Indeed, nothing is more boring to him than the ethical: "The ethical is just as tiresome in philosophy as in life." Whereas in the aesthetic sphere "everything is light, beautiful, transitory, when the ethical comes along then everything becomes harsh, angular, infinitely boring" (1:363). From this perspective, so far from pointing beyond itself to the second volume (*Or,* the ethical), *Either* instates itself as the only volume: What is to

KIERKEGAARD'S SEDUCTIONS ‡ 69

follow, Judge William's treatise on the ethical, is foreclosed in advance as a tedious exercise in the boring.

The figure of Johannes the Seducer is developed in contrast to "A"'s earlier account of the character of Don Juan in his extended analysis of Mozart's opera *Don Giovanni*. We saw in the last chapter that in the aesthete's interpretation, Don Juan seduces as a sheer force of nature; he is "flesh incarnate" (*E/Or* 1:87), and his seduction is simply the elemental, daemonic, musical power of sensual desire itself. Johannes, on the other hand, prides himself on the fact that he is no crude seducer—the search for the experience of sensuous pleasure is far below his talents. No, Johannes is the artist of love. He *creates* Cordelia: "Her development was my handiwork" (*E/Or* 1:439), and "[I] weave her into my plan" (*E/Or* 1:420). He shapes her: "Now write me down as a bungler if I cannot shape the situation as I want it" (*E/Or* 1:318). And not only is he the artist, he is equally the scientist of love: "I am a natural scientist, and I learned from Cuvier[5] how to draw definite conclusions from small details" (*E/Or* 1:310). As scientist of love, he observes, he theorizes, and he calculates: He writes a "Theory of Kissing"; he constantly refines the methods by which to shape Cordelia into an object worthy of his seduction; and he "calculate[s] the developmental history of [Cordelia's] soul; . . . like a physician [he] take[s] pleasure in observing all the symptoms in her case history" (*E/Or* 1:355–56). The scientist and the artist are united so perfectly in the Seducer that he need not merely observe Cordelia's symptoms: He is the physician *as* artist, which enables him to *produce* her symptoms so as to observe them— and just those symptoms he requires for his conquest of her.

Don Juan, as force of nature, loses all possibility of individual personality in his submergence into nature. He is "sheer immediacy" (*E/Or* 1:73), whereas Johannes, by contrast, is sheer consciousness. Indeed, Johannes's attachment to the *reflective* erotic depends on his detachment from his passions. Toward the very beginning of his seduction of Cordelia, Johannes describes himself as seemingly lost to passion: "I scarcely recognize myself. My mind is like a turbulent sea, swept by the storms of passion. If another could see my soul in this condition, it would seem to him like a boat that buried its prow deep in the sea, as if in its terrible speed it would rush down into the depths of the abyss." But if Johannes were to give in to this rush of passion, he would be just another Don Juan. Hence the passage continues: "He does not see that high on the mast a lookout sits on watch. Roar on, ye wild forces, ye powers of passion! Let your dashing waves hurl their foam against the sky. You shall not engulf me. Serene I sit like the king of the cliff" (*E/Or* 1:320).

As detached from the storms of passion that rule Don Juan, Johannes is free to seduce as an artist. The insatiability of Don Juan's desire—that he must continue to seduce again and again, that even when he reaches 1,003 seductions, there is an infinite ellipsis after the number—is the insatiability of desire itself, that it must repeat itself forever. This is just what Johannes knows, and dreads, and seeks to overcome by sitting high on the mast, by becoming pure consciousness, freed from music, from the Siren's song of passion. Now he is able to seduce as only the consummate artist of love can, to seduce not Cordelia herself—what could be more boring, more tiresome, more crude, and ultimately more impossible (since sensuous desire inevitably regenerates itself at the moment of its satisfaction)—but rather the aesthetic idea of Cordelia he crafts her into.

Cordelia becomes merely the mirror for the artwork Johannes is perpetually refining. In a key passage in his diary, Johannes asks, "Do I love Cordelia? Yes. Sincerely? Yes. Faithfully? Yes. . . ." Yes, of course he does, . . . but! The sentence continues: ". . . Yes!—*in an aesthetic sense*" (*E/Or* 1:380, emphasis added). That is, what Johannes really loves is his own artistic re-creation of Cordelia. This unnerving idea is echoed in a passage toward the very end of the diary where Johannes returns to the meaning of his "faithfulness": "Have I been constantly faithful to my pact in relation to Cordelia?" he asks. But again, as in the early passage, Johannes moves quickly to qualify the question: "That is to say, my pact with the aesthetic. . . . Has the interesting always been preserved? Yes, I dare say it freely and openly in this secret conversation with myself" (*E/Or* 1:432).

The intrigue of seduction for Johannes thus emphatically is not the sexual conquest of Cordelia. Leave that to Don Juan; leave that to those who know nothing of the higher pleasures of the aesthetic, nothing of what is truly interesting about love. No, what intrigues Johannes is the shaping of Cordelia into a work of art, the real object

KIERKEGAARD'S SEDUCTIONS ‡ 71

of his desire. To achieve this goal, then just as much as Cordelia, the flesh-and-blood Cordelia, must be removed from the center of attention of the seduction—she is there only as mirror of the aesthetic—so too Johannes, the flesh-and-blood Johannes, must be absent. The exquisitely delicate web of his seduction would completely tear apart should he be required to be present and give in to the storm of passion. Hence Johannes becomes pure "myth," as we learn in the next to last entry of the diary: "Everything is symbol; I myself am a myth about myself, for is it not as a myth that I hasten to this [last] meeting [with Cordelia]? Who I am has nothing to do with it" (*E/Or* 1:439). He is sheer myth not only because he aestheticizes Cordelia, but because he must also poetize himself: "He who does not know how to compass a girl about so that she loses sight of everything that he does not wish her to see, he who does not know how to poetize himself into a girl's feelings so that it is from her that everything issues as he wishes it, he is and remains a bungler," not an aesthete (*E/Or* 1:363).

Here, with the idea of Johannes's seduction as the double poetizing of self and other, we reencounter the paradox of maieutic authorship. Recall that Kierkegaard speaks of indirect communication as an act of fundamental deception ("to deceive belongs essentially to my method of communication," and he "remains faithful to the deception throughout"), just as Johannes defines his "faithfulness" to Cordelia as his faithfulness to his deception of her. Johannes, in fact, is not merely myth about himself, but myth or symbol of the whole project of indirect authorship.

Johannes's art consists in his being absent in his very presence before Cordelia. At the beginning of the seduction, Johannes pretends—and for the sake of an initial experiment (which will later be complicated as we consider the gender issues involved in such an experiment), in what follows substitute for "Johannes," Kierkegaard, and for "Cordelia," yourself as reader—Johannes pretends "to have nothing at all to do with [her], [but] it is readily apparent that Cordelia constantly feels that I am *invisibly present*" (*E/Or* 1:346, emphasis added). Although he sits in the living room, talking with the aunt, "visible to everyone in the living room, still I am really . . . [in] my hiding place, . . . lying in ambush" (*E/Or* 1:344). The author-seducer only appears to be visible to the reader—we have his text before us, after all, just as Cordelia has the Seducer before her: There he is! He's talking with her aunt—but he is in hiding; he is not where we see him; he is waiting secretly in ambush.

Much later in the diary, four months into his nearly six-month seduction, Johannes returns to the theme of his own invisibility. He reflects that he "cannot regret the time that Cordelia has cost me, although it is considerable. Every meeting has demanded long preparation. I am watching the birth of love within her. I am even almost *invisibly present* when I visibly sit by her side. . . . She moves as in a dream, and yet she dances with another, and this other is myself, who, in so far as I am visibly present, am invisible, insofar as I am invisible, I am visible" (*E/Or* 1:376). Everything is shrouded in secrecy: "Love loves secrecy; . . . it loves silence, . . . it loves a whisper"; it hates all "revelation," all "public notice," and all "proclamation from the housetops" (*E/Or* 1:383). It hates, that is, the obtrusive bluntness of *direct* communication. It requires deception: "I should say that it takes something more than honesty to love such a girl. That more I have—it is *duplicity.* And yet I really love her faithfully" (*E/Or* 1:380, emphasis added). The seducer's love of Cordelia, as well as the (Kierkegaardian) author's love of the reader, is always a love that communicates indirectly, an indirect love, a love mediated by a faithfulness to deception and disguise.

SEDUCTIVE AUTHORSHIP AND THE ETHICS OF DECEPTION: "IN THE SERVICE OF A SERIOUS PURPOSE"

If the text of the "Diary of the Seducer" is at least in part the pretext for an exploration of the nature of maieutic authorship—and if, accordingly, it is instructive to read the role of Seducer as the role of the author, and the seduced as the role of the reader—then this seems to raise serious ethical questions about the relationship of author to reader. Many have commented on the misogynistic character of Johannes's seduction of Cordelia.[6] Indeed, the misogyny is quite straightforward: Cordelia is envisioned as the pure object of seduction, pure being-for-Johannes, who will catch her in his web, shape her, create her, transform her into his own artwork. As Leslie Howe suggests, Cordelia has significance only as constructed by Johannes: Seduction "demands that she come to the situation unformed, a *tabula rasa*, in effect. [The only thing truly] interesting [about Cordelia] is [that which] is produced in her by the male's [imagination] acting upon her."[7] And as Jane Duran points out, Cordelia exists only as "Johannes' own creation," so that "the notions of agency and autonomy" are completely "denied her."[8]

An especially stark statement of what Howe calls the "pronounced misogyny" of this attitude toward the feminine[9] can be seen in Johannes's soliloquy about what category of being "woman" should be conceived under. Well, of course, "under the category of being for another," the Seducer proclaims:

[Woman] exists only for an other. In the same way a mystery, a charade, a secret, a vowel, has being only for an other. . . . As being for another, woman is characterized by pure virginity. Virginity is a form of being which, in so far as it is a being for itself, is really an abstraction, and only reveals itself to another. . . . Woman in this condition is *invisible*. . . . This is the contradiction, that the being which is for an other *is* not, and first becomes visible, as it were, by the interposition of an other. . . . The very concept of woman requires that she be the vanquished; the concept of man, that he be the victor. (*E/Or* 1:424–26, emphasis added)

"Poor Cordelia!" "A" sighs in his introduction to the diary (*E/Or* 1:305). Yes, indeed, poor Cordelia, but more: When we effect the substitution of reader for "Cordelia," we must add our own lament—poor reader! The reader: prey and quarry of the author's game of seduction; virgin to be vanquished by the author's act of possession; pure being-for-author, to be ambushed, seduced, ensnared, enthralled, and created in the image of the author's secret designs.

But what then of the idea found throughout Kierkegaard's writings that maieutic authorship has as its goal the liberation of the reader? A strange liberation, this: liberation as effacement of autonomy. Can this be right? What of Kierkegaard's contention that he

practices indirect communication on the model of Socratic mid-
wifery, in the service of allowing the reader to engage in her own
labor of bringing meaning and value to birth? (*PF* 10; *CUP* 74, 222).
I have already cited the journal entry where Kierkegaard declares
that the author "must always express that he himself is not a master
teacher but an apprentice, . . . because ethically the task is precisely
this, that every man comes to stand alone" (*JP* 1:649). As Stephen
Crites puts it, "The pseudonymous writings are designed to throw
every reader back on his own resources. There is not even an actual
author to lay any claim on him. They assign him to himself."[10]

We have seen as well that Kierkegaard returns to the ethics of
authorial indirection in his *Point of View for My Work as an Author*,
and I noted his insistence that although his authorship has been
marked by "ambiguity," "duplicity," and "deception" "from the very
start," he has used this mystification "in the service of a serious purpose" (*PV* 5–6, 10–11, 16). And what purpose is that? To make space
for the autonomy of the reader, "that *individual* whom with joy and
gratitude I call *my* reader" (*PV* 20).

The nature of seduction and deception that govern Kierkegaard's
authorship takes on a new, unexpected meaning with this notion of
mystification as "service" to the reader. In the some one-hundred-
page "Letter to the Reader" that closes *Stages on Life's Way,* Father
Taciturnus reflects on the nature of the authorship of the work and
turns to the idea of seduction. "Ordinarily," he remarks, "one thinks
of a seducer in connection with women"—remember, this is a quintessentially masculine author, as are the authors of all of Kierkegaard's pseudonymous works—"but this is not the [most] dangerous
kind of seducer." Rather, it is the *author,* the narrator or storyteller,
who "with his imagination . . . lures [his listeners] on into seductive
ideals." The danger for the listener is not that somehow she will
become the possession or creation of the speaker—for unlike Johannes, such a seducer "craves nothing for himself." No, what this seducer wants, oddly enough, is to *de*-seduce the listener from a
relation of dependency on the captivating speaker.

This de-seducing seeks "to induce" in the listener the belief "that
the single individual has infinite significance and this is the validity
of life" (*SLW* 491). As Father Taciturnus asks in the diary titled

KIERKEGAARD'S SEDUCTIONS ‡ 75

"Guilty?/Not Guilty? A Story of Suffering" that precedes his "Letter to the Reader"—and that serves as an alternative diary of love (now ethically nuanced) to the narcissistic eroticism of "The Diary of the Seducer"—"Is there not a still higher kind of seduction?" (*SLW* 311).

With this idea of a "higher kind of seduction," a truly surprising reading of "The Diary of the Seducer" suggests itself. For all the misogynistic character of the Seducer's temperament, there is a real sense in which *the Seducer himself shares the nature of "woman."* Recall the sickeningly blithe manifesto of axioms about "woman" we looked at a short time ago:

> Woman exists only for an other. In the same way a mystery, a charade, a secret, a vowel, has being only for an other.
> Woman in this condition [of virginity] is *invisible.*
> This is the contradiction, that the being which is for an other *is* not, and first becomes visible, as it were, by the interposition of an other.

Johannes then adds a conclusion that we have not yet cited: "Man's courtship [of woman]," he suggests, "is a *question,* and her choice only an answer to a question" (*E/Or* 1:426). But like "woman," the maieutic author herself is pure being-for-another—the author has no self of her own, but is a mystery, a charade, a secret, a myth, sheer invisibility, and the author's text becomes visible only as an answer to the question posed by the reader. The reader must court the text, must seduce the seducer.

Consider the brutally misogynistic pronouncement of the Seducer at the close of the diary, as he reflects on his plan to abandon Cordelia: "If I were a god, I would do for her what Neptune did for a nymph, I would change her into a man" (*E/Or* 1:440). But now reconsider, translating Johannes's image of transformed gender into the terms of our analogy: The seducer (author) hopes for the seduced (reader) to assume the role of author. This, finally, is what Kierkegaard views as the fundamentally ethical purpose of indirect communication, that a "reduplication" occur in which the reader frees herself from reliance on the author, assumes her own identity as "that individual" who "stands alone," and appropriates the text as her own, in her own way. "To reduplicate is to 'exist' in what one understands" (*TC* 133).

Robert L. Perkins notes with perfect justice that Johannes "thinks of woman as an imaginative construction, a sexual fantasy, and not as an existent, actual person."[11] But what of Johannes himself? He is only a "creature of fantasy," a "myth." When Johannes asks in his speech at the banquet recounted in the *Stages,* "What else is woman but a dream, . . . outside of time, . . . an illusion?" it is hard not to ask precisely the same question about Johannes, whom "A" describes in his preface to the "Diary" as having "submerged reality in the poetic." Johannes, "A" says, lives in "a world of gauze, lighter, more ethereal, qualitatively different from the actual world." He lives, indeed, "not [in the] indicative but [in the] subjunctive," not in the world of actuality but outside of time, as a dream, in the world of possibility (*E/Or* 1:300–302).

Similarly, when one reads, in one of the many slanderous passages on women in Kierkegaard's journals, that "woman is once and for all a born virtuoso in lying, is really never happy without a little lying, just as it is *a priori* certain that wherever a woman is there is a little lying" (*JP* 4:4998), it is tempting to reflect on the "womanly" character of Søren Kierkegaard himself. For surely this entry on "woman" is equally applicable to Kierkegaard's own authorial program of indirect communication, in which, as we have seen, he "remains faithful to the deception throughout."

COMPLICATIONS

Surprising as it seems, we appear to have arrived at the proposition that Kierkegaard's "Diary of the Seducer" is in certain important ways a feminine text. But there are problems here, problems that are similar to those entailed by readings of the ostensibly feminine character of Nietzsche's authorship. Just as I have sought to tempt my reader into taking seriously the unexpected parallels between Kierkegaard's descriptions of woman and his own authorial values, so too several commentators on Nietzsche tempt us to draw conclusions about the feminine nature of his writings on the basis of the

KIERKEGAARD'S SEDUCTIONS ‡ 77

uncanny closeness of his own descriptions of woman to his authorial style.[12]

I suppose it is not a conclusive counterargument to these readings simply to point to Kierkegaard's and Nietzsche's undisguised misogyny. After all, their texts could in principle point beyond the prejudices of their authors. Or, who knows, there could be an unconscious desire to emulate what consciously they recoil against and marginalize.

In fact, I am half persuaded by these surprising readings of Kierkegaard and Nietzsche as feminine authors: The similarities between their portraits of "woman" and their own styles of writing are without question intriguing. But Kierkegaard's and Nietzsche's misogyny is not the only difficulty for these readings of the feminine character of their authorships. A serious difficulty is the asymmetry between the disguises and deceptions Nietzsche and Kierkegaard ascribe to woman and those they adopt themselves. There are masks and masks, deceptions and deceptions. Both Nietzsche and Kierkegaard tend to conceptualize the masks and deceptions of woman in terms of the categories of superficiality, naïveté, innocence, pettiness, coyness, and pretense, while viewing their own as profound, "in the service of a serious purpose." Kierkegaard's vanishing authors, his "nobodies," are not like the "non-being" Johannes the Seducer ascribes to woman as virgin.

Similarly, there are problems with the reading I have been experimenting with, which seeks to find in Johannes the Seducer a key for decoding Kierkegaard's own seductive style of indirect communication. However tempting the possibilities of this reading, it is important to realize that just as there is deception and deception, there is seduction and seduction. Johannes's seduction of Cordelia is finally a ruthless, if artistically brilliant, act of manipulation. He devours Cordelia so as to re-create her in his own image of the perfect object of male desire. Johannes is Kierkegaard's creation of the consummately pre- (or post-) ethical eroticist, whereas Kierkegaard's own seductive authorship is constructed around an ethics of deception aimed at affirming the other's (reader's) autonomy.

True, Johannes also speaks of the importance of Cordelia's freedom: "She must owe me nothing, for she must be free; love exists only in freedom." But lest we think he has lapsed into ethics, we are immediately reassured of his purely aesthetic credentials. It is not her actual freedom that he wishes for Cordelia, but her *belief* that she is free: "I am aiming at her falling into my arms as it were by a natural necessity, yet I am striving to bring it about so that as she gravitates toward me, it will not be like the falling of a heavy body," but as though she were freely giving herself. "No, when one can so arrange it that a girl's only desire is to give herself freely, . . . when she almost begs to make this free submission, then there is first true enjoyment, but this always requires influence" (1:356, 337). Johannes wants from his prey the simulacrum of freedom, the illusion of freedom, an illusion he has "arranged" and "brought about" through his artistry.

Behind the seductiveness of Johannes's playfulness and brilliance, and the self-assured ease with which he deflects every ethical scruple, lies a cynicism and indifference to the other that is utterly at odds with the stated aims of Kierkegaard's project of indirect communication. Kierkegaard, like the Seducer, is often playful, brilliant, and self-assured—also ironic, combative, and insulting—but never cynical or indifferent. There are, then, two different languages of seduction in the "Diary," that of Johannes the Seducer and that of Kierkegaard, the author behind the author. Both employ deception and the invisibility of the I who speaks, and both seek to lure the other, yet one seeks to devour and the other to emancipate the other.

Or so it seems. This way of sharply distinguishing Kierkegaard from the Seducer leads to one sort of conclusion to this examination of the "Diary," which I will sketch out in the next few pages. But another conclusion is also possible, one that looks with suspicion at the tidy dichotomy of devouring/emancipating seduction. Both conclusions take their point of departure from the act of disappearance of the author.

THE APOSTLE'S CONCLUSION

The author of the Seducer's "Diary" eventually disappears from the text he authors, vanishing into invisibility. Indeed, there is no author to be found: Victor Eremita disavows the diary, "A" disowns it, and the Seducer himself is as insubstantial as gossamer, diaphanous, sheer secrecy, sheer myth, sheer duplicity—insofar as he is visibly present in the diary, he is invisible. As we've seen, Johannes insists that "Who I am," apart from the myth, "has nothing to do with it" (*E/Or* 1:439). In fact, all of Kierkegaard's pseudonyms are invisible in their visibility. All are finally like William Afham, who asks, in introducing a manuscript ("Some Reflections on Marriage in Answer to Objections") by "A Married Man" that Victor Eremita had stolen from the house of Judge William: "Who, then, am I? Let no one ask about that. If it did not occur to anyone to ask before, then I am saved, for now I am over the worst of it. Moreover, I am not worth asking about, for I am the least of all: I am pure being and thus almost less than nothing; I am the pure being that is everywhere present but yet not noticeable, for I am continually being annulled. By myself, I am capable of nothing at all" (*SLW* 86).[13]

Like Don Juan, who "has no stable existence at all, but hurries in a perpetual vanishing, precisely like music" (*E/Or* 1:101), the pseudonymous author has only an apparent self, a self that vanishes into thin air. Every pseudonym creates a seductive world that, as Crites puts it, "like a mirror, reflects its problem according to its angle of vision."[14] But finally, the mirror requires a spectator, and the author must withdraw, be "annulled," become "nobody," leaving only the reader staring into the mirror. As William Afham devilishly puts it in the motto to his contribution to *Stages on Life's Way,* "Such works are mirrors: when an ape looks in, no apostle can look out" (*SLW* 8). What we see, how we read, depends on our courtship of the text. Reflecting in his journal on the meaning of indirect authorship, Kierkegaard writes that "the object of [indirect] communication is not a knowledge [on the part of the reader], but a realization." As such, the ethical goal of authorship is reached only if "the communicator in a sense disappears, steps aside," so that each true reader may "stand alone" (*JP* 1:649, 651).

In the "Diary," the author's disappearance is represented by the Seducer's lack of satisfaction with simply poetizing himself into Cordelia's heart, and his desire to poetize himself *out* of her life: "To poetize oneself into a young girl is an art, to poetize oneself out of her is a masterpiece" (*E/Or* 1:364). Thus at the end of his seduction, as he approaches the moment of consummating his artwork, Johannes wishes for "no farewell with her; nothing is more disgusting to me than a woman's tears and a woman's prayers," and speculates on the possibility of being "able to poetize himself out of a girl, so that one could make her so proud that she would imagine that it was she who tired of the relationship. It could become a very interesting epilogue" (*E/Or* 1:439–40).

Indeed, this is the masterpiece that the text of *Either/Or* is experimenting with—just as Kierkegaard himself was experimenting at this time with poetizing himself out of the heart of his own Cordelia, Regine Olsen—the masterpiece of the "very interesting epilogue" where seduction is consummated in an act of de-seduction. At the end, we are left with the situation "A" describes as the perfect work of theater: "The curtain falls, the play is over, nothing is left except . . . a fantastic shadow-play, which irony directs. . . . The immediately real situation is the unreal situation; behind this there appears a new situation which is no less absurd, and so forth; . . . when it is most reasonable, it appears most crazy; and as the [experience] recedes, . . . so [it] is more and more meaningless in spite of its reasonableness" (*E/Or* 1:275).

Each pseudonymous work ends in meaninglessness, in failure, in craziness—however reasonable, however seductive the artistry of the texts may appear as we read them. Their failure is hardly an aesthetic failure: In fact, it is precisely because the pseudonymous authors and the worlds they depict do succeed so fully as works of art (they are brilliant portraits of "poetized I's," of "phantoms of the imagination," of dramatis personae, but not of persons) that they elude and evade literal meaning and the domain of concrete existential choice we as real human beings must come to terms with. Nor is their failure due to a simple ethical judgment on Kierkegaard's part of the worlds his pseudonyms create—such a judgment would imply an ethical authority, just what the pseudonymous authorship seeks so strenuously to avoid: It is for the reader, not the author, to make such ethical evaluations. It would be better to say that the intentional failure of these works (whether they represent aesthetic or ethical worldviews) is itself an ethical act on Kierkegaard's part, an act of de-seduction and abandonment of the reader to herself. There is no author to be found: Each of the authors disappears, becomes invisible. There are no teachers; no answers except as responses to the questions we pose; no ordained "reality" of the text, but only appearance, only the mirror that reflects ape and apostle alike. Take care, then, reader: What you find is what you are.

THE APE'S CONCLUSION

But if to be the apostle Kierkegaard is looking for who will be his authentic reader requires that the reader be seduced into her own authenticity—albeit through a final act of de-seduction (the "masterpiece") in which the author disappears and leaves the reader on her own—perhaps some would prefer to be the ape than Kierkegaard's masterpiece. Emmanuel Levinas criticizes Kierkegaard for reserving the holiness of absolute otherness to God alone, failing to see that every human individual is also absolutely other. For Levinas, this means that Kierkegaard is incapable of developing an adequate ethics, since all genuine ethics rest on the recognition that the other can never be known. Only as such do we avoid reducing the other to our own projection of her and devaluing her subjectivity.[15]

Yet when we think about the plan of Kierkegaard's indirect communication, it seems that he does in fact relate to the other, the reader, as an absolute other. He does not pretend to know the other in her concrete particularity: As we have seen, "One human being . . . cannot understand [another] except as a possibility" (*CUP* 286). Nor does he seek to display his own self to the reader; on the contrary, he goes to every length to disguise himself. The language of indirect communication is thus a sort of silence, a revocation of what is said as the author disappears into "no one" and "nothing." But it is only *a sort* of silence, since of course something is communicated— but indirectly, through deception. If the seduction is successful, nothing direct will have been said by the author that the reader can rely on. She is abandoned to herself. "The indirect method," Kierkegaard writes in *The Point of View,* "loving and serving the truth, arranges everything dialectically for the prospective captive, and then shyly withdraws (for love is always shy), so as not to witness the admission which he makes to himself alone . . . —that he has lived hitherto in an illusion" (*PV* 25–26).

The apostle's conclusion saw the seduction of Cordelia by Johannes as a sort of devouring and contrasted this with Kierkegaard's ethically motivated, "higher" seduction. But is not the ethics of Kierkegaard's indirect communication—an ethics of evasion and abandonment—also a sort of devouring of the reader, however shy and loving the author assures us he is toward his captive? Interestingly, in his master's thesis, *The Concept of Irony* (defended in 1841, seventeen months before the publication of *Either/Or*), Kierkegaard described Socrates, the primary inspiration for his own maieutic method,[16] as a "privateer" preying on the naive beliefs of the youth, robbing them of all that had given them a sense of orientation and security, and then deserting them (*CI* 205). "He brought the individual under the force of his dialectical vacuum pump, deprived him of the atmospheric air in which he was accustomed to breathe, and abandoned him" (*CI* 203). Socrates is presented as a sort of beast of prey, "consuming" others, becoming "temporarily sated," but continually reawakening to a quenchless thirst for destruction (*CI* 200). Socrates: privateer, vacuum pump, beast of prey—and seducer.

> An eroticist he certainly was to the fullest extent; the enthusiasm for knowledge was his on an extraordinary scale; in short, he possessed all the seductive gifts of the spirit. But communicate, fill, enrich, this he could not do. In this sense one might possibly call him a seducer, for he deceived the youth and awakened longings which he never satisfied, allowed them to become inflamed by the subtle pleasures of anticipation yet never gave them solid and nourishing food. (*CI* 213)

Kierkegaard believes that "the more gifted ones" among Socrates' victims felt "grateful" to him for freeing them from the unsupportable foundations of their former beliefs (*CI* 213, 200). But make no mistake: The ethics of indirect communication is one that seeks victims and is successful to the extent that they are devoured. The aim, to be sure, is that they be born anew, but the beast of prey leaves that to them and their own devices, if they can find the air to breathe in the vacuum of his passing.

And we must wonder not only about how the reader fares, but the author as well. Socrates is satiated by devouring his victims, but only for a moment. There is an eternal return of his hunger. And Kierkegaard? How do we understand his hunger for seduction? Is it a wholly altruistic need, this devouring, a service to God, as he says of his practice of deception in *The Point of View*? (*PV* 6). Or is it perhaps at least in part motivated by a sense of emptiness that simultaneously needs and fears the other and hence imposes a world of disguises and masks between the two? "As far back as I can re-member," Kierkegaard confides in *The Point of View*, "I was in agreement with myself about one thing, that for me there was no comfort or help to be looked for in others." His method for coping with this sense of aloneness, developed already in childhood, is tell-ing: "What reconciled me with my fate and with my suffering was that I, the so unhappy, so much tortured prisoner, had obtained [an] unlimited freedom of being able to deceive, so that I was allowed to be absolutely alone with my pain" (*PV* 79).

Despite his commitment to the ethics of deception, Kierkegaard emphatically does not "remain faithful to the deception" throughout. Many of his pseudonymous works include displays of direct commu-nication where Kierkegaard's own views (evident from his journals) are declared without gloss, not to mention the downright exhibition-istic *Point of View*,[17] which I examine in detail in Chapter 6. These regularly recurring lapses from his pact with indirection and disguise suggest a fundamental desire to be known by the other, to be ac-knowledged, appreciated, and affirmed for who he is. *The Point of View* opens by informing us that "in my career as an author, a point has now been reached where it is permissible to do what I feel a strong impulse to do and so regard as my duty—to explain once and for all, as directly and frankly as possible, what is what: what I as an author declare myself to be." For "I have suffered under much misunderstanding" (*PV* 6, 8).

One of the many splendors of Kierkegaard is that he himself was well aware of these questions. The whole discussion of Socrates in the *Concept of Irony*, in which Kierkegaard takes seriously the idea that Aristophanes' scathing portrait of Socrates in *The Clouds* is not easy to dismiss and that the jury that condemned Socrates to death for corrupting the youth was perfectly reasonable in its judgment, is a haunting prelude to an authorship that will model its own indirect communication on that of the demon lover who has just been so unsentimentally portrayed. And the journals are filled with moments of self-doubt about the cost of the secrecy and disguise that are required by indirect communication, most particularly that his pseudonymity keeps him away from his "own self" (*JSK* 641).

The questions posed by Kierkegaard's ambitious project of indirect communication are fundamental questions of ethics, questions about the relation of the I to the other. To what extent does respect for the radical alterity of the other permit (or even demand) withdrawal into indirection, silence, disguise, and deception on my part? If a direct communication with the other is an ethical impossibility, is there an ethics of seduction by which I might reach the other without eroticizing or manipulating him? May I devour the other's sense of security in order to free her into a more inspired hunger of her own? And what becomes of the I in this process of indirection? What do I make of my own emptiness when my hunger for the other can be satiated only through an act of deception and destruction? Is there room for the encounter with my own intimate "Thou" in a world of fantasy created by these acts? Is intimacy with the self and with the other required by ethics, or are there other requirements that may suspend or sacrifice the goal of intimacy?

The two conclusions, those of the apostle and the ape, circle around two possible points of view to these questions. That Kierkegaard's texts allow each of these contrasting points of view on what it means to read them is a large part of the grandness of his authorship: The ape is given as much room to think for himself as the apostle.

4. Hegel's Seductions

Hegel's narrative is designed to seduce the reader.

JUDITH BUTLER, *Subjects of Desire*

WHETHER WE THINK of Kierkegaard's authorship as seductive in the sense of eroticizing the reader so as to devour her or as an emancipation of the reader into autonomy—the two readings we considered at the close of Chapter 3—there can be no doubt that his authorship undertakes an aesthetically and ethically sophisticated project of seduction. Hegel, though, is alternatively portrayed by Kierkegaard as the most boorish and superficial sort of seducer and as the least seductive author of all.

We noted in Chapter 2, in the context of Kierkegaard's depiction of Hegel's "system" as a form of extraterrestrialism—an "emancipation from telluric conditions" through its abstraction away from the concrete conditions of life—that Kierkegaard acknowledges the irresistibly seductive character of Hegel's philosophy in an age that longs for anything that might make the burden of existence easier. By promising an objective knowledge of existence, "the system" provides a detour around the fear and trembling that attends the uncertainty of subjectivity. "The formulas for pain and suffering are recited by rote," reduced to categories of logic and thus disarmed of their power (*CUP* 229).

DIFFICULTY

If Hegel's only seductiveness is his luring of the reader into a disburdening of her responsibility to confront the "objective uncertainty" of existence (*CUP* 182)—since he supplies an objective explanation of everything, even our suffering and pain—Kierkegaard defines his own project of seduction as one of making life once again difficult. Hence Johannes Climacus, the pseudonymous author of the *Concluding Unscientific Postscript,* seated on a bench in the Frederiksberg Garden, smoking his cigar and ruminating over his life, realizes that he is "going on to become an old man . . . without really [having] undertak[en] to do anything." He recognizes that he does not have the talent of "the many benefactors of the age who know how to benefit mankind by making life easier and easier, some by railways, others by omnibuses and steamboats, . . . and finally the true benefactors of the age who make spiritual existence in virtue of [objective] thought easier and easier." So he takes another puff of his cigar and comes to the insight that "inasmuch as with my limited capacities it will be impossible to make anything easier than it has become, I must, with the same humanitarian enthusiasm as the others, undertake to make something harder." Thus Climacus resolves "to create difficulties everywhere" (*CUP* 166).

Yet what are we to make of this portrait of Hegel as a seducer into the ever "easier and easier" in light of his own description of his philosophy as an entry into "the difficult"? We saw in Chapter 1 that Hegel distinguishes his notion of "thinking philosophically" from "ordinary" thinking in terms of denying us "the use of [our] familiar ideas," so that we "feel the ground where [we] once stood firm and at home taken away from beneath [us]," and we "cannot tell where in the world" we are. So far from seeking to make the reader feel at home in the comforting space of an objective knowledge that relieves us of all burdens, Hegel understands his philosophy as a radical challenge against the commonplace "hankering" (*Sehnsucht*) for comfort (*EL* §3), and as an invitation, for those who choose to accept it, into difficulty and the uncanny sense of *not* being at home.

From Kierkegaard's perspective, though, the difficulty Hegel's philosophy poses for its readers is the inverse of the difficulty Johannes Climacus resolves to dedicate himself to on his bench in the Frederiksberg Garden. Climacus (and Climacus's author, Kierkegaard) will make life difficult by returning the individual subject to the discomfort and anxiety of existence, whereas Hegel magically *produces* difficulty by abstracting away from existence into the fantastic world of his logical categories. The Hegelian "difficulty" is simply the absurdity of his System with its abstruse logicizing of life. And in this sense, although in principle his philosophy is seductive—albeit in a superficial way, as a sinecure for those searching for an easier life—in its actual execution it is a hilariously obscure abracadabra of logical symbolization, the least seductive of all possible texts. It is the purpose of this chapter to argue that Hegel in fact relies on seductive strategies in the service of an ethics of authorship utterly opposed to those Kierkegaard ascribes to him.

Walking on One's Head

The absurdity of the Hegelian system for Kierkegaard is its topsy-turviness, its turning the world upside down, an image often used by Kierkegaard and a favorite of other mid-nineteenth-century critics of Hegel. Feuerbach writes in his *Essence of Christianity* that he will "invert" the Hegelian philosophy, which "reduce[s] real existence to an existence on paper"[1]—echoing Kierkegaard's own reference to Hegel's philosophy as a well-oiled "paragraph machine" for producing a "book world" (*CUP* 376, 224; *JP* 1:649). Engels, in his review of Marx's *Contribution to a Critique of Political Economy,* says that Hegel "reversed the actual relation" of history and ideas "and stood it on its head."[2] And in the first volume of *Capital,* Marx speaks of how "in Hegel's writings, dialectic stands on its head," and of how it is his task "to turn it right way up again."[3]

The following generation of Hegel's critics exploits the same image. To cite just one instance, Heidegger, in his work on *Nietzsche,* remarks that "Hegel himself says that to think in the manner of his system means to attempt to stand—and walk—on one's head."[4] Unlike Kierkegaard, Feuerbach, Engels, Marx, and many others, Heidegger at least acknowledges that Hegel had himself already used the image of inversion later philosophers were to apply to him as though they had thought it up themselves. But Heidegger does not get Hegel's idea about walking on one's head quite right. What Hegel actually says is this: "[My] way of putting the facts is no mere whim, once in a while to walk on one's head for a change, after having walked for a long while on one's legs." Rather, it is because his way of speaking is so contrary to the ordinary way of thinking that it must *appear* to adopt an inverted stance (*PN* §246Z). Similarly, in a letter to his Dutch friend and former student Peter van Ghert, Hegel suggests that "to the uninitiated, speculative philosophy must . . . present itself as the upside-down world, contradicting all their accustomed concepts and whatever else appeared valid to them according to so-called sound common sense" (*Letters* 591).[5] It is thus not that Hegel, out of some sort of metaphysical perversity, determines to write a philosophy that can only be negotiated while walking on one's head, but rather that the world of common sense is itself so upside-down that his philosophy can only appear to make such an outlandish requirement upon its readers.

So far from supporting Heidegger's (and Kierkegaard's) interpretation that Hegel is devoted to a forgetfulness of concrete reality, Hegel's remarks about the upside-down appearance of his philosophy are virtually identical to the spirit of what Heidegger says of the "average everyday" understanding and its essential "forgetfulness" (and one may equally well think here of Kierkegaard's remarks about the "cheap, second-hand" character of common sense in *The Present Age*) (*PA* 58). The everyday understanding, Heidegger writes in *Being and Time,* seeks always "to take things easily and make them easy"; it distrusts any thinking that is unfamiliar and sees it as nonsense. It follow that "that which is . . . closest and well known [for the everyday understanding], is ontologically the farthest and not known at all."[6] Both Heidegger and Kierkegaard, like Hegel, seek to turn our ordinary way of conceiving reality upside down. The question of the possibility of a seductive authorship is not, then, whether one writes a philosophy that inverts the world of common sense, but rather how an authorship that turns everything topsy-turvy can be seductive at all, as opposed to just disorienting and discomforting.

LIVING WITH ONE'S AILMENTS

Kierkegaard himself, while ridiculing the absurdity of the Hegelian System, makes "the absurd" a central category of his own philosophy (e.g., *FT* 48, 51, 57–61; *CUP* 183–84, 188–91). But Kierkegaard's absurd is presented as the opposite (one is tempted to say, the "inside-out" or "upside-down") of the absurdity of Hegel's philosophy. For Kierkegaard, consciousness of the absurd arises when we see the utter incapacity of reason and its pretense to objective knowledge to offer any real understanding of our situation as existing subjects confronting a world that, as Albert Camus puts it, is silent when asked for its "why."[7] Kierkegaard's absurd leads to *faith* as the counterpoint to knowledge: The absurd is the recognition that although human reason is impotent to provide definitive meaning, for God, "all things are possible," even "the impossible" (*FT* 57). The ultimate seduction for Kierkegaard is thus the seductiveness of the Beyond, the Absolute, God, the power of what is outside the human, to save us from our hopelessness.

Even if efforts to read Hegel as a religious philosopher or theologian are plausible,[8] such readings somehow have to accommodate the fact that for Hegel there simply is no Beyond except as the fantasy of the despairing soul, the unhappy consciousness. Long before Nietzsche, Hegel explored the idea that "God is dead": The unhappy consciousness, which projects its yearning for a final sense of reconciliation of itself with the world onto a Beyond, is led eventually to the realization of the incoherency of seeking a reconciliation with the world through what is beyond the world. The unhappy consciousness is "the knowledge of total loss" and "the grief which expresses itself in the hard saying that 'God is dead'" (*PS* 455).

Kierkegaard devotes his entire authorship to a service to God (*PV* 6), seeking to seduce his readers toward a Beyond that might bring them redemption from the sickness unto death that is life. Hegel, though, sees the longing for a Beyond as a form of what Camus would later call "philosophical suicide," the abandonment of "lucidity" when we see that reason can provide no salvation. Camus feels that Kierkegaard more than any other had seen into the abyss of existence, but that finally he was not able to bear it, and took "the leap" into the arms of the Absolute. If for Camus "the important thing, as Abbe Galiani said to Mme d'Epinay, is not to be cured, but to live with one's ailments, Kierkegaard [for his part] wants to be

cured. . . . The entire effort of his intelligence is to escape the antin-
omy of the human condition."[9] Hegel, like Camus, refuses the
cure—the leap into a Beyond—and insists that we must live with
our ailments, with the "pathway of despair," the "Golgotha of the
spirit," and the "slaughterbench of human happiness" that define the
contours of the human situation (PS 49, 493; PH 21).

But how can such a philosophy be seductive? How can an authorship that disdains any extraterrestrial cure (Kierkegaard's portrait of
Hegel notwithstanding) possibly entice any readers at all? In what
follows, I suggest that a close reading of Hegel's proposal for a new
understanding of grammar, his notion of a "philosophic proposition," and his authorial enactment of a form of "spectatorship"
allows us to perceive a style of seduction that serves as an alternative
to Kierkegaard's more obviously seductive authorship.

THE GRAMMAR OF SEDUCTION

In Chapter 1, we alluded to Hegel's idea (and practice) of a "philosophic proposition," which seeks to unsettle our ordinary reading of
propositions where the subject of a sentence "fixes" the meaning of
the predicates. Hegel's proposal for a rethinking of grammar is based
on the idea of replacing—or more strongly, "destroying"—this familiar propositional form (PS 36–40). Like Leibniz, Hegel noted an
important parallel between the grammatical subject-predicate relation and the ontology of the self, the existential subject, as related to
its attributes. The way we speak, right down to the syntax of our
sentences, inherently reflects certain ontological assumptions, in particular, that the self, like the grammatical subject, is simply a collection of its properties. But unlike Leibniz, Hegel challenged the usual
conception of the relation between the subject and its predicates,
which he felt lured us into thinking of subjects as somehow contain-
ing or fixing their predicates, or of predicates as the properties of the
subject, and directly associated this conception with "picture thinking" (or "representational" thinking: vorstellende Denken), which assumes that the meaning of an object of perception is determined
(fixed) by a mental re-presentation of it (PS 18, 479; EL §3). So too,

the ontological subject, the self, does not contain or fix or hold as its property its object by thinking it. In the philosophical proposition, predicates "recoil" back against the subject, casting it into question: The subject "suffers, as we might put it, a counterthrust [*Gegenstoß*]," such that it is displaced. Hegel is searching for what he calls a more "plastic" or "fluid" expression of language that might "destroy" the subject-centered pretensions of ordinary language (*PS* 37–39).

What is particularly misleading about the subject-predicate model of grammar is that it implies that language is the direct, immediate expression of meaning, of subjects that simply enclose their predicates. But language always points beyond the apparently transparent and stable character of signification. Hegel gives the example of the proposition "God is being."

> The predicate is "being"; it has the significance of something substantial in which the subject is dissolved. "Being" is here meant to be not a predicate, but rather the essence; it seems, consequently, that God ceases to be what he is from his position in the proposition, viz. a fixed subject. Here thinking, instead of making progress in the transition from subject to predicate, in reality feels itself checked [*gehemmt*] by the loss of the subject, and, missing it, is thrown back on to the thought of the subject [seeking a new way of understanding it]. (*PS* 38)

It is precisely the "inhibition" (*Hemmung*) of thought effected by the ambiguity and instability of the speculative proposition that Hegel sees as responsible for the sense of obscurity and disorientation people find in reading his philosophy: This "inhibition of thought is in large measure the source of the complaints regarding the unintelligibility of philosophical writing" (*PS* 39). These complaints originate in our commonsense assumption that meaning is directly expressible in propositions, our belief that the proposition is a "firm objective basis" upon which signification is transparently displayed. When in 1805, a year before writing his *Phenomenology,* Hegel wrote a letter to Heinrich Voss, a translator of Homer, that he "wish[ed] to try to teach philosophy to speak German" (*Letters* 107), he was expressing his desire to use the plastic nature of the German language to "destroy" the apparently transparent character of the propositional form.

At the heart of Hegel's new conception of the grammar of the proposition is his commitment to the trope of irony: The ironic figure of speech refuses, or confuses, ordinary expectations. It does not say what it means, just as in the philosophic proposition "we learn . . . that we meant something other than we meant to mean [*die Meinung erfährt, daß es anders gemeint ist, als sie gemeint*], and this correction of our meaning compels us to go back to the proposition and understand it in some other way" (*PS* 39/*W* 3:60). The entirety of Hegel's philosophy is a work of irony, where we discover again and again that the "truth" of a particular form of consciousness, or of a particular category of logic, or of a particular stage of history, is only partial and thus intrinsically a truth that points beyond itself, which does not mean what it appears to mean. As Judith Butler puts it, "Hegel's sentences send us forth into a journey of knowledge; they indicate what is not being expressed, what must be explored." And it is just this ironic withholding of meaning that is seductive: "Hegel's narrative is designed to seduce the reader, to exploit his need to find himself in the text he is reading."[10]

Hegel's extending of his ironic voice to the level of grammar itself, to the very mechanics of how we signify what we mean to say, anticipates Lacan's idea of the "metonymic" structure of the symbolic, where "one signifier constantly refers to another in a perpetual deferral of meaning."[11] There is, for Lacan, an inevitable "*glissement*" or "slippage" in the relation of the signifier to the signified,[12] just as for Hegel the philosophic proposition undermines the fixity of meaning by revealing the fundamental fluidity and restlessness of signification. As Heidegger puts it, "Hegel brings the absolute restlessness of absolvence [*Absolvenz*] into [the] quiet 'is' of the proposition," and "the whole work of his philosophy is devoted solely to making this restlessness real."[13]

The *glissement* and restlessness inherent in Hegel's discourse implies, as Jean-Luc Nancy recognizes, "a new way of reading."[14] Hegel decenters his own voice as the fixed site of signification, since his sentences surrender themselves to a necessary "recoil" or "counterthrust" on the part of the reader, and the seduction of his authorship is precisely that the reader is asked to "go back" to the propositions and find a new meaning.

In many ways, Hegel's exploration of a new grammar foreshadows Heidegger's remarks on grammar in *Being and Time*. For Heidegger, like Hegel, language is constitutive of being human: "Man shows himself as the entity which talks." Yet language has been understood "primarily as assertion," where the relation of subjects to their predicates "is regarded as self-evident." Heidegger then speaks of "the task of liberating grammar from [this] logic" of the assertion,[15] exactly the task Hegel had undertaken a century before in his experimentation with the philosophic proposition.

Central to Heidegger's sense of the importance of this task is his insight that the logic of the assertion implies an utterly traditional and yet profoundly misleading conception of what it means to know. Behind the logic of assertion lies the idea of the subject as a sort of "'inside' and its 'inner sphere' as a sort of 'box' or 'cabinet,'" and the object of knowledge, the signified, as an "outside" that must be appropriated and "brought in" to the enclosure of consciousness in order for it to have meaning. But, Heidegger writes, "When *Dasein* directs itself towards something and grasps it, it does not somehow first get out of an inner sphere in which it has been . . . encapsulated; . . . it is always 'outside' alongside entities that it encounters. . . . The perceiving of what is known is not a process of returning with one's booty to the 'cabinet' of consciousness after one has gone out and grasped it; even in perceiving, . . . *Dasein* . . . remains outside."[16]

Hegel's deployment of the philosophic proposition similarly confounds the ordinary conception of the relation between "inside" and "outside," subject and object—and hence, by implication, between author and reader. Meaning is not fixed "inside" the subject of a proposition or inside the mind of the author, the writing subject, but only in an encounter with the "outside." Indeed, the meaning of the text is always already "outside" it, in the hands of the reader. The seduction of Hegel's authorship is thus its own self-cancellation, its denial of a privileged "inside" meaning, and the consequent beckoning of the reader to enter in to the narrative and make it her own.

THE PHILOSOPHIC SPECTATOR

If Hegel's use of the philosophic proposition, with its new understanding of the grammar of relation between subjects and predicates,
opens the way by extension to a reading of his text as a seduction by
the writing subject of the reader to find herself in the text, his idea
of the author as a "spectator" might at first glance appear to stand at
odds with whatever allure is achieved by the philosophic proposition.
Hegel frequently invokes the language of spectatorship.

> "We [the philosopher] merely look on, as it were, at the object's
> own development, not altering it by importing into it our own
> subjective ideas and fancies" (*PM* §379Z);

> "Philosophy has, as it were, only to watch" (*PM* §381Z);

> "Since what consciousness examines is its own self, all that is left
> for us [the phenomenologist] to do is simply to look on" (*PS* 54).

These passages could be multiplied many times over, since Hegel
regularly refers to "we who contemplate" the process of the development of consciousness, or of "the observer" who "simply takes up
what is there before him" (*PM* §§385Z, 387A; *L* 69).

Alexandre Kojève goes so far as to call Hegel's method "purely
. . . 'positivist': Hegel looks at the Real and describes what he sees."
Hegel fancies himself "the scientist" who restrains himself from any
interpretive work, limiting himself to "purely passive contemplation
. . . and simple description."[17] This reading of Hegel's philosophic
spectator is close to Kierkegaard's portrait of Hegel the scientist, the
one who imagines that existence can simply be observed and neatly
categorized. And what could be less seductive than the image of an
author passionlessly watching and recording the different shapes of
human experience? Hegel would be like the Belgian doctor in Sartre's short story "The Wall," who is sent to the cell of the men condemned to be executed in the morning in order to observe them. "I
felt him watching me," Pablo, one of the prisoners, says. "He never
took his eyes off me. . . . He came to watch our bodies, bodies dying
. . . while yet alive." As Pablo looks into the doctor's "cold blue eyes,"
it occurs to him that the Belgian's "only sin was lack of imagination,"

and yet Pablo hates him: "Bastard, I thought angrily; . . . I wanted to stand up and smash his face"[18]—an impulse we could easily forgive Hegel's readers for sharing if Kojève's interpretation of his passionless witnessing of our "pathway of despair" is correct.

Closer still to Kierkegaard is Gary Shapiro's characterization of "Hegel's philosophical 'we'" as the "foundation of the universalistic ideology of bourgeois culture," to which he contrasts Kierkegaard's "literary mode," which "gives up universalistic aims not only in its explicit and implicit doctrines but in the way it is written and offers itself to the reader."[19] Shapiro nicely captures Kierkegaard's repeated expression of incredulity at Hegel's purported reduction of the multiplicity and specificity of subjective experience into universal categories, as though there were only one "general individual" (*CUP* 106–7, 118–19, 283–89).

BEHIND THE SCENES

Beyond the picture of Hegel the positivist observer is the suspicion that of course this can only be a self-delusion, or perhaps a pretense, a disguise. Behind the mask of the cold blue eyes and the prop of a ledger and pen to record, like the Belgian doctor, with utter lack of imagination, the symptoms of his subject, surely Hegel is stage-managing the story of consciousness that he claims only to be describing. As Butler suggests, "Clearly, Hegel's subject has a very fine director working for him" behind the scenes. "But as Kierkegaard once asked . . . , 'where is the director? I should like to have a word with him.'"[20]

But what sort of directing is Hegel engaged in? Kierkegaard's Johannes the Seducer watches precisely so as to direct—to shape, mold, and ensnare. But Hegel claims to watch as a spectator, as the author of a phenomenology, whose basic commitment is, as Husserl's slogan puts it, to go "back to the things themselves!"[21]—or, as Heidegger says, to allow beings to be, to let them speak for themselves.[22] Hegel's spectatorship is thus meant to reflect the value of an ethic of *listening* rather than imposing his own direction. The story he narrates is the "path of the natural consciousness that presses forward to true knowledge, or . . . the way of the soul which journeys through the series of its own configurations as though they were stations appointed for it by its own nature," and that "will *show itself*" to "lose itself" and "its truth on this path" (*PS* 49, emphasis added).

But what is this "true knowledge" that consciousness presses forward to, and how does Hegel know it? Whatever the seductive attraction of his ethic of listening, doesn't Hegel adopt a sort of Überstandpoint, the omniscient perspective of the Wise Man who stands and waits for us at the end of our journey to congratulate us on our having arrived at what he has known all along? Hegel describes his philosophy as a "circle that presupposes its end," an end that is there already in the beginning (*PS* 10), and he might thus appear as the sage who patiently circles around his novitiates as they struggle to realize the "true knowledge" he could have given them at the very start. As we saw in the Introduction, Foucault writes that "we have to determine the extent to which our anti-Hegelianism is possibly one of his ruses directed against us, at the end of which he stands, motionless, waiting for us."[23] This is just Kierkegaard's frustration with Hegel, that Hegel presents himself as anticipating every possible point of view, absorbing them all and dissolving their critical edge in an Absolute Knowledge that reveals them as mere preliminary stages on the way to a Truth that only he can reveal.

In Chapter 7, we will seek to problematize this portrait of Hegel the Wise Man (the phrase is Kojève's).[24] But for now it is enough to acknowledge that of course Hegel "directs" his narrative. All authorship is directive, even the most indirect: Every author has a plan, a project; every text is a circle whose end is present in the beginning. As Kierkegaard acknowledges in the "First and Last Declaration" he appends under his own name to Johannes Climacus's *Concluding Unscientific Postscript,* he, Kierkegaard, is not the author "properly speaking" of the text, but only a "*souffleur,*" or stage manager (*CUP* 551). The question is not whether there is a director behind the scenes, but what authority he claims, and the extent to which he uses his direction to decenter that authority, to write in such a way that ultimately, as Roland Barthes puts it, a text's meaning "lies not in its origin," its author, "but in its destination," its reader.[25]

Kierkegaard scorns the Hegelian posture of the spectator of the theater of life—we are always in existence and there is no privileged standpoint "outside." Yet in a profound sense, as speakers we always are on the "outside," outside of the inner experience of the other. To watch, then, is not necessarily to adopt a privileged position, but, assuming a commitment to the ethics of listening, can be a form of witnessing and a sign of respect for the inner space of the other, a resolve to let the other speak.

For all the fun Kierkegaard has with the idea of Hegel hovering outside of existence in order to watch it, of course he too adopts a point of view on the multitude of points of view he narrates. Even without considering his *Point of View,* in which he pronounces the truth of his authorship, there is a sense in which we may see his allegiance to "subjectivity" as granting him a license to the grammar of assertion that Hegel's stance of "objectivity" does not. Kierkegaard's declaration that "truth is subjectivity," for example, is ironically an *assertion* of his "pathos of inwardness," what we have seen Hegel call "the oracle within our breast." We can certainly find many propositions in Hegel's writings that also have the apparent form of assertions, and yet the new grammar of his speculative proposition destroys their oracular form, exposing his "assertions" to be unstable, restless, subject to a *glissement,* continually pointing beyond themselves. The philosopher "must beware of the wish to be edifying" (*PS* 6)—with all due apologies to Kierkegaard—not because he lacks passion, but because he must avoid imposing the "law of his heart" on the reader, whose own journey is the true heart of the matter.

WATCHING THE OTHER: SHAME AND LOVE

In *Being and Nothingness,* Sartre explores the meaning of what it is "to be seen by another." He gives the example of looking through a keyhole, surreptitiously observing a conversation. The voyeur is alone in the hallway, utterly absorbed in his furtive act, and as such he has "no 'outside'": He *is* his jealousy, or his curiosity. "But all of a sudden I hear footsteps in the hall. Someone is looking at me!" And now everything changes. There is an "internal hemorrhage" in the voyeur's world. In being looked at, my world "flows toward the other," and "I am for myself only as I am a pure reference to the other."[26] Thus I now have an "outside," which delivers me over to *shame.* Shame is "the feeling of having my being *outside,* . . . without any defense, illuminated by the absolute light which emanates from [the gaze of] a pure subject." In shame, I recognize myself as a "degraded, fixed, and dependent being for the other."[27]

The question for Hegel is that of the possibility of a form of spectatorship, of watching, that is not a form of surveillance, of judgment, of a reduction of the reader to a self of shame. Can there be a watching that is loving, an observation that nurtures autonomy? In the "Diary of the Seducer," Johannes imagines Cordelia looking at herself in a mirror: "She does not reflect on it"—she has no being-for-self, no self-awareness—"but the mirror reflects her"—she is pure reflected being, defined entirely by the image that "catches her" (*E/Or* 1:311), just as the interloper in Sartre's scenario catches the voyeur and gives him an "outside." And Johannes will become Cordelia's mirror, her outside. His seduction will give her "freedom" and beauty only as the one who is reflected by Johannes's own desires.

But can there be a watching that is seductive as a drawing of the other, the reader, into *self*-reflection? Kierkegaard's Johannes hides his act of observation: Cordelia is utterly unaware that she is his spectacle. Although he is "visible to everyone in the living room, still [Johannes is] really . . . [in his] hiding place, . . . lying in ambush" (*E/Or* 1:344). So too Kierkegaard hides himself; he is "a stranger and an alien" to his reader (*CI* 263). Hegel, by contrast, reveals his observation; he announces himself as spectator.

Derrida configures the relation between Kierkegaard and Hegel precisely along these lines of the one who requires "hiddenness" and "secrecy" and the one whose "philosophy represents the . . . demand for manifestation . . . and unveiling."[28] But this is too simple. Kierkegaard's hiddenness is his commitment to the secrecy and privacy of "the inner," which requires his disappearance as author and a seduction of the reader by indirection and subterfuge. But he too unveils himself and emerges into manifestation with his impassioned declarations of "what it means to be an existing individual." His self-manifestation becomes more and more insistent in his later years, when he writes almost exclusively under his own name and publishes a "First and Last Declaration" (the appendix to the *Postscript,* signed S. Kierkegaard), *On My Work as an Author* (published before the *Point of View*), articles in the *Fatherland,* and a series of pamphlets with titles such as "What Do I Want?" "My Task," "Outcry," and "This Must Be Said," all ardently self-declaratory.

Hegel's "demand for manifestation and unveiling" is his refusal to disguise his position as philosophic spectator, so that the reader will not find herself in the position of Cordelia, who has no opportunity to assert herself against Johannes's gaze, which he veils from her. True, Cordelia is spared shame, since the condition for shame is absent: She is unaware of being looked at. But she is also denied freedom, except as an illusion produced in her by her seducer. Hegel's reader is thus undeniably more vulnerable to shame than Kierkegaard's, since Hegel admits to watching her whereas Kierkegaard, like Johannes, makes himself invisible. Hegel seeks to disarm the threat of shame, though, by a practice of observation that denies a position of authority to the one who watches. And this is the sense in which Hegel, the philosopher of "the manifest," is equally a philosopher of concealment and silence.

Kierkegaard is right, then, if not in the sense he meant it, when he writes of how Hegel sought "to transform him[self] into so objective an observer that he becomes almost a ghost" (*CUP* 118). As I will explore more fully in Chapter 7, Hegel is dedicated to his own death as an author; his stance of spectatorship denies him the opportunity for assertion, announcement, and edification; and at just the moment when we might expect him to declare that "This Must Be Said"—when the reader reaches the culmination of the *Phenomenology* in a chapter auspiciously titled "Absolute Knowing"—he is spectral, ghostly, beyond reach, and has precisely nothing to say; he merely asks the reader to reflect back on her own journey and to recollect it.

The seductiveness of Hegel's authorship thus rests paradoxically on the fact that his reader exists in the full awareness of his gaze—in Sartre's words, "illuminated in the absolute light" of his watching. But it is a gaze, unlike that of the voyeur peering through the keyhole, or that of the one who catches him in the hallway and makes him defenseless in shame, which cultivates an ethic of listening and "demands surrender to the life" of the other (*PS* 32). Hegel, as the authorial subject, invites a recoil against himself by the reader, and seeks to enact the basic motion of his alternative conception of "subjectivity": The subject is "not an original or immediate unity," but "is in truth actual only in so far as it is the movement . . . of its self-othering," of its divestment of all pretense to self-sufficiency (*PS* 10). Hegel's watching, his observation and spectatorship, so far from the instantiation of an unassailable position of power, is the surrendering of power and a seduction of the reader into self-empowerment.

5. Talking Cures

Nothing takes place in a psycho-analytic treatment but an interchange
of words between the patient and the analyst.

SIGMUND FREUD, "Psychical Treatment"

FRANZ ANTON MESMER, the early pioneer of hypnotism and animal magnetism, claimed that he once experimented for three months with thinking without words. In Chapter 2 we saw that Sartre's Roquentin conducted a similar experiment in the garden: He "thought without words, *on* things, *with* things." Roquentin, though, however much he yearned to abandon words so as to "touch the thing" in its sheer rawness or "facticity," realized that he had absolutely no comprehension of what he experienced in the garden, and went back to his hotel to write. As for Mesmer, his experiment led him into a state of "obscure rapture" (*un ravissement inconnu*) on the brink of insanity (*la folie*).[1] Some forty years later, Mesmer's experiment caught the attention of the philosopher Hegel, who proclaimed that this was a "manifestly irrational procedure," since it is "ridiculous" to view it as a "misfortune" that thought is bound by language: "For although the common opinion is that it is just the ineffable that is the most excellent, . . . what is ineffable is, in truth, only something obscure, fermenting, something which gains clarity only when it is able to put itself into words" (*PM* §462Z).

THE MAGIC OF WORDS

Hegel's comment on Mesmer's experiment occurs in the same lecture series where he gives his most sustained discussion of insanity or madness (*Verrücktheit*) (*PM* §§406–8), and it is interesting to consider Mesmer's own brush with insanity in the context of Hegel's advocacy of the eighteenth-century asylum reformer Philippe Pinel's "moral treatment" of the insane, which replaced physical remedies with a "gentle" therapeutics based largely on a talking cure.[2] The talking cure, we might say, puts the obscure, fermenting "something" of insanity into words, and in this way gives a sort of clarity that, as Freud saw it, was perhaps the best to be hoped for.[3] In his *Phenomenology,* Hegel refers to the "divine nature" of language (*PS* 66), a comment that foreshadows Freud's idea of the "magic" of words. "Words were originally magic," Freud tells us in the first of his *Introductory Lectures on Psychoanalysis,* "and to this day words have retained much of their ancient magical power," most especially their therapeutic power to treat mental illness.[4] Just as Freud came to replace the hypnotic method of Mesmer and Freud's own teacher Charcot with a talking cure that might finally "strip the manifestations of hypnotism of their strangeness"[5]—replacing the occultness of one procedure with the scientifically superior "magic" of another—Hegel saw the talking cure as a scientific advance over what could appear only as the "incredible miracles" of Mesmer's clinical use of animal magnetism (*PM* §397Z).

But what was the urge that drove Mesmer to his attempt to think without words? And what of Kierkegaard, who in many ways seems to have shared the same urge that motivated Mesmer, luring him toward the ineffable. Although we saw in Chapter 1 that Kierkegaard actually accepts many of the more technical features of Hegel's theory of language, finally he explores *silence* as the passageway to a cure of the torments of existence. From his early pseudonym Johannes de Silentio, who examines the uncanny silence of Abraham as he travels with his son Isaac up to Mount Moriah and the place of sacrifice, to the late "upbuilding discourse" "The Lily in the Field and the Bird of the Air," where Kierkegaard proposes that those seeking the Kingdom of God learn from the lily "to be silent" (*LF* 333), Kierkegaard promotes silence as a demand of faith, which is itself the only cure of despair, the "sickness unto death."

Earlier we mentioned Kierkegaard's fantasy of strip-searching Hegel, removing the "clothes and disguises" of his language so that he would finally be forced to "shut up" and let his life speak for itself (*JP* 3:2334). The fantasy is interesting in at least two ways. First, it suggests that language obscures (clothes over, "disguises") "who you are." That is, it implies that there is a self that is not only not constituted by language but is actually distorted (perhaps even deranged? driven into illness?) by language. This is one of the central differences between Hegel's and Kierkegaard's philosophies of language. Second, the fantasy is poignantly ironic, given that Kierkegaard often described his own existence as being fundamentally determined by his use of language (his authorship). Kierkegaard is thus torn between competing urges, to write and to keep silent, and each simultaneously represents a risk of illness and a promise of cure. Like Mesmer, he is drawn to the wordless, the ineffable—a silent space in which the self may become healed, restored from the disfigurements of language; and yet, as he says in his *Point of View for My Work as an Author,* "This very work of mine as an author was the prompting of an irresistible inward impulse" (*PV* 7). In the same journal entry that begins with the recognition of the therapeutic power of language ("only when I write do I feel well"), Kierkegaard continues: "If I stop [writing] for a few days, right away I become ill. . . . So powerful an urge, so ample, so inexhaustible [is my need to write], . . . subsist[ing] day after day for . . . years" (*JSK* 674). Kierkegaard thus confronts illness on both sides, in speaking too much, like the "mobs of speakers" (*JP* 3:2334), and in the speechlessness of not writing.

The Philosopher and the Clinic

I will argue that Hegel's and Kierkegaard's interest in the relation between language and madness reflects their concern for developing their authorships as competing "talking cures," and this interest opens the way for dialogue with psychoanalytic theory. Here it is important to address an issue raised by James Phillips in his essay "Madness of the Philosophers, Madness of the Clinic."[6] "To what degree," Phillips asks, "has the madness [referred to by] the philosophers always hinged on a *metaphoric* notion of 'madness'—a notion

that fit traditional philosophic conceptions better than clinical phenomena?"[7] That is, are Hegel and Kierkegaard speaking of the same
thing as Freud and Lacan, for example, when they refer to "madness"? One might feel that there is no particular urgency about an-
swering this question: Why not leave the different vocabularies of
the philosopher and the clinician comfortably in their own realms?
But if a meaningful dialogue between philosophy and the clinic is
to arise, then the challenge for philosophers is to show that their
descriptions are not merely metaphoric and that their preoccupation
with the dark side of human experience connects in some way with
the reality of disease, so that there is some way for clinicians to trans-
late their language into the language of psychiatry. Otherwise, philosophers will have only poetic or literary interest for the psychiatrist
or psychologist.

The challenge for clinicians is the extent to which they are open to
moving beyond a reduction of "mental illness" to a purely biological
conception of disease. We needn't go so far—nor should we—as
Thomas Szasz or Michel Foucault in seeing "mental disease" as itself
merely a metaphor.[8] But granting the evidence of underlying organic
disorder, symptoms nevertheless display themselves as mental and
behavioral states (what Hegel calls "shapes of consciousness") that,
as Hegel argued, are paralleled in "normal" experience, so that the
distinction between disease and health is often elusive. Madness "has
the healthy consciousness for its presupposition," Hegel writes, since
the healthy mind is still grappling with the same sorts of contradictions and feelings of alienation, the same "infinite pain" that characterizes insanity. Madness is not the absolute "other" of rationality,
but an echo of it (PM §§382, 408).

Although, to the best of my knowledge, Kierkegaard was silent
on the issue of clinical madness, Hegel himself accepted the medicali-
zation of madness that had begun in the late eighteenth century, and
he rejected the metaphysical and theological categories of what was
called "romantic medicine." But he also cautioned against the nar-
rowness of the "somatic" school that he felt lacked sufficient explana-
tory value if not connected to a "speculative" (i.e., philosophic)
framework.[9]

It might even be argued that every person seeking therapy is first of all suffering from "philosophic" madness, at least in the sense that initially she does not understand her own suffering as "disease," but experiences her torment in the vocabulary of the philosopher. Thus the philosopher's (and the novelist's and the poet's) descriptions are the closest to the subject's own self-understanding, and although the therapist must seek to rephrase these descriptions into the terminology of the clinic (just as Hegel, for example, translated his own philosophic description of the madness of his friend Hölderlin in the *Phenomenology* as the "lost soul" whose "light dies away within it" into the medical category of *Wahnsinn*—mania or frenzy, which today we would call schizophrenia—in the classificatory scheme of mental disorder he gives in the *Encyclopedia*) (*PS* 400; *PM* §408)— there is a real question about which vocabulary is a metaphor for the other.

Lacan, for all his interest in Kierkegaard and Hegel, unfortunately never addresses their conceptions of madness, but it seems safe to say that his own understanding of the clinic was deeply informed by his reading of philosophy. Freud, for all his scorn of philosophy as a *Weltanschauung* closely linked to the "delusions of paranoiacs,"[10] wrote in a letter to his confidant Wilhelm Fliess of "secretly nurs[ing] the hope of arriving by the . . . circuitous route of medicine . . . at my own original, objective philosophy."[11] In a later letter to Fliess, Freud says, "When I was young, the only thing I longed for ·was philosophical knowledge, and now that I am going over from medicine to psychology, I am in the process of attaining it."[12]

Although Freud will appear along the way in my discussion, it is especially Jacques Lacan who will preoccupy us, since it is Lacan above all who thematized the absolutely central place of language in the project of psychoanalysis. Not only is "the Symbolic," the domain of language,[13] the key vantage point from which all other "registers" of psychic life must be approached, but the analyst must be a "linguist"[14] whose aim "it might be said . . . amounts to overcoming the barrier of silence" and "to *get her [the patient] to speak*."[15]

It is perhaps worth noting that Lacan's many comments on Hegel are frequently critical, and his (fewer) references to Kierkegaard entirely positive, but we will see that his own thoughts on a talking cure allow for a complex and nuanced reading of both Hegel and Kierkegaard. Despite some of Lacan's more critical comments about Hegel's conception of the self, for example, we will see that Hegel is tantalizingly close (certainly much more so than Kierkegaard) to Lacan's basic claim that the self is constituted by language,[16] which for Lacan is a crucial assumption of the talking cure. Lacan's theory of the relation between the three orders of psychic life—the Imaginary, the Real, and the Symbolic—also helps us think through Kierkegaard's paradoxical view of language as both responsible for illness, through the interdiction of a more primordial domain of desire, yet also as a necessary (if equivocal) means for the cure of that very illness.

HEGEL'S CONCEPTION OF MADNESS

Although direct references to madness or mental derangement (*Verrücktheit*) are rare in Hegel's writings, it was clearly a topic that interested him. He corresponded with many of the major contributors to the philosophical and medical literature about insanity,[17] and he took an active role in investigating alternative therapies for his own sister Christiane, who spent time in the Zweifalten asylum for treatment of "hysteria" (and who a year after her brother's death would commit suicide).[18] Most important, Hegel made the topic of madness part of a regular lecture cycle he gave at the Universities of Heidelberg and Berlin beginning in 1816 and lasting until just before his death from cholera in 1831. A condensed version of these lectures, along with extensive student notes, was published as part of the *Encyclopedia of the Philosophical Sciences* (first in 1817, with later editions in 1827 and 1830), and show that Hegel had worked out a detailed theory of mental illness, along with an elaborate classificatory system and a theory of diagnosis and treatment.

Moreover, Hegel's lectures on madness are much more important than they might otherwise appear, since they show that a study of madness is essential for an understanding of the "normal" (or "developed" or "rational") consciousness: "Insanity [is] an essential . . . [and] necessarily occurring form . . . in the development of the soul," in the sense that the inner "contradictions" intrinsic to madness—the oppositions between consciousness and the unconscious, between reason and instinct, between desire and its repression, and between the inner world of the psyche and the outer world of social reality—are "still preserved" in the developed mind (*PM* §408Z). Madness and sanity indeed occur on a continuum for Hegel, precisely because the rational mind is vulnerable to illness as a result of retaining its origins in a more primordial domain of instinct and desire: Madness is "nothing else but the extreme limit of sickness to which [the healthy consciousness] can succumb" (*PM* §408Z). In fact, in his lectures on madness Hegel seems to have anticipated by nearly a century Freud's basic principle that "in order to arrive at what is normal and apparently so simple, we shall have to study the pathological with its distortions and exaggerations."[19]

For Hegel, madness is a "reversion" or "withdrawal" or "sinking back" of the rational consciousness into the primitive world of instincts and drives, or what Hegel calls "the life of feeling" (*Gefühlsleben*), which he locates in "the soul," where the "mind is still in the grip of nature" (*PM* §387Z).[20] Hegel's theory of madness is thus grounded, as for Freud and Lacan, in a psychology of the unconscious. The soul is "the form of the dull stirring, the inarticulate breathing of the spirit through its unconscious individuality" (*in seiner bewußtlosen Individualität*) (*PM* §400). In insanity, the "reversion to nature" displaces what Freud calls "the reality principle," or what for Lacan is the rule of the Law of the symbolic, and "the earthly elements are set free." The mind becomes "mastered" by the archaic, unconscious drives of the soul (*PM* §408 and Z).

Hegel's account of the "life of feeling" bears striking resemblance to the description of "primary narcissism" that is so central to Freud's and Lacan's portrayals of the original scene of instincts prior to ego-development. For Hegel as for Freud and Lacan, this play of feelings and instincts allows no distinction between inner and outer realities: The soul is a "differenceless unity," as Hegel puts it (*PM* §398Z), and in this state of "commun[ing] merely with its interior states, the opposition between itself and that which is for it"—the world, or reality—"remains shut up within it" (*PM* §402Z). Reality thus becomes a projected image of the "earthly elements" or drives and desires of the soul, "a shadow cast by the mind's own light—a show or illusion which the mind imposes as a barrier" between itself and all otherness from which it has withdrawn in an attempt to escape some experience of suffering (*PM* §386).

Freud's and Lacan's notions of neurosis clearly echo Hegel's view. Freud speaks of "the low value of reality, the neglect of the distinction between [reality] and fantasy," and the "path of regress" taken by the libido that has been "repulsed by reality" and must seek satisfaction through a "withdrawal from the ego and its laws."[21] Hegel's emphasis on the importance of fantasy in the life of feeling, and thus in the world of illness where the mind reverts to "the grip of nature," is also central to Lacan's account of the unconscious. For Lacan, ego-development—the formation of a rudimentary sense of the I prior to the emergence of a socially and linguistically structured self—begins somewhere between the sixth and eighteenth months of life with the disruption of primary narcissism by the "mirror phase," when the infant first beholds her own image and recognizes it as her own.[22] In becoming aware of herself in her specular image, she becomes doubled, both self and other, looking and looked at, in a single consciousness, simultaneously assured of the primacy of the I and yet confronted with an otherness with which the I can never quite coincide. "This Gestalt . . . symbolizes the mental permanence of the I, at the same time as it prefigures its alienating destination."[23]

The enduring legacy of the mirror phase is the act of projection by the ego onto the image of the other with which it seeks identification. The other becomes part of the ego's "Imaginary," a projected succession of fantasies[24] of the ego's own desire for self-coinciding through mastering the look of the other. Borrowing strongly from Hegel's account of the master/slave relation as a key to understanding the dynamics of desire,[25] Lacan posits that the perpetual and inevitable failure ever to perfectly master the other results in a series of *méconnaissances* (misrecognitions) of the other[26] that confirms a sense of self-incompleteness and yet only the more strongly reinforces the function of the Imaginary to project fantasy-identifications onto the other. The "reality" of the other, for Lacan as for Hegel, thus becomes what we have seen Hegel call "a shadow cast by the mind's own light." Further, just as for Hegel this shadow realm of fantasy is the scene to which we revert in madness, Lacan explicitly identifies the Imaginary order of the I or ego with mental illness: "The ego is structured exactly like a symptom, . . . the human symptom par excellence, the mental illness of man."[27]

As yet, in the Hegelian "life of feeling" and Lacanian Imaginary, there is no developed "self," but only what Hegel calls the prearticulate "breathing" of the "soul," or what for Lacan is the fantasized identifications (always themselves *méconnaissances*) of the I with its projected images of the other. For both Hegel and Lacan, the "self" emerges only with the development of a new order of psychic life, what Lacan calls the "symbolic order." Key to the symbolic order is the repression of the Imaginary. We saw that for Hegel, madness is a reversion to the archaic life of instincts where "the natural self gains mastery over the rational consciousness." One might say that in the symbolic order, this relation of mastery is reversed: The symbolic is the domain of interdiction, of Law, which administers the prohibition of the fantasized identifications of the Imaginary by which the "ego" is constituted, and instead constructs a "self" in and through language. The self, for Lacan, is indeed nothing but "an effect of language."[28]

For Lacan, the intrinsically linguistic character of the self is grounded in a fundamentally Hegelian idea, that the self's very existence is bound up with its being for others. In the words that preface Hegel's introduction of the master/slave dialectic in his *Phenomenology,* "self-consciousness exists in and for itself when, and by the fact that, it so exists for another; that is, it exists only in being acknowledged" (*PS* 111). In Lacan's words, "the subject is a subject only by virtue of his subjection to the field of another."[29] The stance of privacy of the I immersed in the life of feeling, or of the Lacanian ego in the order of the Imaginary, is replaced in the symbolic order by a self that is thoroughly intersubjective, social, and hence linguistic. The talking cure, for both Hegel and Lacan, relies on this basic structural feature of language to integrate (and indeed constitute) the self within the social sphere of signification, and to foreclose the lure of the presocial, private "self" whose only relation to the other is through fantasy.

The shaping of the I into a "self" is already anticipated by the nature of desire itself: For Lacan as for Hegel, desire is the desire for the other's desire.[30] If in the Imaginary order desire relates to the other through a fantasized identification, in the symbolic this mirroring is shattered, and the self emerges not as a coherent subject, but first of all as an *object* of the other's desire.[31] We *are* only insofar as we are acknowledged, seen, and desired by another. For both Lacan and Hegel this is part of the essentially tragic character of the self, that it is constructed on the ruins of the project of self-sufficiency, the impossibility of the stance of "I = I." Moreover, this tragedy of the self is inextricably bound up with the nature of language. For Lacan, to say that the self exists only for an other is to say that the self is a representation or signification of another signifier. Prior to this signification, the subject is only a fiction, a fantasy of autonomy, an "imaginary" unity: again, the subject is "an effect of language."[32]

Hegel's view of language and its constitutive function for the self is remarkably close to Lacan's in several key ways. As for Lacan, Hegel sees language as disruptive of the life of fantasy of the I. The I that is "sunk into itself" in the life of feeling is "still dumb" (*PS* 396), precisely because its relation to the other, which is mediated by language, is not yet truly social; the other is as yet only the shadow cast by the "I." Language, for Hegel, entails that the I "dies away" as it speaks, externalizing itself and therefore negating its position of self-sufficiency (*PS* 309). Hegel's talking cure will thus require death, the dying away of the position of "I am I." His insistence on this death prefigures Lacan's striking phrase that the self is an "effect of language," since it entails that language (by which the self-sufficient subject dies) is the very existence or "being-there" (*da-sein*) of the true self: "We see language as the existence of spirit (*das Dasein des Geistes*). Language is . . . the self that separates itself from itself, . . . existing for others" (*PS* 395).

However substantial the parallels between Hegel's and Lacan's conceptions of the self as linguistically constructed, it needs to be pointed out that Lacan expresses considerable skepticism about Hegel's phenomenology of the self. Most particularly, Lacan argues that Hegel's great "error in the *Phenomenology* . . . [is] the promotion of consciousness as essential to the subject [self] in the historical after-math of the Cartesian *cogito,*" which results in a "misleading em-phasis on the transparency of the I in action at the expense of the opacity of the signifier [namely, in this context, the unconscious] that determines it."[33] That is, Hegel's analysis of the self places too great a faith in the power of reason; the "earthly elements" of the soul that govern the essentially unconscious origin of desire become entirely sublated, *aufgehoben,* in the transition to the symbolic order. For Hegel (or at least Lacan's Hegel), language corrects and transcends the inchoate muteness of the instinctual shape of desire by giving it a rational and social configuration.[34] The Hegelian "'cunning of reason' means that, from the outset and right to the end, the subject *knows* what he wants."[35] With this knowing rela-tion to desire, Hegelian phenomenology abandons any plausible account of the unconscious.

There is an undeniable sense in which Hegel privileges conscious-ness over the unconscious, and the symbolic, linguistic configuration of the self over the "life of feeling," and to this extent there is a real difference from Lacan, who emphasizes the repressive role of the symbolic. It is an ambiguous difference, however, since Lacan too in a sense privileges the linguistic self, in that it is the speaking self that the psychoanalyst must seek to draw out. Indeed, the whole purpose of therapy is "to free the subject's speech."[36] Further, it is misleading to see Hegel's emphasis on reason as a sign of his approval of a Cartesian faith in the transparency of the ego. In the first place, Hegel's phenomenological method is unrelenting in its exposure of the inevitable collapse of the self's subjective feeling of certainty (our "clear and distinct ideas"): The experience of consciousness is one of constant loss of security and continual frustration of the project of satisfying its own desires. We saw in the last chapter how Hegel's own use of language relies on a new grammar, the unconventional grammar of the "speculative proposition," which he develops as an alternative to the grammar of assertion where the subject "fixes" the meaning of its predicates. And we noted how close Hegel's alterna-tive understanding of the "fluidity" of the form of the proposition is to Lacan's own notion of the *glissement* or "slippage" of meaning in language.

In the second place, we could make no sense of Hegel's account of madness if Lacan were right that Hegel's "logocentrism" effects a liberation of the rational self from the influence of the unconscious. Just as Freud adopted as the motto for his *Interpretation of Dreams* Virgil's words that "if I cannot bend the higher powers [reason, consciousness], I will move the infernal regions [the unconscious]," Hegel spoke of madness as a return to the unconscious where "the dark infernal powers of the heart are set free" (*PM* §408 and Z). And this return is an always open possibility for the rational consciousness, precisely because these infernal powers are not eradicated from the ontology of the self as it develops into rationality.

Further, Hegel's explanation of the cause of this reversion of the self to the dark powers of the unconscious in madness is strikingly similar to Lacan's account of illness. Lacan sees the rule of the symbolic, by which the fantasies of the Imaginary are prohibited, to lead to the creation of a nostalgic desire for their recovery. The symbolic is haunted by a lack, a gap, a hole in the fabric of the self, which it constitutes. Hegel says much the same thing. With the "awakening of consciousness" from the dream life of the unconscious—Hegel compares the life of feeling to a "dreaming while awake" (*PM* §408Z)—the self is constituted *not* as a coherent whole, but as a disunity: There is an "inward breach" and "schism" where we "step into opposition" with the life of instinct and are destined to a "severed life" (*EL* §24Z). The self is thus constituted as a fundamental restlessness (*PS* 6, 12) and nostalgic desire[37] for a return to the mythological state of wholeness represented by the fantasies of the unconscious, which is ultimately the desire to be complete unto oneself, to be absolute, to be God.[38] But there is a basic experience of loss, of doubt, of despair at the heart of consciousness, and a recurring experience of "the grief which expresses itself in the hard saying that 'God is dead'" (*PS* 455). The satisfaction of our yearning for self-unification is perpetually deferred. For Hegel, it is just this endless deferral of self-unity that calls for a cure that carries us beyond our attempt to be self-constituting and to embrace language, with all its gaps and lacks and breaches, as the only possible path toward healing.

KIERKEGAARD'S VIEW OF MADNESS

Kierkegaard writes directly about madness even less than Hegel, and he presents nothing like the systematic account that Hegel does in his *Encyclopedia* lectures. But like Hegel and Lacan, Kierkegaard is absorbed with mental anguish and morbid states, and he is also intensely interested in the nature and role of language and communication. What distinguishes Kierkegaard from both Hegel and Lacan in this regard is that he offers a theological account of human despair—what he calls the "sickness unto death," which is a "Christian discovery" (*SD* 145)—and a corresponding therapeutics that depends on faith. It is just this theological situating of sickness and therapy that makes the idea of a talking cure more complex, since faith for Kierkegaard is beyond language. Ethics, the domain of "the universal" (the symbolic) "requires speech," but in faith I "*cannot* speak"; I am "unable to make myself intelligible." Hence, although we will see that Kierkegaard too employs a talking cure—his authorial strategy of "indirect communication," which is designed to lead the reader to take responsibility for self-authorship—it is a cure whose talking will be elusive, strange, and mysterious, what Kierkegaard sometimes calls a "speaking in tongues" (*FT* 123).

Kierkegaard's relatively rare explicit references to madness fall into three categories. First, he often refers to the "objectivism" of Hegelian philosophy as a form of madness (*CUP* 173–75). Not unlike the way Lacan criticizes Hegelian philosophy as effecting a "logicizing reduction" of existence that dramatically exaggerates the power of reason to know its world "absolutely,"[39] Kierkegaard ridicules Hegel's faith in objective knowledge and universal truths. For Kierkegaard, "truth is subjectivity": We cannot abstract away from the sheer particularity that is the fate of each individual self in order to gain an objective vantage point from which to utter universal truths. If Hegel's talking cure is a megaphonic "direct communication," Kierkegaard's will be subtle, evasive, secret, self-concealing, and "indirect."

The second main category of direct reference to madness in Kierkegaard's texts is that of religious faith. Abraham, the father of faith, can appear only as a crazed "monster" and madman ("disordered in his mind") (*FT* 27, 72) to someone who looks at his willingness to "suspend the ethical" by obeying the otherworldly voice that commands him to kill his son. Faith is an abandonment or suicide of reason, a leap into the abyss of ultimate risk where we renounce all that gave us a sense of orientation and sanity in the "finite" world of our "earthly" concerns. "To risk everything [for faith] is the height of madness" (*CUP* 381); madness is God's "blessing and curse" (*JSK* 459); and faith is a sort of "possession" and "tribulation to the point of madness" (*JSK* 525).

The madness of faith is deeply connected with a stance of radical disillusionment with the power of reason to save us from the suffering and sickness unto death that constitutes us all as broken human subjects. As such it is also associated with a suspicion of the symbolic and language. Faith requires silence, since it cuts us off from the world of social, linguistic conventions that regulate our relations to others. We stand alone before God in fear and trembling, shaken loose from the symbolic order, from the entire world of "the finite" in which we are at home in language. Cure cannot be found in speech but only in the inconceivable, absurd power of God's grace: "What is [the despairing soul] to do? Nothing: remain silent and wait in prayer and faith" (*JP* 4:260).

From the perspective of both Hegel and Lacan, such a faith-cure represents the death drive or nostalgic yearning for a recovery of the "life of feeling" or the "Imaginary," the prehistory of the self as a mythically perfect harmony. Hegel thematizes such faith as the projection by "the unhappy consciousness" of its yearning to be healed onto an Absolute that represents the ideal of self-unity that the self finds to be perpetually beyond its own limitations (*PS* 126–38). And Lacan explores the phenomenon of a "*jouissance,*" or drive toward the experience of plenitude, that is beyond speech, ineffable, unsayable, that would be "the God face" of human yearning.[40]

The third and final category of madness in Kierkegaard's writing refers to his own madness, or rather his "partial madness" or "borderline madness," which he diagnoses in several journal entries.[41] In an entry of 1846, at the age of 33, he writes that "I am in the profoundest sense an unhappy individuality that from its earliest years has been nailed fast to some suffering or other, bordering upon madness, and that must have its deeper roots in a disproportion between soul and body" (*JSK* 600). Three years later, in 1849, Kierkegaard writes of his "unhappy melancholy which has . . . been a sort of partial madness." The theme of a disproportionality between soul and body is again prominent in his self-diagnosis. His "sort of" madness is linked to his "operat[ing] purely as spirit"—without a body—in order to "work inhumanly as a spirit, that is, in the third person," risking the "demoniac danger" of this inhuman half-selfhood (*JSK* 938).

We may recall here Kierkegaard's amusement at the Hegelian philosophy's "emancipation from telluric conditions," but it seems that Kierkegaard too, in his own way, seeks a freedom from the gravitational force of the earthly. And if Hegel's philosophy is fit only for "lunar creatures," Kierkegaard's own quest for disembodiment as a preparation of the soul for the madness of faith itself aims at an "inhuman" spirituality.

In a sense, Kierkegaard's project of disembodiment might be seen as a venture to achieve a self purged of desire. Desire chains us to finitude and is the source of the sickness unto death of human existence. To be cured requires a spiritualization of desire through faith in the extraordinary and extrahuman possibilities of divine salvation. But if, as Hegel and Lacan insist, desire is itself constituted by language—since desire is the desire for an other, and language is the very being-there or *da-sein* of the self related to an other—then Kierkegaard's negation of desire would also entail a negation of language. Interestingly, this is the exact opposite of Nietzsche's view of the relation between the quest for disembodiment and language: Christianity, he says in the *Gay Science,* values "desensualization," and is a form of "vampirism," sucking away the lifeblood of the body; its adherents become "ever paler," and are "left *only with words*."[42] For Kierkegaard, though, the lure of disembodiment is precisely that it leaves one silent, without words.

Leaving aside for the moment (if we can!) the fact that Kierkegaard is, after all, an author, and hence devotes his life to language, it is also paradoxically true that he accepts this conclusion about the negation of language. We must learn from the lilies of the field and the birds of the air (but presumably not the "winged creatures" who are attracted to Hegel's fantastic philosophy) the practice of silence.

> From the lily and the bird as teachers, let us learn
>
> > silence, or learn to be silent.
> >
> > > Surely it is speech that distinguishes humanity. . . . But . . . it does not follow that the ability to be silent . . . would be an inferior art. On the contrary, because the human being is able to speak, the ability to be silent is an art, and a great art precisely because this advantage of his so easily tempts him. But this he can learn from the silent teachers, the lily and the bird. (LF 333)

Kierkegaard's ethics of aloneness, his view that "there is only one kind of ethical contemplation, namely self contemplation" and that "ethics closes immediately about the individual" (*CUP* 284), helps explain his attachment to silence. For Lacan, the self is "absolutely nothing" apart from its being constituted by discourse,[43] and for Hegel, the "beautiful soul" who lives "in dread of besmirching the splendor of its inner being" by speech, "is still dumb," a sheer "yearning which . . . finds itself only as a lost soul: . . . its light dies away within it, and it vanishes like a shapeless vapor that dissolves into thin air" (*PS* 400). But for Kierkegaard, language—like desire itself—is a mark of finitude. The value of silence is its protection of the self from the gravitational force of being-for-others, which draws us ever downward into finitude, away from our potentiality for liberation into the infinitude of God's grace.

LANGUAGE AND THE TALKING CURE

For Kierkegaard, like Hegel, language is the expression or externalization of the self. Hegel sees this expression as necessary for the emergence of the true self, the socially, linguistically determined self that leaves behind the inherently unstable and essentially mythic position of the "I am I," the narcissistically enclosed "self" of sheer particularity (see *PS* 43, 105, 109, 395). But for Kierkegaard, it is just this loss of inwardness and particularity through expression that is cause for bereavement. We have seen that Kierkegaard views speech as the "annulment" of reality (*JC* 148), and at least in part, the reality annulled by language is for him the reality of the inward self, the self unmediated by being-for-others.

For both Hegel and Lacan, such a "self" is a myth—"absolutely nothing," a "shapeless vapor." And yet for Lacan, there is a sense in which such a "self" is, as for Kierkegaard, certainly "real." Indeed, Lacan's account of the "the Real," the third "register" or "order" of psychic life (in addition to the Imaginary and the Symbolic), is uncannily close to Kierkegaard's portrayal of "reality" in *Johannes Climacus*. For Lacan, the Real is precisely that which "resists symbolization absolutely";[44] it is the unsayable, the ineffable, the unrepresentable. Thus Lacan shares Kierkegaard's conclusion that "the word "annul[s] reality by talking about it." As Bruce Fink puts it, "That which is named by language and can thus be . . . talked about" is for Lacan a "canceling" of "the real."[45] In this sense, then, Lacan would agree with Kierkegaard that "existential reality is uncommunicable" (*CUP* 320). This clearly raises a question about what a "talking cure" could mean for either Lacan or Kierkegaard. Both, of course, know full well that the Real cannot be expressed, or, therefore, cured—its endless longing for completeness will always haunt us. But, as we will see, both seek indirect methods for a talking cure that, if not ministering directly to our yearning for the Real, our *jouissance,* will at least aid us in coming to terms with its ephemerality.

All three of these authors associate language with death. For Kierkegaard, the word annuls the life of the inner subject; for Lacan, the linguistic symbol is "the killing" of the Real;[46] and for Hegel language entails the "vanishing" and "dying away" of privacy (*PS* 309). Hegel straightforwardly celebrates this death, since for him the inwardly directed "self" is radically incomplete, indeed a mirage of the true self that only emerges in the intersubjective space made possible by language. Madness for Hegel is precisely the regression of the "rational mind" back to this mirage of the self that lingers in us all as the trace of our desire for wholeness, and cure must be sought in a reexternalization (rebirth) of the self into relations with others through a path back to language.

Lacan and Kierkegaard are more ambivalent about the death of the I through language. On the one hand, they both see language (for Lacan, more specifically the symbolic) as the source of a profoundly wounding loss of interiority and "the real." For them, illness is in fact created by language or the symbolic, since it is language that alienates us from the Real. Hence they both, in their own ways, are attracted to silence. Silence for Kierkegaard is the prerequisite for faith, which is the only possible cure of the sickness unto death. For Lacan, silence is an absolutely key strategy of the therapist; silence acknowledges the unutterable (the Real) and the fact that it is the symbolic that represses our most fundamental desires.[47]

On the other hand, both Kierkegaard and Lacan recognize the truth of the Hegelian position that to be a human self is to be a linguistic self: Expression is a necessary condition of our humanity. For Lacan, this is seen in his general theory of the self as an "effect of language," and more specifically in his association of the Real—the unutterable—with the category of "the impossible."[48] Yet more interesting, however, is Kierkegaard's own acceptance of the impossibility of the silent self that he so clearly yearns for. He realizes, as we saw in Chapter 1, that "if man could not speak" he "would be an animal" (*JC* 148). That we *can* speak means that we must speak. The very fact that we are more than animals, that we are *not* birds of the air, means that however much we may seek to practice the art of the bird's silence, it can only always be an imperfect silence, a permeable silence, a silence within speech.

And of course, Kierkegaard does speak. He is an author, and indeed a master of words. But his nostalgia for the interior space of what he terms "reality" leads him to an authorial use of language where language is turned against itself, where words do not mean what they seem, where meanings are concealed beneath disguises, and where he explores the possibility of replacing a literal silence with an indirect silence. Lacan describes the Real as creating "rips" or "tears" in the symbolic[49]—the resistance of the Real to representation and linguistic expression haunts the speaking self with the uncanny realization that whatever and however much it says, there is something missing. Kierkegaard's authorship, by seeking to preserve

his own notion of the Real as the integrity of the subject's inwardness, is itself aimed at effecting such tears in the symbolic. It is the
unsaid, the missing word, that is important, and what appears to be
said is in fact always a deception and a misunderstanding. And, as
we have noted, Kierkegaard is utterly dedicated to being "faithful to
the deception" throughout (*JP* 1:653).

Kierkegaard's practice of indirect communication is thus paradoxically an evasion of communication, a simulacrum of communication, where what is written is to be understood as revoked. The
ethics of authorship that underlies Kierkegaard's use of indirect communication is remarkably close to much of what Lacan says about
the role of the therapist, who, like Kierkegaard's author, plays the
part of "ideal impersonality."[50] The analyst must not seek to direct
the patient and must "ignore what he [himself] knows," maintaining
an "attentive silence" and "keep[ing] quiet" so as to support the
speech of the patient. The analyst thus resists the patient's expectation, indeed "implicit demand," that the analyst supply a cure. But
the analyst must not "answer him, . . . [for] he knows very well that
it would be but words, [and the patient] can get those from whom-
ever he likes." No, the analyst does not and cannot cure: "Rather,
the analyst leaves the subject free to have a go at it"[51]—just as
Kierkegaard and his pseudonymous authors may seek to provoke
the reader, but then "shyly withdraw" so that the reader may author
herself (*PV* 25–26).

But Kierkegaard's indirect communication is not only a talking
cure for the reader. It is clear from his journals that Kierkegaard
sought in his authorship a means of healing himself as well. Lacan
writes that "the symptom [of illness] is first of all the silence in the
supposed speaking subject," and that "analysis consists precisely in
getting her to speak."[52] Kierkegaard too, for all his attachment to
silence, feels an "irresistible impulse" to write; as we have seen, "only
when I write do I feel well." His many pseudonymous works allow
him to people the world with a fantastic cast of characters—the aesthete and the Judge, the Seducer and Cordelia, the Unhappiest Man
and Don Quixote, Constantin Constantius and the young poet, Vigilius Haufniensis and Nicolaus Notabene, Hilarious Bookbinder and
Father Taciturnus, Johannes de Silentio and Johannes Climacus and

Anti-Climacus, and all the others—a world otherwise virtually empty, without love or friendship, all of which Kierkegaard has renounced in his project of disembodiment and detachment from the finite.

Kierkegaard's pseudonyms are not so much alter egos as they are what Lacan calls "imagos": fantasy images of others by which the self seeks to experience itself, which "appear in the human being [. . . as an effect] of the subject's alienation."[53] Both the sense of alienation and of release through fantasy that are central to Lacan's idea of the imago are present in the memorable passage from Kierkegaard's journal we have alluded to more than once, where he writes of how his invention of pseudonyms has allowed him to travel through "a whole world of fantasy" yet also "kept me away from my own self" (JSK 641).

Hegel's analysis of this diary entry, I am afraid, would have been quite pitiless. Kierkegaard's attempt at a talking cure for his own illness, the unhappy home of his melancholic withdrawal into himself, can only fail, leaving him yet further away from himself. For his whole authorship is predicated on a model of communication in which both the author and the reader are left alone in their privacy, without any genuine dialogue, and it is only through such dialogue that a self can be constituted. This attenuation of language, found also in Lacan, by which the author/analyst revokes her own speech and withdraws into silence so that the reader/patient may speak her own soliloquy (the classic model of the psychotherapist who nods sagely at every request that she offer an opinion and says, "Well, what do you think?"), is fundamentally opposed by Hegel, whose talking cure and whole theory of the emancipatory power of language is based on the need for genuinely dialogical speech.

Kierkegaard's exploration of a form of authorship that will assure that both the author and the reader are left "free" to "stand alone" (JP 1:649) reflects both his conviction that the true self is the self of subjective inwardness and his corresponding disillusionment with the nature of language to externalize this self, to make it public, and thus to "distort" it. For Hegel, though, language is not a "distortion" of the inner—what we have seen Kierkegaard call an "annulment" of inner "reality"—but an emancipation from the inarticulable, inchoate particularity of the "I."

Judith Butler refers to the "romantic symbolism that governs" Hegel's philosophy of language, and contrasts Hegel's optimism in the power of language to express the True with Lacan's recognition that "to be in language means to be infinitely displaced from original meaning."[54] But Hegel's philosophy of language is in many ways ruthlessly anti-Romantic. It is not, after all, as though Hegel somehow forgets or ignores this "original meaning," or that he is oblivious to its lure. Rather, it is our sentimental attachment to it, however powerful its attraction, that is the source of our illness, our entrapment within a prehistorical, atavistic "self." Hegel's talking cure is thus based on the idea that the merely "meant"—that which cannot be expressed—is but an empty word, a blank space, and the yearning to preserve or somehow recover this meaning is a sentimentalizing of the space of the interior: *This* is romanticism, and this is what Hegel's talking cure calls on us to renounce as the necessary condition for health.

Lacan himself, for all the importance he places on the role of the symbolic in repressing the Real, sees that therapy must seek "to treat the real by the symbolic." Indeed, silence is a symptom of illness, and the purpose of analysis is getting the patient to speak, to overcome the barrier of silence.[55] More generally, despite his obvious fondness for Kierkegaard, Lacan articulates a theory of the self that is implicitly critical of Kierkegaard, in much the same way that Hegel's philosophy is. "The subject goes far beyond what is experienced 'subjectively' by the individual," Lacan writes, and the "truth of his history is not all contained in his [own] script," for although "he knows . . . his own lines," in fact the subject *is* "the other's discourse." The other is indeed "the locus in which is constituted the I who speaks, . . . the other deciding . . . whether the one has spoken or not." Finally, it is only "in the disintegration of the imaginary unity" of the ego (Kierkegaard's "inward self") that "the subject finds the signifying material of his symptoms."[56]

THE INEFFABLE

It is true, as Butler says, that Lacan emphasizes the cost of the talking cure much more than Hegel does: Entry into the symbolic alienates

us from the Real and explains the human need for imaginary projec-
tions that seek to supply what language can never give, the sense of
the complete coinciding of the self with itself. This explains Lacan's
fondness for Kierkegaard, whose authorship is a fascinating experiment with the Imaginary. As for Hegel, there is no doubt that he
values the linguistic over the reticence of silence: In madness, there
is a withdrawal into the interior where speech is felt to fail us, where
we feel essentially alone and therefore mute, and where we are not
fully free rational subjects. But even here, Hegel's celebration of
speech is more complicated than it seems.

Louis Sass, in his essay "Madness and the Ineffable," argues that
Hegel's valorization of language entails a corresponding failure to
acknowledge the value of the ineffable. As Sass puts it, for Hegel
"that which seems to be 'murdered' by language is actually of little
value." Kierkegaard, in Sass's reading, holds virtually the opposite
position, that it is the prelinguistic and ineffable that is "absolutely
real."[57] Lacan, for Sass, offers a more nuanced position: Although
he certainly acknowledges, even insists on, the inescapability of the
symbolic and linguistic, he also sees madness, where the symbolic is
disrupted, as presenting an insight into the dominating and repressive role of language. By relegating madness, and its affinity for the
ineffable, to the realm of illusion and mere fantasy, Hegel misses the
possibility of "an appreciation of the potentially satiric vision of the
mad person."[58]

Certainly Lacan looks more critically at language than Hegel, and
Sass points to the central difference when he notes that "from Lacan's point of view," and in distinction to Hegel, "the psychotic is
not merely *deprived* of conventional linguistic abstractions, but is in
some sense *alienated* from them—in the sense of having a certain
awareness of their arbitrariness and possible absurdity."[59] Hence the
mad person's silence is not merely a protest against the dominating
and stultifying potential of linguistic and social norms but suggests a
superior insight into the inadequacy of these norms: What for Hegel
is the life of illusion of madness is for Lacan in principle the recognition on the part of the psychotic of the illusions of the social order
itself.

Sass is on to a very important difference here between Lacan and Hegel, and he points to what is undoubtedly an undervaluation of the "abnormal" on Hegel's part, and with it, an insufficiently critical account of the liberating power of language. But the contrast between Hegel and Lacan in this regard is not as stark as it seems. Hegel is hardly unaware of the experience of loss entailed by language. He is eloquent in his portrait of the loss of innocence implicit in the fall into language, which is a fall into the path of doubt and despair. The entry into the social world of language is experienced by consciousness as a "violence" against itself, entailing a "sundering" of the self's sense of harmony with itself and a sense of being destined forevermore to a "severed life" (*PS* 51; *EL* §24). Finally, Hegel too knows full well that something is lost by speaking, and that however much language makes possible a community—and therefore for the first time the possibility of a self—there always remains a space of difference between the self and the other. The whole *Phenomenology of Spirit* is a narrative *not* of successive triumphs of the human spirit to achieve a fulfilled harmony, but on the contrary, a narrative that exposes the ephemerality of all such "triumphs."

Thus however much it is true that Hegel celebrates the passage of the self into the realm of the symbolic and views the presymbolic as the underdevelopment or even the derangement of reason, it is equally important to stress that he envisions this passage as one that places the human spirit into a life of sheer "negativity," "devastation," and "dismemberment" (*PS* 19)—hardly the world of complacency and "herd happiness" Kierkegaard associates with the symbolic order and to which Nietzsche, for example, opposes the insight made possible by his own illness.[60] Lacan may be right that Hegel fails to investigate adequately the dominating role of the symbolic order, yet Hegel's emphasis on the negativity of the life of the "normal," "rational" consciousness does lead him to acknowledge the tremendous power, and in this sense the great importance, of our nostalgia for the prelinguistic, of silence, the ineffable, of what cannot be said.

Sass writes of Lacan (and this is true of Kierkegaard as well) that "unlike Hegel, he is not inclined to treat [the symbolic] system as instantiating *truth*."[61] This is another important point of contrast, yet just as Hegel fundamentally complicates the conception of the "normal" and the "rational"—which have nothing to do with common sense, quotidian reality, since for him rationality entails the constant loss of any sense of security, the recurring experience of not being at home in the world, and the continual frustration of consciousness's project of mastering its own contents—so too the truth that belongs to the symbolic sphere is for Hegel not monolithic. As seen in Chapter 1, for Hegel truth is rather a "Bacchanalian revel in which no member is not drunk" (*PS* 27). The symbolic order for Hegel thus is hardly the domain of fixed laws and uniform, uncontestable institutions of domination, but rather it is fundamentally disorienting. Meanings are never "at rest" (*HP* 1:33) but perpetually "dissolve and pass over" into new configurations (*W* 3:593).

This "passing over" (*übergehen*), we might say, is the reality of death (the passing away, *vergehen*) at the heart of Hegel's conception of the symbolic, social order: Truth is always open to subversion, to dissolution, to dismemberment, and to experimentation and reconfiguration. Hence the role that Lacan (and Kierkegaard and Nietzsche in their own ways) see for madness as a privileged insight into (and thus as a privileged space of resistance to) the limitations of language and the symbolic is incorporated by Hegel into the symbolic sphere itself. This is not by any means to undermine Sass's point that Hegel dismisses the value of the ineffable, since even when we see Hegel's conception of rationality and truth in a "bacchanalian" light, he is uncompromising in seeing the self as inescapably linguistic and in rejecting silence as a flight into nostalgia for a mythic private reality. Equally important, even if we can read Hegel as integrating the role of subversion and resistance into the symbolic order itself, this does not diminish Sass's insight that Hegel's attachment to language leaves out of account much more radical and fundamental possibilities of subversion that may be possible only within the space of madness and the ineffable. For all his sensitivity to the darkness and sorrow that mark the path of consciousness—and for all the personal pain and empathy he experienced at the descent into madness of his sister Christiane and his friend Hölderlin—Hegel was perhaps in the end too much the "rationalist" (albeit with the caveat mentioned earlier about Hegel's distance from any sort of

Cartesian faith in the transparency of the mind) to accept the view of someone like Kierkegaard, who gave thanks to God for his madness (*JSK* 459).

At the end, Hegel proposes that "the wounds of the spirit" must be "healed" by language through the act of *forgiveness* (*PS* 407). His account of forgiveness occurs toward the close of his portrait of the "Beautiful Soul," the shape of consciousness he associates with Romanticism (and perhaps specifically with his friend Hölderlin, the poet who burned himself out into madness).[62] The "beautiful soul" has withdrawn into itself and become paralyzed by the impossibility of expressing itself, since all expression comes hard up against the wall of an alien reality, the reality of the other. It recognizes "evil" in itself, since all its actions will fail to express "the universal"—it can only express its own individual self, what Kierkegaard calls the "passion of inwardness" (*CUP* 177–82). And it recognizes evil in the other, for it is the very existence of the other that prevents the self from realizing its purely individual reality (*PS* 401–2). "In order to preserve the purity of its heart, it flees from contact with the actual world" (*PS* 400). As Kierkegaard might put it, it renounces "the finite." But just as Mesmer's effort to live without words led him to the brink of insanity, the beautiful soul's renunciation and inability to speak entails madness: The beautiful soul is "entangled in the contradiction between its pure self and the necessity of that self to externalize itself" through expression, and becomes "disordered to the point of madness, wast[ing] itself in yearning" (*PS* 406, 407).

This is a madness that is an ever-present risk for us all, since it represents the basic predicament of the doubleness of human existence, that we are both inner and outer beings, beings who long to preserve the specificity of our subjectivity and who yet must speak and thus become determined by others. For Hegel, such madness can be cured only by an act of "forgiveness which [the self] extends to the other" and by which it therefore forgives itself as well (*PS* 407). Forgiveness is a resolve to let go of our obsession with the evil that prevents a perfect coinciding of inner and outer, of self and other. It is an acknowledgment and acceptance of difference: The other will always escape me, and I her—there will always be a *méconnaissance,* a misrecognition, to speak with Lacan, between self and other—and we will both always be guilty of constituting each other and thus reshaping the other's self. Finally, we must choose between madness or "the word of reconciliation" (*PS* 408)—the "Yes!" by which we say "I accept you as such, as the one who reshapes me, as the one who I can never reach in your interiority, and who can never reach my own interiority." This is the "reconciling *Yea* in which the two I's let go their antithetical existence" and that makes possible "the existence of the I which has expanded into a duality" (*PS* 409).

For Kierkegaard, duality is horror. "Can you think of anything more frightful," Judge William asks his young friend the aesthete, "than that it might end with your nature being resolved into a multiplicity, that you really might become many, . . . and you thus would have lost the inmost and holiest thing of all in a man, the unifying power of personality?" (*E/Or* 2:164). Yet Kierkegaard's authorship is precisely a "polynymity" of the self (*CUP* 551), and more, this polynymity is the inevitable fate of all who speak: We all enter into duality, indeed multiplicity. We all face the frightful prospect the Judge warns the aesthete of, of becoming many, for to speak is to relate ourselves to others, who in interpreting us, double us. Duality, the constitution of the self by an other, may be frightful, but it is a necessary horror, a horror that harbors the only possibility of a cure.

All of us stand in need of cure. We all suffer, and often enough to the point of illness, because we are finite, forever incomplete unto ourselves, destined to a desire for wholeness that we cannot achieve on our own. For Hegel, Kierkegaard, and Lacan alike, the cure must be sought in language. This is relatively straightforward for Hegel: Language liberates us from what is the main cause of human illness, our attachment to the privacy of the "I." For Kierkegaard, things are more ambiguous, since cure rests ultimately in an act of faith in God, our ultimate communicant, for whom we must sacrifice any direct relation to or communication with others. But even in this sacrifice, Kierkegaard devotes his life to an indirect communication with others, a communication replete with deception, evasion, self-concealment, and silence, to be sure, all in the hopes of preserving and respecting the ultimate privacy of both author and reader—but it is a communication nonetheless. For better or worse, we are what we say, and what others say to us. As Lacan says, we are an "effect of language." However fraught with danger is our immersion in the world of language—however much we must sacrifice our image of the "self" as "standing alone"—and thus however ambiguous the cure, the only cure of the despair that is the fate of our human condition is to talk. And perhaps, as Hegel recommends, the most important word we say might be the word of forgiveness: "Yes!"

6. A Penchant for Disguise: The Death (and Rebirth) of the Author in Kierkegaard and Nietzsche

Such a dubious author . . . I am, one who does not have a single reader.

SØREN KIERKEGAARD (William Afham), *Stages on Life's Way*

Sing! Speak no more! Are not all words made for the grave and heavy? Are not all words lies to those who are light? Sing! Speak no more!

FRIEDRICH NIETZSCHE, *Thus Spoke Zarathustra*

ON OCTOBER 2, 1855, at the age of forty-two, Søren Kierkegaard, returning from the bank with the last installment of his inheritance, collapsed on the street in Copenhagen. He was brought to Frederick's hospital, paralyzed, where he refused medical attention: "The doctors do not understand my illness," he told a childhood friend; "it is psychical, and now they want to treat it in the usual medical fashion."[1] He died forty days later.

Some three and a half decades later, on January 8, 1889, at the age of forty-five, Friedrich Nietzsche collapsed on the street in Turin, after throwing his arms around the neck of a horse that was being beaten (as one common story has it). He was brought to Basel by his friend Franz Overbeck for treatment, then by his mother to a clinic in Jena, and later, after all attempts at treatment had failed, to her home in Naumburg, and eventually to Weimar, under the care of his sister Elisabeth Förster Nietzsche, where he lived, irretrievably insane, until his death in 1900.[2]

Long before Kierkegaard and Nietzsche collapsed on their respective streets, "Kierkegaard" and "Nietzsche" had died. Long before

1968 when Roland Barthes proclaimed the "death of the author"—
and a year later when Michel Foucault announced that the author
"must assume the role of the dead man in the game of writing"[3]—
Kierkegaard and Nietzsche had enacted this death in their own authorships. Barthes says that "writing is the destruction of every voice,
of every point of origin. . . . As soon as a fact is narrated no longer
with a view to acting directly on reality but intransitively, that is to
say, finally outside of any function other than that of the very practice
of the symbol itself, this disconnection occurs, the voice loses its origin, the author enters into his own death."[4] Kierkegaard's and Nietzsche's authorships are precisely about this intransitivity, this practice
of the symbol that silences the voice of the speaker in the very instance of its speech, this absence of the author's imprint on his own
work.

John Searle writes of speech acts such that "in speaking a language
I attempt to communicate things to my hearer by means of getting
him to recognize my intention to communicate just those things,"[5]
but Kierkegaard and Nietzsche seek rather to negate their own effect
on their texts. They have a "penchant for disguise," as Lou Andreas-
Salomé, Nietzsche's erstwhile lover, put it of Nietzsche,[6] concealing
themselves behind masks and evasions and deceptions with a view
to effacing all trace of intentionality.

We have seen that Kierkegaard writes constantly of how the art
of his "indirect communication" consists in "reducing oneself, the
communicator, to *nobody*" (*TC* 132), and of how the ironic author
lives as "a stranger and an alien, . . . and he too, to a certain extent,
has become unreal" (*CI* 263, 276). And not only does the communicator "Kierkegaard" disappear, but the pseudonyms themselves, who
are fantastic and unreal, vanish as well. As William Afham, one of
the pseudonymous authors of *Stages on Life's Way,* puts it, "By myself
I am capable of nothing at all" (*SLW* 86).

For his part, Nietzsche says (in the voice of his Zarathustra) that
"I am not one of those who may be questioned about their Why."[7]
The "Why," the intention behind the author's words, what is so
essential to communication for Searle, is simply ruled out of order.
Speaking in a letter to the composer Peter Gast, Nietzsche writes
that "I am one of those machines that may explode," and in a letter

to the church historian and his close confidant Franz Overbeck, he says of his *Zarathustra* that it is "an explosion of forces; in such explosions the author himself may easily be blown up."[8] The text explodes the possibility of an author, becoming an autonomous entity. As Barthes says, there is only the text—the practice of the symbol itself[9]—and the voice loses its origin: The death of the author is a "substitut[ion] [of] language itself for the person who until then had been supposed to be its owner. . . . It is language which speaks, not the author."[10]

Nietzsche asks in *Beyond Good and Evil*, "Why couldn't the world that concerns us—be a fiction? And if somebody asked, 'but to a fiction there surely belongs an author?'—couldn't one answer simply *why*? Doesn't this 'belongs' perhaps belong to the fiction, too? Is it not permitted to be a bit ironical about the subject no less than the predicate and object? Shouldn't philosophers be permitted to rise above faith in grammar?"[11] The very idea of authorship, whether of the world or the text, is a fiction: There are no gods, no authors, except as illusions of grammar. To rise above faith in grammar is to see the text as a predicate with no authorial subject.

This idea of the author as an illusion of grammar is analogous to Judith Butler's argument that gender is only an appearance without an underlying reality, a "fabrication" and "parody" and "hallucinatory effect." Gender is not an essence, a substance, but a certain "style of the flesh" that is "performatively produced."[12] Butler in fact cites Nietzsche's criticism of the "metaphysics of substance"—the myth of a stable subject or I underlying its attributes or actions—as an inspiration for her own subversion or "troubling" of the analogous metaphysics of gender.

> The challenge for rethinking gender categories outside of the metaphysics of substance will have to consider the relation of Nietzsche's claim in *On the Genealogy of Morals* that "there is no 'being' behind doing, effecting, becoming; 'the doer' is merely a fiction added to the deed—the deed is everything."[13]

Thus just as for Butler "there is no gender identity behind the expressions of gender,"[14] for Kierkegaard and Nietzsche we may say that there is no author behind the performances (the texts) that constitute the appearance of an "author." If for Butler gendered bodies are so many "styles of the flesh,"[15] for Kierkegaard and Nietzsche the "author" exists only as the mimicry or parody of an Author, as so many styles of enactment. The "author" is always only a disguise or costume.

The purpose of this chapter is in part to trace out the strategies by which Kierkegaard and Nietzsche use this parodic practice to pursue their own deaths as authors. Beyond this forensic analysis, I will argue that Kierkegaard and Nietzsche each experienced a fundamental ambivalence about their authorial deaths. Neither was able to fully share the celebratory tone of Barthes's and Foucault's requiems. Their uneasiness is evident in the notorious parallel texts they produced toward the end of their lives (Kierkegaard's *Point of View for My Work as an Author* and Nietzsche's *Ecce Homo*), works in which they each come out of hiding, as it were, and seem intent on undoing their deaths, resurrecting themselves by pronouncing with almost unbearable earnestness—what Carl Pletsch, in reference to *Ecce Homo,* calls something "akin to the obscene"[16]—the true meaning of their authorships that had hitherto been carefully obscured and disguised. Even if these are read as ironic texts, at the very least they are highly theatrical performances of the idea of the author's resurrection that call for some explanation.

In fact, signs of Kierkegaard's and Nietzsche's ambivalence toward the death of the author are present all along, not just at the end. Foucault speaks of how the text "creat[es] a space into which the writing subject constantly disappears"[17]—a space like a grave, perhaps, into which the corpse of the author is lowered. But we find in the death of the authors "Kierkegaard" and "Nietzsche" that the tombs are (sometimes) empty. With every intention of dying, Kierkegaard and Nietzsche have recurring second thoughts: At the entrance to the tomb they hesitate; they experience a certain nostalgia for the privileged position of the author. Thus their authorships present us with the uncanny spectacle of a ghostly, spectral passing back and forth between the grave and life, between the dead and the undead.

The death of the author in Kierkegaard and Nietzsche is a consequence of several shared commitments: An epistemology and ethics
of subjectivity that has the effect of dissolving the authority of the
author; a philosophy of language that sees language as inherently
falling short of expressing "the real," so that speech is infinitely interpretable according to the "reality" occupied by the reader; and a
personal inclination to solitude and self-concealment that entails that
the author always remains a stranger, and hence undecipherable, to
the reader. In looking at these related themes, I pay particular attention to the spaces where their ambivalence over this death appears,
spaces where the dying resist interment.

It should be noted here at the start that Kierkegaard's extensive
use of pseudonyms and Nietzsche's pseudo-pseudonymity in *Thus
Spoke Zarathustra*—a text authored by "Friedrich Nietzsche" but
narrated by Zarathustra, himself a homonym who simultaneously
appropriates and transgresses against the historical Zarathustra/Zor-
oaster—are certainly marks or signs of their deaths as authors: Pseudonymity is an obvious act of disappearance of the author of the
author. But in a profound sense, every author is a pseudonym (consciously or not), irreducibly other than the self who writes. "*Je est
un autre*" (the I is an other), as Rimbaud famously put it.[18] Indeed,
Kierkegaard's pseudonymity and Nietzsche's radical experimentation with authorial voices (which amounts to pseudonymity) are only
rather incidental signs of the project Barthes and Foucault later the-
matize as the ethical project of the dislocation of the author. This
dislocation may be aided tangentially by pseudonymity, but Kierkegaard's and Nietzsche's strategies of death rely on a much deeper
and more extensive commitment to disguise and deception as the
means to their gifts of death.

Another important preliminary note is that Kierkegaard's and
Nietzsche's dedication to the erasure of the author is of course not
new with them. Barthes and Foucault both mention Mallarmé
(1842–1898, contemporary with Nietzsche), and Foucault refers to
Marx (1818–1883, born five years after Kierkegaard). But we can go
back at least as far as Plato, who notably insisted (if we can accept
the authenticity of his second and seventh letters) that the dialogues
bearing his name (dialogues in which the reader is virtually forced

to enter in to the text, given the typical shallowness of Socrates' interlocutors and Socrates' own reticence and "ignorance") were not "his
own": "No writing of Plato exists or ever will exist."[19] The first-
century-BCE Roman poet Catullus expressed his displeasure (with
some gusto: "I'll fuck you in the ass and fuck you in the face," he
tells his meddling interpreter Aurelius) at confusing him with his
poems:

[You] who size me up as indecent

On the basis of my poems

Because they're naughty

[Are too dim-witted to realize that] the devoted poet must
live an upright life himself

But not so his verses.[20]

In the early seventeenth century, Cervantes claimed to have translated *Don Quixote* from a manuscript by the "true author," the Moor
Cid Hamet Ben Engeli;[21] in the eighteenth century Diderot wrote his
celebrated *Lettre sur les aveugles* ("Letter on the Blind") anonymously
while under police surveillance, only to be immediately identified as
the author and imprisoned;[22] and in the early nineteenth century
the romantic composer and author of fantasy and horror, E. T. A.
Hoffmann, pretended to be merely the editor of the *Six Canticles for
A Cappella Choir,* which he attributed to one Johannes Kreisler (and
Hoffmann's biography of Kreisler, *The Life and Opinions of the Tom-
cat Murr,* he claimed to have been authored in part by his cat and in
part by some anonymous biographer).[23]

I am not enough of a historian of literature and literary theory to
decide whether Barthes and Foucault are right to argue that the
sustained preoccupation with the death of the author is a phenomenon of late modernity and early postmodernity (they focus on writers
such as Proust, Brecht, Becket, Freud, and the surrealists, and speak
more vaguely of writers of "today").[24] But even if this is a misleading
claim, there is little room for doubt that Kierkegaard and Nietzsche

(although not figures of interest in Barthes's and Foucault's texts on the death of the author) stand as the two writers historically poised as anticipatory forerunners of the postmodernity Barthes and Foucault celebrate for its dedication to conceptualizing and carrying out the practice of authorial death.

Kierkegaard's and Nietzsche's shared commitments to death aside, there is of course one glaring point of difference between them: Kierkegaard's insistence that he be read as a Christian author and that all of his writing is "in the service of God" (*PV* 6) evidently will entail a different sort of conception of the author (and his death) from Nietzsche's, which is an experimentation with what it means to be an author (and to die as an author) in the aftermath of the death of god. Barthes writes that "by refusing to assign a 'secret,' an ultimate meaning, to the text (and to the world as text), [writing] liberates what may be called an anti-theological activity, an activity that is truly revolutionary since to refuse to fix meaning is, in the end, to refuse God."[25]

Kierkegaard would have an interesting response to this, though, since in a sense he models his own indirect communication, and hence death, on God's own practice of indirection (and hence, in a sense, death): "For no anonymous author can more cunningly conceal himself, no practitioner of the maieutic art can more carefully withdraw himself from the direct relationship, than God. He is in creation, and present everywhere in it, but directly He is not there" (*CUP* 218). Thus Kierkegaard's authorship presents us with an attempted counterexample to Barthes's equation of the death of the author with the refusal of God, since faith in God in no way "fixes" meaning for Kierkegaard, but on the contrary only intensifies the sense of the elusiveness of meaning. As Josiah Thompson puts it, for Kierkegaard "God is *deus absconditus*, never present, always absent, an inhabitant of dark places"[26]—perhaps even graves. Hence even at the site of Kierkegaard's and Nietzsche's major difference, the either/or of faith or its refusal, there is more in common than one might suppose. The world with God and the world without God are equally worlds in which the author may refuse to assign a secret, ultimate meaning to the text.

THE LONELINESS OF THE AUTHOR

The death of the author is ultimately based on an ethics of authorship that resolves to cancel out the authority and indeed the very personality of the author. But well before either Kierkegaard or Nietzsche formulated such an ethic—well before they published their first works—each had developed personalities that predisposed them to this death. Already as youths, friends perceived in them something uncanny, strange, unreachable, just as later they would adopt an authorial position as absolute strangers to the reader, opaque and incomprehensible. One of Kierkegaard's schoolmates said of him that "to the rest of us who led a genuinely boyish life S.K. was a stranger, . . . wrapped in a mysterious half-darkness of severity and oddity."[27] Reflecting back on his childhood in his *Point of View for My Work as an Author,* Kierkegaard writes that "from a child I was under the sway of a prodigious melancholy, the depth of which finds its only adequate measure in the equally prodigious dexterity I possessed of hiding it under an apparent gaiety and *joie de vivre*" (PV 76).

Both the sense of strangeness and the habit of self-concealment beneath a public façade of sociability are present in the young Nietzsche as well. Erwin Rohde, a friend from Nietzsche's youth, speaks of him as "surrounded by an indescribably strange atmosphere, something that seemed really weird to me at that time, . . . as though he came from a land where nobody else dwelled."[28] Yet as with Kierkegaard, Nietzsche also developed a certain doubleness, a mask of normality beneath which he remained a stranger. In a letter to Overbeck he speaks of his "weirdly concealed life" where "all my human relationships have to do with a mask of me."[29] And in *Ecce Homo,* Nietzsche refers to himself as a doppelgänger: "I have a 'second' face in addition to the first. And perhaps also a third."[30] Lou Salomé, whom Nietzsche became close friends with for a few months when he was thirty-eight and she was twenty-one, describes this doubleness in reflecting on her first meetings with him.

> Something concealed, an intimation of an unspoken loneliness—that was the first strong impression that gave Nietzsche's appearance its captivating power. . . . His eyes spoke a revealing

language: . . . they seemed like guardians and keepers of inner treasures and mute secrets. . . . [His] overt behavior, too, conveyed the impression of things concealed and unspoken. In everyday life he showed great courtesy and an almost feminine gentleness—a constant, good-hearted equanimity. . . . But in it all lay a penchant for disguise. . . . I recall that when I spoke to him for the first time, his deliberately formal manner shocked and deceived me. But I was not deceived for long by this lonesome man who only wore his mask as unalterably as someone coming from the desert and mountains wears the cloak of the worldly-wise.[31]

Nietzsche speaks of himself in much the same way that Lou does. In his *Genealogy of Morals,* he writes of living in a different world from others, a "strange, questionable, terrible world, . . . an as yet undiscovered country whose boundaries nobody has surveyed yet."[32] Finally he created his own alter ego, whom he called "the last philosopher," so that he could have someone to speak with—this after having written two works (*The Birth of Tragedy* and *Untimely Meditations*), so that presumably he did not consider his authorship to constitute a "speaking with" anybody: "Terrible loneliness of the last philosopher! . . . I call myself the last philosopher because . . . nobody talks to me but myself, and my voice comes to me like that of a dying person! . . . Through you [my alter ego], I conceal my loneliness from myself and make my way into the multitude and into love by lies, for my heart . . . cannot bear the terror of the loneliest loneliness and compels me to talk as if I were two."[33]

Kierkegaard too speaks of himself as utterly apart from others. In a journal entry he says that "I understand myself in my heterogeneousness, my unlikeness to others. . . . I shall never know the security which consists in being like others. No, I remain in unlikeness."[34] And like Nietzsche, he has no one to talk to: "Alone in dialectical tensions which (without God) would drive any man with my imagination to madness; alone in anguish unto death; alone in the face of the meaninglessness of existence, without being able, even if I would, to make myself intelligible to a single soul" (*PV* 71), he creates a mask by which to live a public life through deception, just as Nietzsche "makes his way into the multitude" by lies.[35]

This doubleness of character that bifurcates the self between a public and a private persona becomes the model for Kierkegaard's and Nietzsche's authorships. In an early journal entry of 1836, seven years before his first major work (*Either/Or*), Kierkegaard recounts that "I have just come from a party of which I was the soul: witticism flowed from my mouth, all laughed and admired me, but I went (here indeed the dashes should be as long as the radius of the earth's orbit) –away and wanted to shoot myself."[36] And indeed when he becomes an author he does shoot himself, as does Nietzsche. The "author" is a fabrication, the public mask, visible to all through the signature on the title page. But the signature is a forgery; the author is a complete stranger and fades into invisibility. The author remains utterly lonely by refusing to become intelligible: He writes in such a way that he has "no one to speak to." "Incommunicability is in truth the most terrible of all forms of loneliness," Nietzsche writes in a letter to his sister, "and difference"—the radical separation of self and other, author and reader—"is the mask that is more iron-like than any iron mask."[37]

The writing of Kierkegaard and Nietzsche is devoted from the beginning to the cultivation of masks, disguises, and concealment of the author's intentions. Their texts are, as Kierkegaard puts it about his own, a "speaking in tongues" (*JSK* 2333) that rigorously excludes direct communication. We have seen that Kierkegaard describes his authorship as an "enigmatic mystery," filled with "*double entente*," "ambiguity," "riddle," and "duplicity" (*PV* 5, 8, 10), and he serves notice to his reader (even if this "notice" is only given in his private journal) that "there will come moments . . . when I . . . must set between ourselves the awakening of misunderstanding" (*JP* 1:662). The reader's expectation that the author says what he means, that he is accountable for his text, that the reader's job is to decipher the author's point of view, is all a misunderstanding. The author is a fictional character who perpetually revokes his ownership of the text.

Nietzsche too speaks of the deliberate nurturing of misunderstanding: "The writer—wishes to be *not* understood"; "every profound thinker is more afraid of being understood than of being misunderstood"; and "every word" of the author "is also a mask."[38]

The author is "a concealed man who instinctively needs speech for silence . . . and who is inexhaustible in his evasion of communication, wants and sees to it that a mask of him roams in his place through the hearts and heads of his friends [readers]." The author's speech is actually a nonsaying, a silence, a negation of its own voice, and this silence prepares the author's death, his "burial in silence."[39]

With this commitment to deception and miscommunication, we reach the heart of Kierkegaard's and Nietzsche's ethics of authorship. To deceive—on the face of it an ethical transgression—is for Kierkegaard and Nietzsche an ethical imperative of authorship. Without deception—the provocation of misunderstanding of the author's intentions—the reader is left to the mercy of the author, tied fast to the idea that to discover the writer's meaning is to discover the Truth of the text. But then the reader is disburdened of the responsibility to determine meaning on her own, as it applies to her own life. *This* deception, *this* devotion to the lie, is the opposite of Plato's infamous "noble lie," the lie the ruler devises precisely so as to manipulate his subjects into conforming to his ingenious plans.[40] Rather, it is a lie that consciously renders the author "ignoble," unworthy of authority, and that therefore empowers his or her "subjects"/readers, opening the space for the reclaiming of their own subjectivity.

Just as early in their lives Kierkegaard and Nietzsche had developed impersonal public personalities, masks concealing every trace of personal identity, they construct authorial voices that are also, beneath the brilliance and passion of their styles, entirely impersonal. Foucault says that "the writing subject cancels out the signs of his particular individuality,"[41] and Barthes asserts that "to write, is, through a prerequisite impersonality, . . . to reach that point where only language acts, 'performs,' and not 'me.'"[42] In his *Gay Science,* Nietzsche speaks of "the inner craving for a role and mask, for *appearance,*" and of "the delight in simulation exploding as a power that pushes aside one's so-called 'character,' flooding in and . . . extinguishing it."[43]

This extinction of the author's character is echoed by Kierkegaard in the "First and Last Declaration" he appends to the *Concluding Unscientific Postscript*—which was authored not by Kierkegaard but by Johannes Climacus, who has already added his own appendix in which he "revokes" everything that he has said in the text. In Kierkegaard's "Declaration," he disavows the work as in any way his own: "There is not a single word which is mine; . . . I am impersonal, or am personal in the second person, a *souffleur,*" or stage manager (*CUP* 551). According to Joakim Garff, Kierkegaard even went so far as to "intervene surgically" upon his journal by cutting out pages, "presumably because they did not further Kierkegaard *the myth* but merely exhibited *the man* of the same name."[44] It is as though Kierkegaard were operating forensically as an autopsist, cutting away at "the man" so as to leave only the fiction of the author.

AUTHOR AND READER

Kierkegaard's and Nietzsche's projects of authorship are thus paradoxically an evasion and simulacrum of communication. The therapeutic function of the death of the author—recall Lacan's principle that the analyst must not seek to direct the patient but rather maintain an "attentive silence"—is one of three basic rationales for this evasive style. The others, which I explore in the next section, are an ethics of subjectivity that isolates the author and reader in their inwardness and a philosophy of language that sees speech as effecting an unbridgeable gap between meaning and expression. The therapeutic function is more prominent in Kierkegaard than in Nietzsche. Both regularly renounce authority over the meaning of their texts, just as Lacan says of the therapist that he must not answer the patient's questions and must ignore what he himself knows, thereby leaving the construction of meaning to the devices of the reader. "I want no 'believers,'" Nietzsche says in *Ecce Homo*: "I think I am too ironic to believe in myself; I never speak to masses. I have a terrible fear that one day I will be pronounced holy."[45] And Kierkegaard, as we have seen, renounces any privileged knowledge of the meaning of his own works, insisting that it is only a prejudice that "an author [is] . . . the best interpreter of his own words, as if it could help the reader [to know] that an author had intended this or that" (*CUP* 551, 225).

But much more clearly than Nietzsche, Kierkegaard conceives of his authorship as fundamentally serving a maieutic purpose, aiding the reader to think for herself (*PF* 10; *CUP* 74, 222; *JSK* 1291). Nietzsche is much more ambivalent about performing such a service. For Kierkegaard, the first goal of the author is to "seduce" the reader into self-questioning, but ultimately the ethical goal of indirect communication is a *de*-seduction of the reader that leaves her no longer the object of the author but her own autonomous subject (see *SLW* 311, 491; *E/Or* 1:364, 439–40). As Lacan says, it is not the analyst's function to supply a cure: "Rather, the analyst leaves the subject free to have a go at it" (*Écrits* 641).

Kierkegaard is thus entirely aligned with Barthes's idea that to "suppress the author . . . is to restore the place of the reader."[46] Nietzsche, though, often seems rather indifferent to his reader. "If you misunderstand the singer, what does it matter? That is the 'singer's curse.'" He knows that his works will remain utterly "silent for them (these good people)," but if there are none who hear him, well, that "is not only understandable, it even seems right."[47] Nietzsche's Zarathustra abandons his solitude atop his mountain to "go down" to the village of men; he is "overflowing" and is like the "great star" whose "happiness [depends upon] those for whom [he] shine[s]." But he returns to his mountain in disgust. "In solitude, all being wishes to become word, to learn to speak," Zarathustra says, but "down there, all speech is in vain."[48] Like Zarathustra, Nietzsche finds that his own "life does not reach men's ears; [his] life is silent for them, and all the subtleties of its melody . . . remain hidden from them."[49]

Kierkegaard certainly also often expresses an impatience and irritation with his readers, and "nothing is done to minister to a reader's indolence" (*CUP* 265). But Nietzsche is much harsher: He suffers from a "great nausea" and "contempt for man," and in "intercourse with men" he "glisten[s] in all the colors of distress, green and gray with disgust."[50] Kierkegaard will abandon his reader, but by "shyly withdraw[ing] (for love is always shy)" (*PV* 25–26); Nietzsche orders his erstwhile disciples to "Go away!"[51] Kierkegaard masks himself as an author as a gift to the reader: "The fact that there is no author is a means of keeping the reader at a distance" from the author's own point of view, so as to invite her own point of view. But when

Nietzsche speaks of the "pathos of distance" that separates him from the other, it is generally to "prevent people from doing mischief with me."[52] And Nietzsche's masks are as often as not unwittingly supplied by the reader himself: "Every profound spirit needs a mask: even more, around every profound spirit a mask is growing continually, owing to the constantly false, namely *shallow,* interpretation of every word, every step, every sign of life he gives."[53]

In this sense, there is a real difference in the manner of death of "Kierkegaard" and "Nietzsche" as authors. Barthes and Foucault speak of the death of the author as an historical event emerging in modernity and becoming a fact of the postmodern literary temperament, and tend to write as though this death was a single phenomenon. The contrasting maieutic and agonistic, mocking styles of Kierkegaard's and Nietzsche's respective deaths show, however, that there is no uniform shape of the death of the author, but that a typology is necessary, a forensic analysis, a necropsy or autopsy of the particulars of demise.[54]

Still, even within Nietzsche's more hostile relation to the reader one can find instances of something approaching a maieutic purpose, albeit more muted and infrequent than in Kierkegaard. Nietzsche's Zarathustra is above all a "gift-giver," which is "the highest virtue,"[55] and although he continually retreats back up his mountain to solitude, just as continually he goes back down again to seek a way to give. In his "Night Song," Zarathustra sings of his desire to give, and to love, through his speech:

Night has come: now my craving breaks out of me like a well; to speak I crave.

Night has come; now all the songs of lovers awaken. And my soul too is the song of a lover.[56]

The gift-giving implicit in the authorial strategies of both Kierkegaard and Nietzsche is a "gift of death," to use Derrida's phrase that serves as the title for his reading of Kierkegaard's (Johannes de Silentio's) *Fear and Trembling.* Derrida is concerned with the ethics of Abraham's sacrifice of Isaac, but for own purposes we may see the gift of death more generally as concerned with an ethics of author-ship in which the author dies to the reader. Kierkegaard and Nietz-sche perform their deaths through a double act of sacrifice: The author sacrifices himself by vanishing beneath his disguises and so preserving his privacy; but the reader is also sacrificed, in the sense that she is removed from the life-support supplied by the author, who abandons her to herself.

What is left as a result of this series of sacrifices that constitute the author's gift of death is a relation between "author" and reader as between utter strangers. The between-space of author and reader becomes a shadow world, a nocturnal dreamscape of vanishing shapes, ephemeral meanings, and mis-sightings of the author, who is perpetually wandering away into the mist of the text. In *The Hollow Men,* Eliot writes that

> Between the idea
> And the reality
> Between the motion
> And the act
> Falls the Shadow

(5.5–9)

So too in Kierkegaard's and Nietzsche's texts there is a shadow that falls between the idea or the motion (the author's meaning) and the reality or the act (the text), a darkness that obscures all sight of the author. In the "Shadowgraphs" section of *Either/Or,* a lecture delivered before the Symparanekromenoi, the fellowship of the dead, the speaker remarks that "the day" is "communicative, social, . . . and desires expression"; the night, though, is "secretive, silent, soli-tary, and seeks to retire into itself." Kierkegaard's and Nietzsche's authorships "herald the approaching victory of night," as the lecturer puts it to his fellowship; they shun the day, shun communication, shun sociability and the clarity of expression, seeking secrecy, self-withdrawal, death. "Death," the members of the Symparanekro-menoi are told, "is for us the greatest happiness" (*E/Or* 1:165).

One of Nietzsche's early works was *The Wanderer and His Shadow,* and the theme of shadows and wandering remain recurring motifs of his later works. The wanderer is the experimentalist, the inventor of unexpected perspectives, who plays with the construction of ever new voices, personas, and "truths" (or "errors"). Here is Nietzsche's (nonliteral) pseudonymity or polynymity, equal in inventiveness to Kierkegaard's production of literal pseudonyms: His texts are all authored by wanderers; although signed by "Friedrich Nietzsche," each is an experimentation with new voices. The shadow is the barely decipherable, ephemeral trace left by the wanderer's experiments—the text itself, as the effect of the author who has wandered away and is no longer present; the sign that is illegible in itself without interpretation (and there are "infinite interpretations" possible);[57] the question mark, that twisted shape of punctuation awaiting the reader's response; the ellipsis; the blank space following a dash; the nocturnal, ghostly, uncanny, raspy whisper of the wanderer who, when asked "Wanderer, who are you? . . . What [do you] seek?" responds "Another mask!"[58]

ISOLATION, LANGUAGE, LAMENT

This eerie world of wanderers and their shadows that emerges with the death of the author is not simply a result of the maieutic project of emancipating the reader from the tyranny of the author—a gift of autonomy to the reader—but is equally a consequence of a radically subjectivist epistemology and ethics that precludes the possibility of any genuine meeting between self and other. As such, the author's meanings are never within reach of the reader, any more than the perspective of the reader is ever available to the author.

Derrida centers his *Gift of Death* on the idea that "*tout autre est tout autre*"—every other is entirely other: Every other is "as inaccessible to me, as secret and transcendent, as Jahweh," the absolute other. The other is always out of reach.[59] We have noted Johannes Climacus's conviction that every other is "isolated and compelled to exist for himself."[60] So too for Nietzsche, "every person is a prison" and "we are always only in our own company."[61]

Jean-Paul Sartre writes of the "impossible ideal" of love, namely that a self exist simultaneously for-itself and for-another,[62] and we may say that for Kierkegaard and Nietzsche (as for Barthes and Foucault) this is precisely the impossible idea of any direct relation of author to reader. Their solutions to this riddle will thus seek an indirect relation, an indirect "love," we might say. They will seek to provoke the reader, but then, like Kierkegaard's God, desert the scene, becoming an *auctor absconditus,* leaving the reader to herself.

This ethics of isolation and separation is reinforced in Kierkegaard and Nietzsche by their views of language. Since, as Nietzsche says, "In the end one experiences only oneself,"[63] the project of direct communication with another becomes as impossible an ideal as the ideal of love itself. In Barthes's words, language is a system of "perpetual misunderstanding" that is "exactly the 'tragic'" character of speech.[64] For both Kierkegaard and Nietzsche, language is an expression or externalization of the self, a making public of the private, which inevitably effects a tragic loss of the inner reality of the subject. "We are none of us," Nietzsche writes, "that which we appear to be in accordance with the states for which alone we have . . . words. . . . [Words] make us *misunderstand* ourselves."[65]

As noted, for Kierkegaard speech is inherently untruth, an act of almost offhanded destruction of the real: "The Word annul[s] reality" simply "by talking about it" (*JC* 148). In his *Gay Science,* Nietzsche presents a similarly tragic view of language. He speaks there of the development of language as intimately linked to the development of consciousness, much as Lacan sees the "symbolic order" of language to be what makes the constitution of an I possible.[66] "Consciousness is really only a net of communication between human beings," Nietzsche says, and yet this linguistically constructed consciousness is a fundamental falsification and simplification (just as for Lacan the symbolic relentlessly represses the "Real"): "Consciousness does not really belong to man's individual existence [i.e., his inner, private existence] but rather to his social or herd nature." As such, "the world of which we can become conscious"—the linguistically constructed world—"is only a surface- and sign-world, . . . shallow, thin, relatively stupid, . . . a corruption, falsification, [and] reduction to superficialities."[67]

Derrida writes in *The Gift of Death* that "as soon as one speaks, as soon as one enters the medium of language, one loses [one's] . . .

singularity. . . . The first effect . . . of language therefore involves depriving me of, or delivering me from, my singularity. . . . Once I speak I am never and no longer myself, alone and unique."[68] This exactly captures Kierkegaard's and Nietzsche's sense of the tragic character of language, its power to effect the loss of self. Yet both devote their lives to writing. For Kierkegaard, authorship is "the prompting of an irresistible impulse" (*PV* 7). Nietzsche too feels a "compulsion" to write, even though he feels that "my 'philosophy,' if I have the right to give this name to that which maltreats me down to the roots of my being, is no longer communicable, at least not in print."[69] Being compelled to write and yet tormented by the sense of the incommunicability of their thoughts, they devote their lives to their own deaths, to their burial in silence, to depriving themselves of their own singularity. But as can be seen from their portraits of the nature of language, their devotion to writing is accompanied by lamentation, a nostalgia for the interior space of their singular selves that is lost when they turn to their calling as authors.

Foucault, we saw, writes of how the text "creat[es] a space into which the writing subject constantly disappears."[70] Barthes also speaks of the empty space of the author, of how "the author is never more than the instance [of] writing," so that "this [writing] subject [is] empty outside of the very enunciation which defines it."[71] But neither Kierkegaard nor Nietzsche happily accepts his emptiness as a subject, however much they both toil precisely at effecting emptiness. They are inexhaustible in creating masks that conceal themselves from their readers, and in ensuring that, for the reader, beneath the veil is nothing. But really there *is* something, at the very least a longing for what has been lost.

Nietzsche writes in a letter of February 1888, a year before his collapse, that "I myself have unwittingly turned into something like a cave—something hidden that could no longer be found even if one went out to look for it."[72] The tone of melancholy Kierkegaard expresses at his loss of intimacy with himself by having voyaged "through a world of fantasy" in his authorship (*JSK* 641) is mirrored in Nietzsche's letter: He has "unwittingly" turned into a dark place, perhaps like a grave, which has swallowed him up and hidden him from himself. There is a sense of yearning in both cases, to return home from the fantasy world of authorship in which the author must die, to emerge from the cave, to come back from the grave.

CORDELIA'S CURSE AND THE RESURRECTION OF THE AUTHOR

This nostalgia for the lost self of the author can be seen most glaringly in the positively exhibitionistic autobiographical texts *The Point of View for My Work as an Author: A Report to History* and *Ecce Homo: How One Becomes What One Is.* Both were published posthumously, the *Point of View* at Kierkegaard's request and *Ecce Homo* due to Nietzsche's sister Elisabeth's decision to withhold it for sixteen years after her brother's collapse into insanity in January 1889, just a day after he had requested his publisher to return two poems he wished to revise in order to complete the work to his satisfaction.[73]

The irony that these works, which seem to enact the resurrection of Kierkegaard and Nietzsche from their authorial deaths, awaited publication until several years after their actual deaths is poignant. That Kierkegaard consciously decided to have the *Point of View* published posthumously perhaps indicates his own ambivalence over his resurrection: He will remain dead (as an author) until he has died (as a person), and only then be reborn (as an author). "There shall not be any direct discussion of myself . . . until after my death," he writes in his journals just after finishing the *Point of View,* "because I am . . . essentially a poet; but there is always something enigmatical in a poet's personality, and above all he must not confuse himself with an [actual] character" (*JP* 6:6383). In Nietzsche's case, the evident desire for authorial rebirth during his life (as a person) is foiled by his breakdown and eventual death, almost as though his authorship (in which he had died) were preventing his resurrection (as an author) until he had died (as a person) and until the whims of his sister finally resolved on publication.

Indeed both Kierkegaard and Nietzsche expressed hesitation about publishing these works. This is especially true of Kierkegaard, who wrote in his journal that "the *Point of View* must not be published, no, no. And this is the deciding factor: . . . I cannot tell the full truth about myself" (*JP* 6:6327). In the same entry he alternatively considered publishing the work under the pseudonym Johannes de Silentio, which would have converted the I of the text into a fictional character. In another entry he toyed with making this conversion explicit by writing a foreword in the voice of the pseudonym "A-O," who tells us that the author of the *Point of View* (Søren Kierkegaard) "speaks in the first person; but one will, I hope, remember that this author is not Magister K but my poetic creation" (*P X 2 A 171*).[74] Finally Kierkegaard abandoned these subterfuges, leaving himself as the author of his own "Report to History" and thus emerging at the (near) end of his authorship as himself. Nietzsche went through no such tortured process over the publication of *Ecce Homo,* but he did express a certain tone of self-doubt in the preface to the work, explaining that although he feels it his duty to reveal himself to his readers, it is "a duty against which my habits, even more the pride of my instincts, revolt at bottom."[75]

Here then are the opening lines of these parallel texts, announcing, one might say, Kierkegaard's and Nietzsche's renunciations of their membership in the Symparanekromenoi, the fellowship of the dead, and leaving behind their allegiance to the night, secrecy, and silence, entering for the first time in their authorships into the day, which we may recall is "communicative, social, . . . and desires expression." First, then, Kierkegaard:

> In my career as an author, a point has now been reached where it is permissible to do what I feel a strong impulse to do and so regard as my duty—namely, to explain once for all, as directly and frankly as possible, what is what: what I as an author declare myself to be. . . .
>
> There is a time to be silent and a time to speak. So long as I considered the strictest silence my religious duty I strove in every way to preserve it. . . . [But] what I have done in that way has been misunderstood, . . . [and now I must] affirm what I truly am. (*PV* 5)

And now Nietzsche:

> Seeing that before long I must confront humanity with the most difficult demand ever made of it, it seems indispensable to me to

say *who I am*. . . . The disproportion between the greatness of my
task and the *smallness* of my contemporaries has found expression
in the fact that one has neither heard nor even seen me. I live on
my own credit; it is perhaps a mere prejudice that I live.

I only need to speak with one of the "educated" who come to
the Upper Engadine for the summer, and I am convinced that I
do *not* live.

Under these circumstances I have a duty against which my habits, even more the pride of my instincts, revolt at bottom—namely,
to say: *Hear me! For I am such and such a person. Above all, do not
mistake me for someone else.* (*Ecce Homo*, 673)

Kierkegaard and Nietzsche had so successfully hidden themselves
that it is as though they were dead, living only through a prejudice,
an error of reasoning. But this "not living" delivered them over to
misunderstanding, to being mistaken for someone else. Notwithstanding the fact that they had conceived the ethics of their authorships to rest precisely in the desire "*not* to be understood" (Nietzsche)
and in the "awakening of misunderstanding" in the reader (Kierkegaard), the time has come to fulfill the duty of throwing off their
masks and to emerge from the camouflage of their authorial personas
as "Kierkegaard" and "Nietzsche" into who "they truly are,"
Kierkegaard and Nietzsche.

There may well be intricate ways of explaining these texts away,
readings that show that Kierkegaard and Nietzsche actually remain
only "Kierkegaard" and "Nietzsche"—that their insistence to be delivered from misunderstanding is really only a particularly devilish
way of producing further masks, of perfecting the fictions of themselves. As Henning Fenger puts it of Kierkegaard, his authorship
was "a gigantic play in which [he] acted a profusion of roles, among
them that of Søren Kierkegaard in countless versions."[76] Kierkegaard himself actually says the same thing in a "Preface" for the
Point of View authored by "A-O": "I now dare to make this poetic
venture [the *Point of* View]. . . . The author himself is not K., but
my poetic creation.—I must certainly beg the pardon of Mr. K. for
venturing right under his nose, so to speak, to understand him poetically." But then Kierkegaard decided not to publish this "Preface,"

leaving his own interpretation of the pseudonymity of the author of the work, "Søren Kierkegaard," in doubt.[77]

Louis Mackey says that "when a man fabricates as many masks to hide behind as Kierkegaard does, one cannot trust his (purportedly) direct asseverations. And when he signs his own name, it no longer has the effects of the signature."[78] Derrida expresses the same view about Nietzsche, writing that Nietzsche's "[auto]biographical desire" is "beyond the mythology of the signature, of the theology of the author,"[79] and Carl Pletsch views *Ecce Homo* as "the most silent of Nietzsche's books."[80]

But even if such intricate interpretations are convincing, so that Kierkegaard and Nietzsche really do preserve their deaths as authors even as they implore their readers to "Hear me!" at the very least they are playing with the idea of the resurrection of the author, tempting the reader to reassert the customary and comfortable relation to the author as an authority. Their frequent expressions of distaste and resentment over the reader's power to misunderstand them leads them to publish works that (again, at the very least) act out the role of the affronted author.

Well before the *Point of View* and *Ecce Homo,* Kierkegaard and Nietzsche yearn for readers who will be worthy of their gifts, who will understand them—Kierkegaard's "imagined reader" who "understands [him] at once and line by line" (*CUP* 548) and Nietzsche's reader who will "have the ears" to hear "my truths."[81] Thus at times the death of the author appears to be intended as a death only for unworthy readers. "A writer wishes to be *not* understood," Nietzsche says, but then adds, "by just anybody."[82] In one of Kierkegaard's earliest works, *Repetition,* the pseudonym Constantin Constantius writes in a similar vein that "not everyone [can be] a reader; the author does well to write like Clemens Alexandrinus[83] in such a way that the heretics cannot understand what he writes" (*R* 131)—but presumably in a way that nonheretics can. As we have seen, another pseudonym, William Afham, uses as the motto for his essay "In Vino Veritas" the saying of the satirist Lichtenberg that "such works are mirrors: when an ape peers into them, no apostle can be seen looking out" (*SLW* 8). But of course it is just the idea of seeking apostles that Barthes and Foucault—and Kierkegaard and Nietzsche in many

other places—are so intent to relegate to a bygone era in their an-
nouncements of the death of the author.

Nietzsche's readers are also too often only apes—also donkeys,
flies, cows, leeches, fire hounds, ghosts and apparitions, the sick and
decaying, pale criminals, scholars, cripples, beggars, priests, gravedig-
gers, and a whole host of other creatures who crowd around Zarathustra but are incapable of understanding him. His readers are also
fish, and he is a fisherman, like Kierkegaard trolling for apostles
(and like Christ, one may note in passing, who tells the fisherman
Simon that if he becomes a disciple, "henceforth thou shalt catch
men," Luke 5:10): "All of my writings are fish hooks," Nietzsche
says in *Ecce Homo*. "Perhaps I know how to fish as well as anyone?—If nothing was caught, I am not to blame. *There were no
fish.*"[84] Kierkegaard fishes as well, seeking to catch the right sort of
reader: "This is what is achieved by the indirect method [of author-
ship], which, loving and serving the truth, arranges everything dialectically for the prospective captive" (*PV* 25).

What emerges in this recurring quest for the true reader, a quest
that culminates in Kierkegaard's and Nietzsche's direct instructions
to the reader in the *Point of View* and *Ecce Homo* about how to
correctly understand them, is not simply a lament over the loss of
self entailed by language. For this loss is compensated for by the
mask beneath which the self still lives, the inner sanctum in which
Kierkegaard and Nietzsche preserve their private individualities
carefully hidden from their readers. No, something more is present
here: a sense of bitterness over the idea that it is *not* finally their
masks (their own handiwork) that constitute them as authors, but
rather the *reader* who constructs the author, in a sense stealing their
souls.

In "Writers, Intellectuals, Teachers," Barthes writes that "it suf-
fices that I speak, that my speech flow, for it to flow away."[85] Sartre
puts the point more harshly: All language is a "stealing of thought,"
a robbery of the speaker's being-for-self by the other's appropriation
of my meanings.[86] The stealing of the author's thoughts is the reader's curse that caused Kierkegaard and Nietzsche second thoughts
about maintaining their deaths, however strong their commitments
were to this death in principle. The *Point of View* and *Ecce Homo*

are the culminating expressions of these second thoughts, texts where the author turns back from his grave and seeks to reappropriate his stolen soul.

It is interesting that both Kierkegaard and Nietzsche had women as their imagined readers: Regine Olsen and Lou Andreas-Salomé. This is particularly interesting given Kierkegaard's and Nietzsche's well-known misogyny. They conceive of woman as sheer being-for-other, existing only to be formed by male imagination and desire; she is pure surface, superficiality, shallowness. In the "Diary of the Seducer," Kierkegaard's master eroticist Johannes writes that woman is "characterized by pure virginity: . . . the very concept of woman requires that she be vanquished; the concept of man that he be the victor" (*E/Or* 1:424–26). Nietzsche echoes the seducer in the *Gay Science:* "For it is man who creates for himself the image of woman, and woman forms herself according to this image."[87] Woman is thus like the reader in a particularly cynical version of the traditional (patriarchal) model of authorship, dependent on the authority of the author, incapable of assuming authorship of the text herself. The resurrection of the author in Kierkegaard and Nietzsche is the mark of their reservations about the emancipation of woman, of the reader, from her properly "feminine" (dependent) position.

But woman is not simply all surface: She is dangerous. Like all surfaces, she hides a depth; she is the "beast of prey, the tiger's claw under the glove."[88] Woman represents the frightening capacity for independence.[89] Nietzsche often expresses his fear and disgust at the idea of "woman's emancipation," a "defeminization" that threatens woman's natural dependence on man.[90] This potential for independence is hinted at even in the outlandishly misogynistic "Diary of the Seducer" in Kierkegaard's *Either/Or,* in the ambiguous letters that Cordelia sends to Johannes after he abandons her. Although Kierkegaard is carefully four times removed from the Seducer (Kierkegaard creates Victor Eremita, who edits the papers of "A," who in turn steals the diary of the Seducer), the diary nevertheless is an allegorical exploration of the ethics of authorship, just as Kierkegaard himself is experimenting with myriad versions of authorship in *Either/Or,* his first pseudonymous work. Johannes returns the letters unopened (his abandonment of Cordelia must be perfect), but we learn from "A," Cordelia's intermediary with Johannes, who has opened the letters and copied them for publication along with the diary, that Cordelia has placed a curse upon her seducer: "Johannes! . . . I realize very well that you have never been mine . . . and yet I call you mine; my seducer, my deceiver, my enemy, my murderer, the cause of my unhappiness, the grave of my joy, the abyss of my destruction. Flee where you will; . . . love a hundred others, I am still . . . *thine,* thine, thine, thy curse" (*E/Or* 1:307).

Here then is the reader's curse upon the author. But the curse is ambiguous. The male paradigm of authorship would see Cordelia's pleasure in her "slavery" as confirming the reader's utter dependence on the author, her complete incapacity to exist for herself. The author has given the gift of death; he is the reader's murderer, the grave of her joy, the abyss into which she has sunk and lost all autonomy. But there is another register to Cordelia's voice: Yes, she calls herself *his,* but she also calls Johannes *hers:* "You are mine." She is his grave.

"Woman," we might say, represents for Kierkegaard and Nietzsche the potential of the reader's gift of death to the author. The author becomes the possession of the reader; he cannot escape her love, her construction of him; she is the one who determines the meaning of his seduction, and who thus reverses the relation of authority. It is just this reversal that helps explain Kierkegaard's and Nietzsche's exhibitionistic reassertions in the *Point of View* and *Ecce Homo* of their autonomy and the injustice of the reader's appropriation of them.

Although Kierkegaard broke off his engagement to Regine Olsen almost as soon as he had made it, he dedicated his "whole authorship" to her.[91] His work is meant "to accentuate her as [his] one and only" reader (*JP* 6:6473). Later he made her his sole heir.[92] "It was she who made me a poet,"[93] just as the Young Man in *Repetition* is made a poet by the woman he loves but then must abandon, for to be a poet is to die to the particular person one loves and to love rather "the idea" (*R* 87–89).

Nietzsche also broke off his relationship with Lou Andreas-Salomé after just a few months. Lou represented for Nietzsche the possibility of "becoming a human being," of being saved from his terrible loneliness. But "as soon as I had merely dreamed this dream of not being alone, the danger was frightful," and "I commit nothing but follies: I realize more and more that I no longer fit among human beings."[94] Lou was to be Nietzsche's true reader; he writes to her a little more than a month into their acquaintance that "I should like very much to be permitted to be your teacher. I am looking for human beings who could become my heirs."[95]

Both affairs were colossal failures. Kierkegaard's ended with an excruciatingly convoluted and continually bungled plan to de-seduce Regine,[96] just as Johannes the Seducer imagines the "masterpiece" of a de-seduction of Cordelia in the "Diary" published at just the time Kierkegaard was seeking to mastermind the collapse of his own affair with Regine (*E/Or* 1:364). Nietzsche's affair with Lou ended with his challenging his former friend and now perceived rival Paul Rée to a duel.[97] In Nietzsche's case, Lou could not satisfy his desire for her to be a disciple: She was much too independent. In Kierkegaard's case, he himself could not satisfy the demands of a relationship: He could neither imagine his own dependence on another nor bear the responsibility of hers on him. Both retreated back into loneliness. But Regine and Lou remained, haunting their authorships as a curse, or as a cross, the sign of their burial—reminders of the failure of their "attempts to become human" and of the frightening independence of a reader who cannot be possessed, who remains for-herself.

GRAVE SITES

Carl Pletsch writes that in the *Point of View* and *Ecce Homo,* "Kierkegaard and Nietzsche were working out a fantasy that Nietzsche had recorded in an adolescent sketch of an autobiography: 'to write a book and read it myself'" (no ref.). He notes that "Nietzsche expresses this remarkably innocent narcissistic fantasy again in an epigram that he placed at the front of *Ecce Homo* thirty years later: 'how could I fail to be thankful to my whole life?—and so I tell my life to myself.'" Pletsch remarks that "this is the onanistic pleasure of the self-sufficient text."[98] Kierkegaard expresses this same fantasy at the very beginning of his pseudonymous authorship, in the voice of "A" in *Either/Or,* in one of the "Diapsalmata" (musical interludes) written *"ad se ipsum"* (to himself). "A" writes of his grief as being "like an eagle's nest upon the peak of a mountain lost in the clouds" so that "no one can take it by storm." There he "live[s] as one dead," telling the stories of his life to himself "in a voice as soft as a whisper," so soft, perhaps, that no one else can hear him (*E/Or* 1:41).

The fantasy of the self-sufficient text is the paradoxical fantasy of a perfected death of the author that at the same time achieves the author's perfect resurrection. The author becomes utterly opaque to the reader, foiling the reader's curse (that she steals the author's thoughts, his soul, by being the arbiter of meaning) by entirely cutting the reader out—the text is written only for the author, *ad se ipsum.* But in this death to the reader the author is also reborn: He is pristine, unencumbered by the other, pure transcendence; he exists for himself alone.

Although this fantasy is brought to fruition in the *Point of View* and *Ecce Homo,* it is anticipated provisionally in earlier works, as the entry from the "Diapsalmata" shows in Kierkegaard's case (or rather "Kierkegaard's" case, since it is A's fantasy). In his own voice, Kierkegaard reiterates the fantasy in the very last sentence of the epilogue he appends to Johannes Climacus's *Postscript,* the "First and Last Declaration": "And, oh, that no half-learned man would lay a dialectic hand upon this work, but would let it stand as now it stands!" (*CUP* 554). The work must remain his alone, uncontaminated by the hand of any reader—here, not a woman, but an equally superficial and dangerous type, the "half-learned man." Nietzsche's Zarathustra also fantasizes about the self-sufficient text in the plaintive lines we have already cited, after he has returned to the solitude of his mountain (like A's eagle's nest) in despair and disgust over his failure to communicate his gift of wisdom to those who live below: "In solitude, all being wishes to become word; to learn to speak. Down there, all speech is in vain."[99] Zarathustra seeks a miraculous speech, a speech that might circumvent the tragedy of language, that, in Derrida's words, "once I speak I am never and no longer myself, alone and unique,"[100] a self-sufficient speech addressed to oneself in solitude.

But of course this narcissistic fantasy must fail. The self-sufficient text, where the author is his own reader, is a structural contradiction. The I of the author is no more the very same I as the one who reads his text than is the I of the "other" reader/s "down there" in the shadow of the author's mountain. The self-sufficient text is never self-sufficient; in reading what I write I am not "myself." As Rimbaud says, "*Je est un autre.*" In my speech I become other to myself, I become "only a reader," a "third person," with no privileged access to "the aim" of the author, as Kierkegaard says of his own authorship (*PV* 13, 15; *CUP* 225). When I read what I write, I am, like Nietzsche, a doppelgänger: "I have a 'second' face in addition to the first, and perhaps also a third."[101]

As Hegel argues, the standpoint of narcissism, the dream of the self-coinciding "I = I," is inherently unstable and hollow, unsettled by desire, by the need of an other. "Self-consciousness exists in and for itself when, and by the fact that, it so exists for another; that is, it exists only in being acknowledged" (*PS* 111). Hence notwithstanding their desire to preserve an "inner sanctum" for themselves in their writing that "prevents all access," Kierkegaard and Nietzsche desire readers; they desire love. As Nietzsche writes to Overbeck less than two years before he succumbs to insanity, it "*hurts* frightfully that in these fifteen years [of my authorship] not one single person has 'discovered' me, has needed me, has loved me."[102] This desire is the source of Kierkegaard's and Nietzsche's "irresistible impulse" and "compulsion" to write, as it is the source of each of our compulsions to speak. And however much Kierkegaard and Nietzsche may at times succumb to reveries about controlling how they should be recognized by their readers, giving instructions about how the reader ought to understand them "at once and line by line," it is the saving grace of their authorships that their texts revoke this control—even against their authors' conflicting desire to maintain their authority—ensuring their burials as authors and the autonomy of the reader. Their lapses into "speaking plainly" were a nostalgic return to the commonsense ethics of authorship, an ethics without deception, without miscommunication and disguise, an ethics where textual meaning is the author's private property. But, as we have seen, an authorship without deception is an abandonment of an alternative ethics that is, to quote Socrates out of context, a "practice in the art of dying."[103] Socrates is speaking of dying away from the body, which traps the soul. In the context of the death of the author, the task is to die away from the personality of the author itself, which traps the soul of the reader.

In *Ecce Homo,* Nietzsche says of his Zarathustra that he is a "seducer,"[104] just as Kierkegaard's authors are all seducers. But Zarathustra is a different sort of seducer, one who desires the other to escape the seduction. Nietzsche quotes from *Zarathustra* (that is, he quotes himself, but not onanistically; on the contrary, he quotes his doppelgänger, Zarathustra, who beckons beyond himself to the one who ceases to revere him).

> Now I go alone, my disciples. You, too, go now, alone. Thus I want it. . . .
>
> One repays a teacher badly if one always remains nothing but a pupil. . . .
>
> You revere me; but what if your reverence *tumbles* one day? Beware lest a statue slay you. . . .
>
> Now I bid you lose me and find yourselves.[105]

Zarathustra thus gives his gift of death: He becomes a mere statue, like the sentinel at a grave site, so that his disciples may be released from his seduction.

As for Kierkegaard's most notorious seducer, Johannes, the murderer of Cordelia, we saw in Chapter 3 that he ends his diary with a last wish (couched in the misogynistic language that characterizes his understanding of woman): "If I were a god, I would do for her what Neptune did for a nymph, I would change her into a man" (*E/Or* 1:440)—that is, the author wishes, as he leaves town and vanishes from the reader's life, for her to become an author.

As Barthes says, "A text's unity lies not in its origin [author] but in its destination [reader]."[106] The reader is the grave site of the author. Nietzsche's and Kierkegaard's own grave sites, in church cemeteries in Röcken and Copenhagen, bear metaphoric witness to this. Nietzsche's sister Elisabeth made plans for a gargantuan memorial site, complete with several buildings and a sports stadium.[107] Although her plans never materialized, she did have an impressive tombstone laid over his grave, next to which she later took up residence after her own death. Before he was interred, Elisabeth orchestrated an elaborate funeral with full Lutheran rites for the famous atheist— Kierkegaard, the Christian author, for his part refused last rites[108]— and his friend Gast pronounced "Holy be thy name to all coming generations,"[109] evidently forgetting that Nietzsche had sent him a draft of his *Ecce Homo* in which he wrote of his "terrible fear that one day I will be pronounced holy."[110] Thus Nietzsche went to his grave cursed by his readers (his sister and his friend), mistaken for who he was not.[111]

Kierkegaard's grave was left unmarked for almost twenty years, after which no one could remember where he was buried, so a simple slab was made with his name on it that now leans against his father's monument.[112] By leaning against his father in death, Kierkegaard returned to the man who had tutored him in the life of fantasy that came to define his authorship. In his unpublished *De Omnibus Dubitandum Est*, Kierkegaard allows Johannes Climacus to describe his relationship with his father when he was a young boy. Rather than taking Johannes out for a walk, his father would take his hand and "go for a walk up and down the room" of the house, transporting him to far corners of the earth and making up stories of their adventures. "For Johannes it was as if the world was being created as they conversed," and he "soon learned from his father how he, too, could exercise this magic power" in order to "construct everything" out of the imagination (*JC* 105–6).

But what makes the tableau of Kierkegaard's grave marker leaning against his father's monument perfect is that it does not locate Kierkegaard at all. The exact location of Kierkegaard's burial site remains obscure; it is only "Kierkegaard" who lies beneath the slab bearing his name—that is, really no one at all—so that even in death he retains the anonymity he sought so hard to preserve in his authorship. In both cases, then, Kierkegaard's and Nietzsche's actual graves pay homage to the projects of their authorships, that they remain "strangers and aliens" to their readers, without definite location, their "holiness" only an ironic misunderstanding.

7. Passing Over: The Death
of the Author in Hegel

The acceptance without reserve of the fact of death is
the final source of all of Hegel's thought.

ALEXANDRE KOJÈVE, *L'introduction à la lecture de Hegel*

Death . . . is of all things the most dreadful, and to hold fast to the
work of death requires the greatest strength.

G. W. F. HEGEL, *The Phenomenology of Spirit* (translation modified)

SURELY NO MAJOR PHILOSOPHER has been as criticized, scorned,
lampooned, dismissed, dismantled, and deconstructed as Georg Wilhelm Friedrich Hegel. Already in 1819, during the height of Hegel's
fame, Arthur Schopenhauer was writing in his *World as Will and
Representation* that "the greatest effrontery in serving up sheer nonsense, in scrabbling together senseless and maddening webs of words,
such as had previously been heard only in madhouses, [has] finally
appeared in Hegel."[1] Later Schopenhauer described Hegel as "a
commonplace, inane, loathsome, repulsive and ignorant charlatan,
who with unparalleled effrontery compiled a system of crazy nonsense that . . . [has] completely disorganized and ruined the minds of
a whole generation."[2]

Not to be outdone, Otto Gruppe, a philosopher, poet, and secretary of the Prussian Academy of Art, a year before Hegel's death
wrote a savagely satirical play about Hegel worthy of Aristophanes'
Clouds (in the vivacity of its invective if not in its aesthetic achievement). Written under the pseudonym Absolutus von Hegelingen,

Gruppe's *Die Winde* (*Winds,* perhaps even *Clouds,* or less elegantly but closest to the spirit of the play, *Flatulences*) presented Hegel as a bombastic lunatic.[3] In another work, just weeks before Hegel succumbed to cholera, Gruppe described Hegel's philosophy as a "pathological abscess" and his own duty as "to use the knife."[4]

Death may have liberated Hegel the man from his critics, but if possible, things only got worse in his posthumous existence for the reputation of his philosophy. Ten years after Hegel's death, the newly crowned King Friedrich Wilhelm IV proclaimed his desire to "expunge the dragon's seed of Hegel's pantheism" from the minds of Prussian youth,[5] and invited Hegel's former friend and college roommate (and later bitter enemy) Friedrich Schelling to Berlin to carry out the task. The young Friedrich Engels was present—along with Otto Gruppe, by the way—in the packed Lecture Hall No. 6 where Schelling gave his lectures. Engels reported on the lectures in a local newspaper under the pseudonym Friedrich Oswald with the headline "Schelling's death sentence on Hegel's system."[6] Although in this article Engels strongly defended Hegel, he would later come to his senses and join with Feuerbach and Marx in the effort of turning Hegel's "topsy-turvy" world back on its feet.[7] Also present at Schelling's lectures, sitting in the seat next to—who else?—Otto Gruppe,[8] was Søren Kierkegaard, who would soon devote a considerable portion of his life's work to the exposure of the dangers and absurdities of Hegel's philosophy.

More recently, the project of resistance to the Hegelian system has become a focal point of critical theory, deconstruction, Lacanian psychoanalytic theory, and Foucauldian "archaeology." Although there are of course many important differences and nuances of approach to Hegel in the work of Derrida, Foucault, Lacan, Barthes, Bataille, Lyotard, and Deleuze, there are some generally shared strands to their critiques. The French critics share with the earlier critics Gruppe, Kierkegaard, Feuerbach, Marx, and Engels the sense that Hegel's philosophy abstracts away from what Deleuze calls "the concrete richness of the sensible"[9] into, in Bataille's words, "the aprioristic clouds"—or to recall Gruppe, the winds or flatulence—"of universal concepts."[10] (Schopenhauer's and Schelling's criticisms are somewhat different.) Such an abstraction entails an abandonment of the particularity and subjectivity of the lived experience of the self, and indeed a leveling of difference between self and other. "One of the profound defects of Hegel's thought," Jean Hyppolite says, is that it "lead[s] us to a *universal subject* . . . which tends to eliminate *specific existents.*"[11]

Although these criticisms were already well rehearsed by Hegel's earliest opponents, and should certainly sound familiar to us after our examination of Kierkegaard's critique, what is largely new in the French critics is the idea that Hegel betrays his own philosophy of negativity—his reliance on a dialectical method that mercilessly exposes opposition, contradiction, and rupture at the heart of every supposed certainty and every yearned-for state of unity—by finally resolving all oppositions in an ultimate grand synthesis. Hegel's philosophy portrays spirit as perpetually riven: "The life of spirit is not the life that shrinks from death and keeps itself untouched by devastation," he writes in the *Phenomenology of Spirit,* "but rather the life that endures it and maintains itself in it. It wins its truth only when it finds itself in utter dismemberment." Yet behind the scenes he is desperately seeking a therapeutics in which, as he says toward the end of the *Phenomenology,* "the wounds of the spirit heal and leave no scars" (*PS* 19, 407).

But, as Lacan insists of therapy, there is no cure.[12] Judith Butler writes of Derrida and Foucault (and her comment holds good for the whole generation of French "postmodern" thought) that they "theorize from within the tradition of a dialectic deprived of synthesis,"[13] deprived, we might say, of the possibility of cure. William Desmond speaks similarly of this tradition as one that is committed to "difference, sheer difference, . . . multiplicity without an enjoining unity, . . . the reduction of univocity to the equivocal," with no "center or unity" and no "central meaning."[14]

Finally, a major source of preoccupation of postmodern critics of Hegel is how his longing for synthesis, his inability to endure the anxiety and "unhappy consciousness" that inevitably accompanies spirit's dismemberment, leads him to adopt the authorial stance of what Bataille calls "Sovereignty"[15] and Kojève "the Wise Man,"[16] the one who claims a privileged position of authority beyond all subjectivity, culminating in an "Absolute Knowledge" in which the author makes transparent the unity underlying the mere show of difference and negativity that has glided along the surface of the text. Hegel "has become . . . wise, very wise," Kojève writes[17]—so wise, in fact, that he has become God-like, and his writing, therefore, holy scripture. As Stanley Rosen says, "Absolute knowledge is the thinking of totality," yet totality can only be fantasized by human beings. Hence "if we achieve the Hegelian science of totality we must cease to be human or become genuinely divine."[18] Bataille puts the point more succinctly: With his claim to absolute knowledge, Hegel becomes "everything, i.e., God."[19] Bataille's point is reminiscent of Kierkegaard's (or Johannes Climacus's) claim in the *Postscript* that "reality itself is a system—for God; but it cannot be a system for any existing spirit" (*CUP* 167). Hegel, for Kierkegaard as for Bataille, has somehow forgotten that he is not God but merely a human being.

HEGEL AND HIS CRITICS: A LIFE-AND-DEATH STRUGGLE

It is this last theme of Hegel's purported authorial arrogance, his assumption of sovereign authority, that is the focus of this chapter. In a way, the struggle against Hegel on the part of his critics has been a "life-and-death struggle," as Hegel famously described the master-slave dialectic in his *Phenomenology*, a struggle to define the terms of domination and submission between author and reader. Hegel the Wise Man implies the death of the reader: In assuming an absolute position, the author achieves the absolute subjection of the reader. The slave of Hegel's *Phenomenology* gains an awareness of the potential for freedom through the activity of labor on the material world—by reshaping nature, the slave recognizes his own creative power (*PS* 116–18). Hegel's critics labor as well: They labor on his text itself, as an assertion of the power of the reader and hence of the rights of the multiplicity of interpretation over the monological meanings of the author. As Roland Barthes says, "The birth of the reader must be at the cost of the death of the author."[20]

In what follows, I hope to show that this relentless life-and-death struggle against Hegel is profoundly ironic, since long before Schelling had pronounced his "death sentence" on Hegel's philosophy in

Lecture Hall No. 6, Hegel had himself effected his own death as an author. We saw in the last chapter that Michel Foucault speaks of how the author "must assume the role of a dead man in the game of writing" and of how in this game the text "create[s] a space into which the writing subject constantly disappears."[21] It will be argued that the role of the Wise Man, of the absolute authority, is in fact an elaborate mask in Hegel's game of writing, covering over a project whose goal is the same as that of Kierkegaard and Nietzsche, that of the disappearance of the author, by which it becomes the reader who is left to author the text.

Unlike Kierkegaard, who explicitly pursued his death as an author—who, as we have seen, wrote of his effort to reduce himself, "the communicator, to *nobody*" (*TC* 132)—Hegel is less obvious about his death, which is unaccompanied by the incessant ceremonial of calling attention to it. His demise is less obtrusive, quieter. This is wonderfully ironic, since Kierkegaard portrays Hegel as the quintessentially *loud* philosopher, the one who shouts from the rooftops and expounds upon the soapbox. Yet, as we will see, Hegel was the consummate philosopher of the mask and disguise, of evasion of communication and indirection. To recall Judith Butler, "Hegel's sentences are never completed; they never offer up 'what is meant' in some final . . . form; . . . Hegel's text does not address the reader directly; [his] narrative strategy . . . is to implicate the reader indirectly."[22]

It is Kierkegaard, after all, and not Hegel, who writes a *Point of View for My Work as an Author* in which he proclaims his "strong impulse" and "duty" to "explain once and for all, as directly and frankly as possible, what is what: what I as an author declare myself to be" (*PV* 5). For Hegel, though, there is no "*my*" work as an author and hence no impulse or sense of duty to proclaim it. In a letter of 1819, the same year Schopenhauer wrote of Hegel's unbearable arrogance, Hegel addressed his friend Hermann Hinrichs's intended compliment that "the Absolute has first comprehended itself only in your [Hegel's] philosophy." Hegel replies that "in speaking of philosophy as such, one cannot be speaking of *my* philosophy. For every philosophy is the self-comprehension of the Absolute"—every philosophy "is in turn . . . the one and true philosophy," as he says in another place (*HP* 1:17–18). "But," he tells Hinrichs, "it is of course impossible to prevent misunderstandings by those who in the face of such ideas cannot rid themselves of the standpoint of the particular individual person" (*Letters* 478).

In what follows, I explore Hegel's commitment to his own death as an author—his disappearance as a "particular individual person" who might claim ownership and unique insight into the meaning of his philosophy—in a variety of contexts: in his invention of a new method of demonstration in which truth is not proclaimed by the author but rather discovered in the evolving experience of consciousness itself; in his epistemology, where knowledge is not the passive reception of the "given," but the process by which the subject alters the given through her interpretive acts; in his philosophy of language, which denies any privileged position to a speaker's intentions but rather locates meaning in the response of the other; in his theory of desire, which establishes the emptiness of the self apart from its constitution as being-for-other; and even in his notorious invocation of "absolute knowledge," which, far from establishing the authority of the author, will be seen to acknowledge his death and to defer to the experience of the reader.

In exploring these themes, we will be led to cast a new light on the long history of combat with Hegel's ghost. The three waves of Hegel's critics—Schopenhauer, Schelling, Kierkegaard, and Marx; Kojève, Hyppolite, and Sartre; Bataille, Lacan, Lyotard, Deleuze, Foucault, and Derrida—have sought their own identities in large measure in the negative space surrounding the apparitional figure of Hegel, the author who will not die but who, improbable as it may seem, was dead at his own hand long before he met his end at the hand of cholera.[23]

METHOD: DISORIENTATION, SURRENDER, AND PASSING OVER

Hegel claims to have discovered an "altogether new concept of scientific procedure" (*L* 27). It is a method designed to provoke the reader to learn to think differently, where, as we have seen, we must "become acquainted with [things] in a new way, quite opposite to that in which we know them already," so that we will "feel the ground where we once stood firm and at home taken away from beneath [us], and . . . cannot tell where in the world we are" (*EL* §§3, 19). Hegel's method is not only a disorientation of the reader, whose familiar expectations about how a philosophic text will proceed are thrown into confusion, but also a disorienting and confusing of the very relation between author and reader.

Hegel's dislocation of our familiar ways of thinking is suggestive of the way that Heidegger would later question the familiar, "average everyday" understanding of things, and underlying both projects of disorientation is a critique of what both authors call "representational" thinking, which involves, as Heidegger phrases it, the "tyranny" or "dominance" of the subject over the objects it thinks.[24] For Heidegger, the most decisive moment for the peculiarly modern expression of this form of thinking occurred in the post-Greek "epoch" of the history of philosophy initiated by Descartes. In Descartes's philosophy and physics, nature is conceived of simply as *res extensa,* extended matter, that which is constantly available for use by the self-constituting ego, *res cogitans.*[25] Essential to the Cartesian viewpoint—and all subsequent metaphysics—is a representational theory of meaning: Beings have a value only insofar as they are represented (*vor-gestellt*) by consciousness, which thus stands over against them as their real meaning and truth. This representational thinking (*Vorstellungsdenken*) ushers in the age of technology, which is itself an "enframing" (*das Ge-stell*), a "setting-upon" (*stellen*) the world that allows beings to become present only as "mere things." To represent the world means that "what is, in its entirety, is now taken in such a way that it first is in being and only is in being to the extent that it is set up [*aufstellt*], . . . represent[ed] [*vorgestellt*] and set forth [*setzt*]" by the thinking subject.[26]

Interestingly, Heidegger sees (I am tempted to say "represents") Hegel as himself the representationalist par excellence, speaking of the "absolute representing" of Hegel's metaphysics.[27] It would require much too long an aside to investigate Heidegger's argument here, but whatever its merits, it must be said that it does not come to terms with the fact that Hegel goes at least as far as Heidegger's own uncovering of connections between the essentially destructive, nihilistic trinity of *Vorstellen, Gestell,* and *stellen.* Hegel associates representational thinking (*Vorstellen*) with *Verstellung,* a fundamental dissemblance that is equally a shifting or misplacing or displacing of the world (*verstellen*): Representational thinking "sets up" (*aufstellt*) or "posits" or "sets forth" (*setzt*) a world that is really an act of dissemblance (*Verstellung*), since the place (*Stellung*) of this world is radically displaced (*versetzt, verstellt*) into a mere representation (*Vorstellung*) of consciousness (*PS* 374–83/*W* 3:453–64).

Hegel speaks of representational thinking as a sort of "apprehension" (*Auffasung*) of things that is very close to Heidegger's description of representation as an "enframing" and "setting upon" things. To apprehend things is to "hold them fast" (*festhalten*) in our representation of them. Like Heidegger, Hegel also implies an inherent violence to this act: "To confine [the thing] to a pure apprehension," Hegel writes, consciousness "has only to take it" (*es hat ihn nur zu nehmen*). Representational thinking "degrades" the being of things into "something therefore that is dead and cannot be [authentically] known" (*PS* 61, 70/*W* 3:86, 96). It is precisely in Hegel's rejection of this dominating, violent model of representational thinking that we can locate his commitment to a reconceptualization of his own authorship as a refusal to confine and set upon the reader, to render her something that is dead.

And just as Hegel's critique of *Vorstellungsdenken* reconfigures the role of the author, so too it reimagines the reader. His alternative to representational thinking, where we "take" things and "hold them fast," is what he calls authentic "thinking things over" (*Nachdenken*) (*EL* §§1, 3, 5). *Nachdenken* literally means "thinking after," or "after-thinking," and implies that meaning is never fixed in a simple representation but must be sought in thinking "after," or in response to, what is presented. Just as the reader's identity is no longer fixed as a representation of the author, so too the reader's agency is not simply to re-present and submissively "hold fast" to the meaning set forth by the text, but to engage in after-thinking, a reply in which she makes it her own. Thus Hegel describes his own philosophic method as a "replacement" of all representational schemas of the experience of consciousness with a phenomenology in which consciousness "presents itself" (*W* 3:593).

Above all, Hegel's style of authorship is one that declines "bare assurances," notwithstanding Kierkegaard's depiction of his form of communication as that of "direct assertion." It is utterly "inappropriate and misleading" for an author to offer any "explanation of [his] aim" (*PS* 1), just as we have seen that Kierkegaard believes the author's own interpretation of his world should be a matter of complete indifference (*CUP* 225). Rather, the author's role is to take the ground away from beneath the reader precisely by his (the author's) withdrawal: The author, the one who we count on for assertions and edifications, must not be "at home."

Thus the world the reader enters into in Hegel's texts is not one where truth will be found "like a minted coin that can be pocketed ready-made."[28] Hegel's critics aside, there simply is no such truth for Hegel. As Richard Rorty puts it,

> Hegel left Kant's ideal of philosophy-as-science in shambles, . . . [and] created a new literary genre, a genre that exhibited the relativity of significance, . . . the bewildering variety of vocabularies from which we can choose, and the intrinsic instability of each. He made unforgettably clear the deep self-certainty given by each achievement of a vocabulary, . . . each new style, each new dialectical synthesis—the sense that now, at last, for the first time, we have grasped things as they truly are. He also made unforgettably clear why such certainty lasts but a moment.[29]

Rorty's description of Hegel's style is reminiscent of what Lacan says about "*points de caption*," "quilting" points where there is a moment of rest in "the otherwise endless movement of signification,"[30] points that provide what Dylan Evans refers to as "the necessary illusion of a fixed meaning,"[31] the semblance of stability, a semblance that inevitably falls apart. Hegel's famous aphorism that truth is "a "Bacchanalian revel in which no member is not drunk" (*PS* 27) entails that meanings are never "at rest" but perpetually "dissolve and pass over" into new configurations (*HP* 1:33; *W* 3:593). And this passing over (*übergehen*) is equally the passing over, the dissolution and death, of the author as the arbiter of meaning.

Hegel's "passing over" is at the heart of his dialectical method, which has as its basic law the destabilization of all fixed meanings, "the dynamic of the self-transcendence of things" (*EL* §81Z) and thus the experience of the self being "driven beyond it[self], and this uprooting entails its death" (*PS* 51). The author too must pass beyond himself, must die, uprooting himself from any privileged authority, submitting his text to a dialectic of self-transcendence as it passes over to the reader.

Epistemology: Contesting the Anxiety of Infidelity

Hegel's methodological commitment to the death of the author is paralleled in his epistemology. Hegel challenges the traditional correspondence theory of truth, the theory that true knowledge requires some sort of agreement between our conceptions and external reality (see *HP* 2:150f; *HP* 3:312; *EL* §41). Interestingly, this is precisely the model of "objective truth" that Kierkegaard argues against (e.g., *CUP* 169: Objective truth is the "conformity of thought and being"). Yet Hegel is as critical of this sort of "objective truth" as is Kierkegaard. In the first place, Hegel proposes that we cannot meaningfully refer to an entirely external object at all: The object as "given" is always already an object of consciousness and hence an *internal* object (*PS* 54). But Hegel also criticizes Kant's solution to what they both believe is the fatal flaw of the correspondence theory, that there is no way to inspect the external object in order to determine an agreement with our conception of it, since we cannot voyage outside of our minds into an external space of objects.[32] Kant concludes from the fact that consciousness necessarily alters or reshapes reality by its very act of receiving it into thought that all we can ever know is the appearance of things: Reality in itself is left outside and beyond us, unreachable and unfathomable. Our knowledge "has to do only with *appearances*," Kant writes in the *Critique of Pure Reason*, "and must leave the thing in itself as indeed real *per se*, but as not known by us."[33] The thing in itself haunts Kant's philosophy, and indeed the whole history of philosophy, as the inscrutable Real hovering just past the reach of thought.

Hegel's response to Kant is to question the coherence of the idea of a reality that is in principle radically other to appearance: Reality "does not linger behind or beyond appearance" (*EL* §131Z). Long before Nietzsche's scandalous claim in his *Twilight of the Idols* that he has "abolished" the "'real' world,"[34] Hegel had spoken of the "vanishing" into "emptiness" of reality conceived as a "pure beyond" "on the other side" of the "curtain" of consciousness (*PS* 88, 103)— just as his authorship seeks to effect the vanishing of the reality of the author conceived of as a pure essence. The source of Kant's positing of the unattainable Real is, Hegel suggests, a fundamental anxiety or "fear of falling into error," given his conception that knowledge involves an unavoidable shaping, and hence *mis*-shaping or distortion, of what it perceives. But for Hegel the "fear of error is . . . just the error itself": Reality, in any meaningful sense, *is* only as it is shaped by thought (*PS* 47). As he writes in his *Encyclopedia,* "An alteration must be interposed before the true nature of the object can be discovered" (*EL* §22). Prior to this alteration, or interpretive act, the "thing in itself" is a "*caput mortuum,*" a "formless lump," a "spectral . . . abstract shadow divorced from all content" (*HP* 3:427; *FK* 76; *L* 47).

Kant's fear of error is an anxiety over infidelity, the betrayal of reality by our very act of experiencing it, and this fear is also the anxiety deep at the heart of the traditional conception of the relation between the author and the reader. The author's text is the thing in itself whose Real meaning is always vulnerable to the distortions of the reader. The virtuous reader must, then, restrain herself from altering the text by imposing her own interpretations—every interpretation is a mere appearance and disfiguration of the text—and must demonstrate fidelity by deferring to the authority of the author, remaining passive, without voice, silent, inert, and obediently receptive. Hegel's own authorship, though, must be seen in the same light as his critique of Kant. "Hegel," as the thing in itself, is only a *caput mortuum,* a dead thing, and the reality of the text is a production of the reader.

Hegel writes in the *Encyclopedia* about the nature of "reflection" in a way that directly expresses his response to Kant's anxiety about the distortion of the real and that indirectly underscores his resolve to die as an author.

The word "reflection" is originally applied when a ray of light in a straight line impinging upon the surface of a mirror is thrown back from it. In this phenomenon we have two things—first an immediate fact which is, and secondly the deputed, derivated, or transmuted phase of the same.

Something of this sort takes place when we reflect, or think upon an object; for here we want to know the object, not in its immediacy, but as derivative or mediated.

The problem or aim of philosophy . . . is the ascertainment of the essence of things, a phrase which only means that things, instead of being left in their immediacy, must be shown to be mediated by or based upon something else. (*EL* §112Z)

The text, no less than reality itself, cannot be left in its "immediacy," as a simple given. As such it is empty, a spectral shadow divorced from all meaning. Rather, it must be based on "something else," the activity of reflection, the labor of the reader. Only with the reader's "transmutation" of the text does meaning arise.

Hegel's ethics of authorship is grounded in the larger goal of his philosophy, "the awakening of consciousness" from passivity, the invitation to enter into "the struggle for liberation which the soul has to wage" against its inclination to take things in their "immediacy, . . . in order to become completely master of itself" (*PM* §402Z). This invitation to the reader's mastery is a gift of death, but unlike Abraham's sacrificial gift of Isaac to the Lord, Hegel's gift of death is a gift of his own death, the death of the father so that the other may live.

LANGUAGE: HONESTY, DESIRE, AND DYING AWAY

Hegel's gift of death as an author is intimately connected with his philosophy of language, which I have already examined in some detail. For Hegel language is the performative act by which the self comes to exist or "be there" in the world: "In speech, self-consciousness . . . comes as such into existence, so that it exists for others. Otherwise the I, this pure I, is non-existent, is not there." Thus while Hegel the author certainly comes to "be there" through the language of his texts, it is an existence that entails the negation of his private reality as a "pure I." Language is "at once the externalization and the vanishing of this particular I," and this I "dies away" (*verhallt*) as it comes to "pass over" (*übergehen*) into a being-for-others (*PS* 308–9/*W* 3:376). In the very act by which the author comes to be, to reveal himself in language, he vanishes. His externalization is the dying away and passing over of his inward particularity and the revealing that he "is there" only as existing for another. As such, the site of meaning is shifted from the author, whose speech points beyond itself, to the response of the reader.

For Hegel as for Derrida, it is true that "as soon as one speaks, as soon as one enters the medium of language, one loses [one's] . . . singularity. . . . Once I speak I am never and no longer myself, alone and unique."[35] Similarly, for Hegel as for Sartre, language is a "flight outside myself" in which there is a "stealing of [my] thoughts" by the other's appropriation of my meanings.[36] Finally, for Hegel as for Kierkegaard, language is an "annulment" of the particularity and inwardness of the I by which the self becomes fatefully public. Kierkegaard's own death as an author, unlike Hegel's, is based on an experimentation with a way of writing in which the subjective inwardness of both author and reader are preserved, allowing each to remain "isolated and compelled to exist for himself" (*CUP* 287).

But unlike for Derrida, Sartre, and Kierkegaard, for Hegel the death of the author has nothing to do with preserving the isolation of the author or the privacy of his meanings. "Language is more truthful" than private meanings. Far from losing his freedom in the act of speaking, for Hegel the author is actually freed by his death: As the I "dies away" in language, the author for the first time "is there" in a meaningful way, made present through the interpretations of his readers.

The sense of tragic loss of the self at the hands of language that Kierkegaard and Sartre and Derrida express implies a nostalgia for an ideal of selfhood that is prelinguistic, where one might retain one's singularity, untouched by the unforgiving gaze of the other—his gaze, or, as we have seen, his hands: "And oh, that no half-learned man would lay a dialectic hand upon this work, but would let it stand as now it stands!" (*CUP* 554). Kierkegaard's words here seem to express a fear of (authorial) death, a fear of the hands (and mishandlings) of the reader, precisely the fear, which we saw in the last chapter, that induced him to pause at the entrance to the tomb, a fear of the reader that leads him to reassert his authority over his authorship.

For Hegel, the very idea of a self unconstituted by language is a fantasy. Hegel defines self-consciousness as *desire,* which originates in the sense of lack that haunts every effort of the self to constitute itself alone. Desire requires the other, so that the self "exists in and for itself when, and by the fact that, it so exists for another; that is, it exists only in being acknowledged" or recognized (*anerkennt*) (*PS* 105, 111). Language is precisely the medium in which the self comes to exist for another and hence comes to exist as a self at all.

In speaking, though, the mythological idea of a self complete unto itself, the narcissistic "I = I," is exposed as an impossible fantasy. As Derrida says, in speaking I am never and no longer alone and unique. My lack requires that I speak to the other, but as such I become subject to the other's desire and her own lack, my identity is no longer my own, but shaped by her. As Kojève remarks in his reading of Hegel's dialectic of desire, the other's desire operates "only by the 'negation,' the destruction, or at least the transformation, of the desired object. . . . Far from leaving the given as it is, action destroys it, if not in its being, at least in its given form."[37] The author's speech, his text, is his gift of death, indeed a double gift: The author gives himself over to his own negation and simultaneously gives the "givenness" of his text over to its transformation through the action of the reader.

Bataille, in speaking of surrealism, praises Breton for his project of seeking everywhere "to annihilate or 'reduce to nothingness,'"[38] but claims that this cannot be achieved through "poems, pictures, and exhibitions,"[39] for "true poetry is beyond the use of words."[40] Kierkegaard too, we have seen, attempts to break the curse of words by seeking an "inner sanctum" of silence, not unlike Mesmer's and Roquentin's desperate experimentations with thinking without words. Silence cuts us off from the public world of social, linguistic conventions that regulate our relations to others. Cure for the lack that defines us as finite creatures cannot be found in speech, which makes us the object of another's lack, but only in the absurd power of God's grace: "What is [the despairing soul] to do? Nothing: remain silent and wait in prayer and faith" (*JP* 4:260).

The urge for silence, for thought without speech, for a poetry beyond words, is a longing for the obscure rapture and *jouissance* of a self-fulfillment without death. Putting oneself into words is indeed the death of the I = I, but the devotion to a faith in the ineffable is for Hegel a yet more profound form of death, a shadowy life in a dreamworld of fantasy and fear. What the silent author *does* write is never the Real text, but "merely" the text for the other—which for Hegel is the only text there is. For Kierkegaard, there is always a "secret writing," as he puts it in his journal, that he keeps hidden "in my inmost parts" and that no one else can discover.[41] But as Barthes says, with the death of the author, "There is nothing beneath": The author's death is precisely a "refus[al] to assign a 'secret,' an ultimate meaning, to the text."[42] I am what I say, and the author is what she writes. Yet the author is not the judge of meaning of what she writes; what she writes, what she *is*, is always determined by the reader.

The End: Absolute Knowledge

Behold, I will make thee know what shall be in the last end . . . ;
for at the time appointed the end shall be.

Daniel 8:19

Hegel's philosophy of negativity, his portrayal of the self as "restless mutation and change" set upon a "road of doubt" and a "way of despair" (*PH* 72; *PS* 49), improbably reaches its conclusion with a healing of the wounds of spirit. If Hegel's philosophy is "a philosophy of death," as Kojève has called it[43]—of sheer negativity, devastation and dismemberment, the "slaughterbench" of human happiness and the "funeral pyre" that spirit "eternally prepares for itself" (*PH* 21, 73)—it is so, or so his French critics see it, only up to the denouement, the fifth act, where Hegel descends deus ex machina to arrange a happy ending. The "tremendous power of the negative" that dislocates consciousness from every possibility of lasting satisfaction is finally subdued by a yet greater power, "absolute knowledge," where the "labor" of spirit comes to an end (*PS* 19, 486).

On the one hand, this denouement is seen by Hegel's critics as a cheating of death—the wounds of the spirit heal and leave no scars, and the phoenix arises from its ashes back into life. But on the other, it enshrines a different sort of death, or rather a series of deaths: the death of desire, since satisfaction "signals death" by putting to rest the restlessness of desire (*PH* 75); the death of history, since history is sheer negativity, a slaughterbench; and the death of language, since the word destroys the unity of the speaking subject, casting it into otherness and alienation. "Absolute knowledge" is the Last Word, and then . . . silence. Hegel is the "megalomaniacal sorcerer," Eric Voegelin asserts, driven by a "*libido dominandi*" and messianic need to become the "Last Great Man," the man who "gains power over history by putting an end to history."[44]

Hegel describes absolute knowledge as the "last shape" of spirit, where "the work of spirit" comes to "completion" in a "perfect knowing of what it is." The goal of absolute knowledge is simply the recollection (*die Erinnerung*) of the historical unfolding of consciousness into its various shapes and through its various struggles. The "content" of recollection is thus "the self-alienating self," spirit's "own restless process of superseding itself, or negativity." The very nature of spirit is "action," the "self-sundering" of consciousness as it "steps forth into existence" and into time, which is "the destiny and necessity of spirit that is not yet complete within itself." Time is the very "existence" or "being there" of spirit; it is spirit "that *is there*" in the world, and spirit "necessarily appears in time," but only "just so long as it has not grasped its pure notion," reaching a complete knowledge of itself. With such a knowledge, time is "annulled" (or even "annihilated": *tilgt*). The only work left for spirit is to recollect itself, an act of "withdrawal into itself in which it abandons its outer existence. . . . Thus absorbed in itself, it is sunk in the night of its self-consciousness; in that night its vanished outer existence is preserved . . . [and] reborn of spirit's knowledge [of itself]" (*PS* 484–93).

Hegel's description of recollection as a sinking of consciousness into the shadow world of the night, where it preserves its vanished life only as the trace of memory, is strikingly similar to the eerie description Kierkegaard (or rather "A," the author of the first volume of *Either/Or*) gives of his grief.

> [Grief] is my . . . castle. It is built like an eagle's nest upon the peak of a mountain lost in the clouds. No one can take it by storm. From this abode I dart down into the world of reality to seize my prey; but I do not remain down there, I bear my quarry aloft to my stronghold. My booty is a picture I weave into the tapestries of my palace.
>
> There I live as one dead. I immerse everything I have experienced in a baptism of forgetfulness unto an eternal remembrance. Everything temporal and contingent is forgotten and erased. Then I sit like an old man, grey-haired and thoughtful, and explain picture after picture in a voice as soft as a whisper; and at my side a child sits and listens, although he remembers everything before I tell it. (*E/Or* 1:41)

Hegel is the old grey-haired man, the Wise Man, living as though dead—"death living a human life," as Kojève puts it[45]—immersing all of experience in a baptism of forgetfulness, erasing time itself and all outer existence, but unto an eternal remembrance. Next to him a child listens: the reader, indeed the perfect reader, remembering everything just as Hegel tells it, just as we have seen that another of Kierkegaard's pseudonyms, Johannes Climacus, writes that his own "imagined reader" is the one who "understands [him] at once and line by line" (*CUP* 548, "For an Understanding with the Reader").

In his *Encyclopedia,* Hegel explores the story of the Fall of Man as an allegory for the human situation, in which we are destined to lose our original innocence, our sense of harmony with the world, and to become "severed" from this Edenic fantasy, cursed to "labor and bring forth in sorrow" (*EL* §24Z). It is just this portrait of the tragic character of spirit, consciousness fallen into a world in which its sense of certainty, its "innocence," is constantly undone, in which it is destined never to be at home, but to exist forever in estrangement and uncanniness (*umheimlichkeit*, not-at-homeness), that Hegel's French critics admire about his philosophy. What troubles them is that he supposedly loses the courage to "tarry with the negative," to use Žižek's phrase[46]—a phrase that pays homage to a key passage in the preface to the *Phenomenology*, where Hegel writes that spirit is "power, not as something positive that closes its eyes to the negative, . . . [but] only by looking the negative in the face and tarrying with it" (19). But (so the criticism goes) Hegel finally flinches from this power of negativity and looks away from its face. Hence his telling of the story of the Fall does not end with the curse of never being at home in the world, but with a "second harmony" at the "end" of our path of sorrow, a "final concord" and "restoration" of our sense of unity with the world. As Hegel says later in the *Encyclopedia*, the aim of his philosophy is ultimately to "divest the . . . world that stands opposed to us of its alien character, [so that we may] find ourselves at home in it" (*EL* §§24Z, 194Z).

For Hegel's critics, though, we can never find ourselves at home. Bataille speaks of how absolute knowledge suppresses the fundamental "irrationality" (*déraison*) and endless "anxiety" of life,[47] and Derrida writes of the Hegelian *Aufhebung*, or annulment of negativity, as a "re-stricture" and "repression" of the irreducible nature of difference, rupture, and alienation.[48] Lyotard warns us to beware of Hegel's "nostalgia of the whole, . . . the one, . . . [and] reconciliation: . . . let us [rather] wage war on totality; . . . let us [re]activate difference."[49] Foucault resists Hegel's teleology, his need to find a final End to the process of becoming;[50] Hyppolite laments the collapse of Hegel's commitment to "a tension" of alienation "inseparable from existence" into an "immobilism" of perfected knowledge;[51] and Barthes speaks of how the very idea of a closure of the dialectic is an effort to "master" the inherently "unmasterable" character of reality.[52]

What Hegel's French critics seek is not, it seems, so much to leave Hegel behind as to reappropriate Hegel the dark philosopher, the philosopher of negativity, uncanniness, and sorrow, unencumbered by Hegel the philosopher of light, of resolution, and "final concord." In Derrida's words, we need a "Hegelianism without reserve," a

dialectic of movement without rest, division without *relève* or reconciliation, lack without closure and without ultimate meaning.[53]

This sort of criticism has important implications for how we think
about the relationship of the author to the reader. For the French
critics, a philosophy of sheer difference without synthesis is necessary
to preserve the autonomy of the reader. As Barthes puts it, without
this "tragic" character of communication, the "perpetual misunderstanding" that separates author and reader, the reader remains sub-
servient to the author's authority.[54] A philosophy of synthesis implies
a co-option of the reader, a suppression of particularity, a vow of
obedience to the author's desire—and hence the impossibility of any
meaningful death of the author. The challenge for Hegel's critics,
which we have already partially examined with respect to Kierkegaard, is how to imagine the possibility of communication across an
abyss of absolute difference, what Kierkegaard views as the utter
unreachability of the other (*CUP* 287). The challenge for Hegel, on
the other hand, is how to imagine synthesis without effacing otherness, to imagine an ethics of authorship that genuinely empowers the
reader.

Key to assessing how well Hegel meets this challenge is to note a
striking peculiarity about the nature of "absolute knowledge,"
namely that it has *no content* of its own. Its "content," Hegel writes,
is the history of the "self-alienating self's" own "restless process of
superseding itself," or the sheer "negativity" of the experience of
consciousness (*PS* 490–91), the history, that is, of the perpetual failure
of achieving any deliverance from the path of sorrow that is life. As
Žižek puts it, "Far from being a story of [the] progressive overcoming [of opposition], dialectics is for Hegel a systematic notation of the
failure of all such attempts—'absolute knowledge' denotes a subjective position that finally accepts contradiction as an internal condition
of every identity."[55] In this sense, the purpose of the Absolute Knowing chapter is to provoke the reader into a recollection of her path,
so that she may tell her own story, a story that refuses the comfort
of a happy ending provided by the author. Indeed, from Hegel's
perspective, no happy ending is possible: The story of spirit, he
makes clear in the "Absolute Knowledge" chapter, is the story of
Calvary, or Golgotha, the place of crucifixion, the scene of the death

of satisfaction (*PS* 493). This, according to Engels, is "the true significance and the revolutionary character of the Hegelian philosophy, . . . that it once and for all dealt the deathblow to the finality of all productions of human thought and action."[56]

Mary O'Brien remarks on the frustrations of Hegel's friends early in his academic career over his slowness to publish. Finally in 1807, at the age of thirty-seven, Hegel completed his *Phenomenology*. O'Brien writes, "It does not appear to have been the case that Hegel did not want to publish until he had *something* to say, but that he did not want to publish until he could say *everything*."[57] In fact, what is remarkable about the *Phenomenology* is that when Hegel finally does assume his own voice, the voice that articulates the structure of "absolute knowledge," it is a voice of silence. Rather than waiting to publish until he could say everything, he waited until he had nothing to say, until, we might say, he was prepared to die. Absolute knowledge has no insights and no wisdom to impart other than to beckon us to reflect back on our own experience. It has no past and no future of its own, and in this sense it is a *Tilgung* or annihilation of time and history, the annihilation of any claim to possess a voice of its own. This explains, according to Robert Solomon, "why the last chapter of the *Phenomenology* is so short and so unsatisfying; it does not state a final thesis so much as it tells us that there can be no final thesis, only a certain humility."[58] So far from expressing Hegel's "*libido dominandi*"—his ambition to become the Last Great Man or the Wisest Man—absolute knowledge expresses a fundamental humility, a lack of voice, a refusal of edification and assurance. If language is the very existence—the *Da-sein,* or being-there—of spirit, then Hegel, as the voice of the author that silences itself in "absolute knowledge," is not there: The author disappears. There is, as Gertrude Stein would say, no "there" there.[59]

Hegel's silence as an author is not like the silence he associates with "pure insight"—the authoritarianism he sees as a central characteristic of the Enlightenment. "Pure insight" is "comparable to a silent expansion or to the diffusion, say, of a perfume in the unresisting atmosphere. It is a penetrating infection, . . . [and when we finally become aware of it] the struggle is too late, and every remedy only aggravates the disease, for it has laid hold of the marrow of spiritual life." "Absolute knowledge" is also silent, but rather than a "silent expansion" it is a silent contraction, more like the "non-knowledge" Bataille proposes as a supposed antidote to Hegel.[60] "Pure insight" produces silence by silencing the voice of the other, which it dismisses as mere "superstition." The other becomes a "dead form" "preserved only in memory," and "the new serpent of wisdom raised on high for adoration has in this way cast merely a withered skin," the discarded husk of the superstitions of those who oppose its enlightened insights (*PS* 331–32).

Hegelian absolute knowledge also brings about a sort of death by an act of memory, as we have seen—this knowledge is "sunk in the night of its self-consciousness," a night in which "its vanished outer existence is preserved" in recollection. But this act of recollection is the very opposite of "pure insight," which preserves the "dead forms" of opposing viewpoints as "mere" memories of discredited "falsehoods." Hegelian recollection is the gathering up and "inward-izing" (*Er-innerung*) of the experience of consciousness (*PS* 490), not its negation and relegation to superstition. Hegel's silence, then, is not a disease, infecting and killing the spirit of the other, the reader; it is not the effect of a new serpent of wisdom raising itself on high for adoration, deadening opposition. Rather, it is the silence of the author who gives his own death to the other, so that the reader may recollect and speak her own story.

It is in this gift of death that Hegel sees a way for "the wounds of the spirit [to] heal." We have already explored the context in which this maxim occurs, the discussion of the "beautiful soul," the shape of consciousness in which the self is reduced to speechlessness, since all expression places the self in subjection to the other. Thus "in order to preserve the purity of its heart, it flees from contact with the actual world," but this flight is madness, a "wast[ing] itself [away] in yearning" (*PS* 400–407).

This madness hovers around every act of authorship, since it has its origin in the competing desires of the self to be the master of its own meanings but also the need for a reader and hence the loss of mastery. We have seen that Hegel's "talking cure" relies on the ne-cessity of an act of forgiveness—a forgiveness of the self for its inabil-ity to constitute itself without the other, and a forgiveness of the other precisely for her becoming the site of signification of what I am.

This healing act of forgiveness is anything but the *Aufhebung* of difference and the absorption of the other (the reader) into the sway of the self's (author's) "pure insight." On the contrary, it is a reconciliation that insists on difference: Spirit "lives in this diversity alone" (*PS* 22). But for Hegel this difference is not inevitably a Derridean tearing apart or *déchirement* of the author and reader by an "implacable" antagonism that perpetually defers any possibility of meaningful connection,[61] by a Sartrean "insurmountable nothingness" or a Kierkegaardian "barrier of isolation" or a Nietzschean "iron-like mask" of "incommunicability" that is "the most terrible of all forms of loneliness and difference."[62] Authorship for Hegel is ultimately a unity-in-difference, a meeting of self and other, of author and reader, on the ground of a death that liberates. The death of the author is an act of forgiveness of the inevitable "particularity" of the reader's appropriations of the text, and an act of self-forgiveness for the author's own particularity, which, in writing, the author dies away from in a passing over of the text to the reader.

Conclusion: The Melancholy of Having Finished

Whatever begins, also ends.

SENECA, *On Consolation, ad Polybium*

You're searching, Joe, for things that don't exist; I mean beginnings.
Ends and beginnings—there are no such things. There are only middles.

ROBERT FROST, "In the Home Stretch," in *Mountain Interval*

AT THE END OF Nietzsche's *Beyond Good and Evil* (or rather the
provisional end: Nietzsche then adds an "Aftersong," the poem
"From High Mountains"), he expresses his melancholy at having
finished.

> Alas, what are you after all, my written and painted thoughts! It
> was not long ago that you were still so colorful, young, and mali-
> cious . . .—and now? You have already taken off your novelty, . . .
> [you] already look so immortal, so pathetically decent, so dull! And
> has it ever been different? What things do we copy, writing and
> painting, . . . we immortalizers of things that *can* be written—what
> are the only things we are able to paint? Alas, always only what is
> on the verge of withering, . . . and feelings that are autumnal and
> yellow! . . . We immortalize what cannot live and fly much
> longer—only weary . . . things! And it is only your *afternoon,* you,
> my written and painted thoughts, for which alone I have colors
> . . . : but nobody will guess from that how you looked in your
> morning, you sudden sparks and wonders of my solitude, you my
> old beloved—*wicked* thoughts! (§296)

This beautiful, haunting closing to Nietzsche's text is a dirge to the tragic nature of language and authorship. To author—to write, to paint, to compose—is precisely to fail, inevitably to fall short of the morning of solitude where everything is a sudden spark and wonder, and to fall into the afternoon of language where our words transform our thoughts into a November colorlessness. It is almost as though Nietzsche's inordinate use of exclamation points in this last breath of his book was one last attempt to reanimate the thing that is fading and dying even as he writes it.

Nietzsche's dirge is Kierkegaard's as well. Kierkegaard's authorship, like Nietzsche's, is an annulment of his true self, which is fully alive only in the pathos of inwardness that precedes speech. Their dirge is the grief and longing of the despairing soul, the unhappy consciousness, which experiences total loss, the cruel knowledge that God is dead. However poignant, the dirge testifies to a reluctance to forgive—both to forgive the self for its need for speech, its irresistible impulse to write, which is a betrayal of the morning and springtime of solitude by the afternoon and autumn of expression, and of the reader, who can at best only constitute the author as withered, weary, pathetically decent, without the wickedness his private thoughts deserve.

Hegel could never have written such a dirge, which contradicts his entire philosophy of language and style and ethics of authorship. The author is not betrayed either by his own flight outside himself in his text or by the reader's appropriation of the text. Rather, the author paradoxically first comes to exist only in his double experience of loss, the loss of the prelinguistic I and the loss of his ownership over what he says. Life is revealed in loss, in death, which is not an occasion for melancholy, but for celebration: In death the true meaning and miracle of authorship is discovered—the birth of the reader, and thus of the text itself.

Aftersong: From Low Down

THIS POEM is in dialogue with the final section of Nietzsche's *Beyond Good and Evil* and his "Aftersong," "From High Mountains."

I am
—no: I forget so easily—am not I.
Am I another? *Ein Andrer ward ich?*
Did I elude myself? *Mir selbst entsprungen?*
I seek:
forgiveness; I seek to forgive.

I
who yearn to remain,
yearn also to surrender,
to give up my morning for my afternoon,
to die,
to speak not from on high mountains
but from low down,
from the grave.

Where are you, friends? *Kommt!*

NOTES

Introduction: Rorschach Tests

1. Aristophanes, *The Clouds,* trans. Alan H. Sommerstein (New York: Penguin, 1983), 117, 122, 125, 129, 145.

2. The story is told by Aelian (c. 170–c. 235) in his *Historical Miscellany (Varia Historia),* ed. and trans. N. G. Wilson (Cambridge: Harvard University Press, 1977), 85 (2.13). Aelian's interpretation is that Socrates' act was one of defiance, demonstrating his "contempt for comedy and the Athenians" (85).

3. Jon Stewart, *Kierkegaard's Relations to Hegel Reconsidered* (Cambridge: Cambridge University Press, 2003). Main representatives of Danish Hegelianism were Johan Heiberg, Hans Martensen, and Adolph Adler.

4. See Jean Wahl, *Études Kierkegaardiennes* (Paris: Fernard Aubier, 1938); Stephen Crites, *In the Twilight of Christendom: Hegel vs. Kierkegaard on Faith and History* (Chambersburg, Penn.: American Academy of Religion, 1972); Stephen Dunning, *Kierkegaard's Dialectic of Inwardness: A Structural Analysis of the Theory of Stages* (Princeton: Princeton University Press, 1985); Stewart, *Kierkegaard's Relations to Hegel Reconsidered;* Mark C. Taylor, "Aesthetic Therapy: Hegel and Kierkegaard," in *Kierkegaard's Truth: The Disclosure of the Self,* ed. Joseph H. Smith (New Haven: Yale University Press, 1981), 343–80; Mark C. Taylor, *Journeys to Selfhood: Hegel and Kierkegaard* (Berkeley: University of California Press, 1980); and Merold Westphal, "Kierkegaard and Hegel," in *The Cambridge Companion to Kierkegaard,* ed. Alastair Hannay (New York: Cambridge University Press, 1998), 101–24.

Of course, there are others who explore genuine dialogue between Hegel and Kierkegaard but not in as sustained a way as those mentioned. Paul Ricoeur is a good example: "It is not just a biographical trait or a fortuitous encounter but a constitutive structure of Kierkegaard's thought that it is not thinkable apart from Hegel." "Two Encounters with Kierkegaard: Kierkegaard and Evil; Doing Philosophy after Kierkegaard," in *Kierkegaard's Truth:*

The Disclosure of the Self, ed. Joseph H. Smith (New Haven: Yale University Press, 1981),336.

5. All references to Hegel's works will be given parenthetically in the text. See Abbreviations.

6. All works of Kierkegaard and his pseudonyms will be cited parenthetically in the text. See Abbreviations.

7. Roland Barthes, "The Death of the Author," in *Image, Music, Text,* trans. Stephen Heath (New York: Hill and Wang, 1977), 148.

8. Niels Thulstrup, *Kierkegaard's Relation to Hegel,* trans. George Stengren (Princeton: Princeton University Press, 1980), 12.

9. Richard Kroner, "Kierkegaard's Understanding of Hegel," *Union Seminary Quarterly Review* 21, no. 2, part 2 (1966): 234. See also Kroner's "Kierkegaard or Hegel?" *Revue Internationale de Philosophie* 19 (1952): 79–96.

10. Paul Ricoeur, "Two Encounters with Kierkegaard," in *Kierkegaard's Truth: The Disclosure of the Self,* ed. Joseph H. Smith (New Haven: Yale University Press, 1981): 335–36.

11. Judith Butler, *Gender Trouble: Feminism and the Subversion of Identity* (New York: Routledge, 1999), xviii–xix.

12. William Faulkner, interview with Jean Stein vanden Heuvel, *The Paris Review Interviews* 12 (Spring 1956): 4.

13. Quoted in Walter Lowrie, *A Short Life of Kierkegaard* (Princeton: Princeton University Press, 1965), 81. The letter, which may or may not have been sent—see Joakim Garff, *Søren Kierkegaard: A Biography,* trans. Bruce Kirmmse (Princeton: Princeton University Press, 2005), 53—is preserved in Kierkegaard's journals (*P* 1 A 75).

14. Franz Kafka, quoted in "Poetry Critical: Online Poetry Workshop," http://poetrycritical.net/read/56256/. The quote may be apocryphal; I have been unable to locate the original source.

15. Alfred Kazin, quoted in *Think* (February 1963).

16. See *PV* 20, and the two "Notes" appended to the *Point of View,* "Concerning the Dedication to 'The Individual'" and "A Word about the Relation of My Literary Activity to 'The Individual'" (109–20, 121–36). See also Lowrie, *Short Life of Kierkegaard,* 162.

17. Friedrich Nietzsche, *Beyond Good and Evil,* in *Basic Writings of Nietzsche,* trans. and ed. Walter Kaufmann (New York: Random House, 1968), §289.

18. Friedrich Nietzsche, *The Gay Science,* trans. Walter Kaufmann (New York: Random House, 1974), §213.

19. On Kierkegaard's claim that Hegel had no ethics, see Paul Cruysberghs, "Hegel Has No Ethics: Climacus' Complaints against Speculative Philosophy," *Kierkegaard Studies: Yearbook* (2005): 175–91.

20. A philosopher "must beware of the wish to be edifying" (*PS* 6).

21. Jean-Paul Sartre, *Nausea,* trans. Lloyd Alexander (New York: New Directions, 1964), 39.

22. Barthes, "Death of the Author," 142.

23. Michel Foucault, *The Archaeology of Knowledge,* trans. A. M. Sheridan Smith (New York: Pantheon, 1972), 235.

24. Jacques Lacan, T*he Seminar of Jacques Lacan,* book 11: *The Four Fundamental Concepts of Psychoanalysis,* trans. Alan Sheridan, ed. Jacques-Alain Miller (New York: Norton, 1981), 11; Jacques Lacan, *Écrits,* trans. Bruce Fink (New York: Norton, 2006), 351. References to the *Écrits* are to the pagination in the margin of the complete French edition (Paris: Éditions du Seuil, 1966).

1. A Question of Style

1. The first description is from the novelist and playwright Karl Gutzkow, *Lebensbilder* (1870), 2:105–6; the second from H. G. Hotho, who later edited the three volumes of Hegel's lectures on aesthetics, *Vorstudien für Leben und Kunst* (1835), 383–99. Both are cited in Walter Kaufmann, *Hegel: A Reinterpretation* (Notre Dame, Ind.: University of Notre Dame Press, 1978), 357, 368.

2. See T. H. Croxall's note on the publication date in his "Assessment" of *De Omnibus* in Søren Kierkegaard, *Johannes Climacus, or De Omnibus Dubitandum Est,* trans. T. H. Croxall (Stanford: Stanford University Press, 1967), 17.

3. As Charles Taylor puts it, "I cannot know even what I mean if all I can say is 'this' or 'here.' . . . For it to mean something for me, and not just be an empty word, there must be something else I could say to give a shape, a scope, to this 'now.'" Charles Taylor, "The Opening Arguments of the *Phenomenology,*" in *Hegel: A Collection of Critical Essays,* ed. Alasdair MacIntyre (Notre Dame: University of Notre Dame Press, 1972), 165.

4. See also *PF* 84: "I cannot immediately sense or know that what I immediately sense or know is an effect, for immediately it simply is." In his analysis of the *Philosophical Fragments,* W. S. K. Cameron points out how "strikingly similar to Hegel's 'Sense-Certainty'" account of language Kierkegaard is. "[Writing] about Writing about Kierkegaard," *Philosophy Today* 39 (Spring 1995): 58.

5. See Cameron: "Why is authorial intent not decisive" for Kierkegaard? "His reason is Hegelian: an author is 'only a reader' on par with others because all human understanding is mediated by the shared resources of language. . . . If we communicate through public media of interpretation and evaluation, no author . . . can claim a private relation to a text." Cameron, "[Writing] about Writing about Kierkegaard," 59.

6. See Daniel Berthold-Bond (now Berthold), *Hegel's Theory of Madness* (Albany: State University of New York Press, 1995), 202–6.

7. Jean-Paul Sartre, *L'être et le néant* (Paris: Éditions Gallimard, 1943), 422.

8. Jacques Derrida, *The Gift of Death,* trans. David Willis (Chicago: University of Chicago Press, 1995), 77–78.

9. Martin Heidegger, "Letter on Humanism," in *Basic Writings,* ed. David Farrell Krell (New York: Harper, 1977), 198, 199.

10. Martin Heidegger, "The Question concerning Technology," in *Basic Writings,* ed. David Farrell Krell (New York: Harper, 1977), 298–301.

11. Heidegger, "Letter on Humanism," 199.

12. Ibid., 198.

13. Martin Heidegger, "Building Dwelling Thinking," in *Basic Writings,* ed. David Farrell Krell (New York: Harper, 1977), 327.

14. Heidegger, "Letter on Humanism," 199. On the importance of silence for Heidegger, see also Martin Heidegger, *Being and Time,* trans. John Macquarrie and Edward Robinson (New York: Harper, 1962), 161, 164, 273, 277, 296. All references to *Being and Time* are to the marginal numbers, representing the pagination of the seventh (final) German edition.

15. Heidegger, "Letter on Humanism," 199.

16. G. W. F. Hegel, "Rede zum Schuljahresabschluß am 14. September 1810," in *Werke,* ed. Eva Moldenhauer and Karl Markus Michel (Frankfurt am Main: Suhrkamp Verlag, 1970–79), 4:332. This comment is substantially repeated, with some elaboration, in a long chapter on Pythagoras in Hegel's later *Lectures on the History of Philosophy (HP),* trans. E. S. Haldane and F. H. Simson (New York: Humanities Press, 1974), 1:202–3.

17. See *JP* 1:650: "My service in using pseudonyms consists in having discovered . . . the maieutic method."

18. See Heidegger, *Being and Time,* 32–36.

19. Joseph Flay, *Hegel's Quest for Certainty* (Albany: State University of New York Press, 1984), 187.

20. Hegel, as quoted in an ad in *Intelligenzblatt der Jenaischen Allgemeinen Litteraturzeitung,* October 28, 1807.

21. Paul B. Armstrong, "Reading Kierkegaard—Disorientation and Reorientation," in *Kierkegaard's Truth: The Disclosure of the Self,* ed. Joseph H. Smith (New Haven: Yale University Press, 1981), 23, 48.

22. See Joseph Flay's discussion of irony as lying at the heart of Hegel's dialectic. "Hegel, Heidegger, Derrida: Retrieval as Reconstruction, Destruction, Deconstruction," in *Ethics and Danger: Essays on Heidegger and Continental Thought,* ed. Arleen Dallery and Charles Scott (Albany: State University of New York Press, 1992), 202.

23. There are several fine discussions of Hegel's "speculative proposition." See, for example, Theodor Bodammer, *Hegel's Deutung der Sprache* (Hamburg: F. Meiner, 1969); Daniel Cook, *Language in the Philosophy of Hegel* (The Hague: Mouton, 1973); Dietrich Gutterer, "Der Spekulative Satz," *Kodikas/ Code* 1 (1979): 235–47; Jean-Luc Nancy, *La rémarque speculative* (Paris: Editions Galilée, 1973); Jere Paul Surber, "Hegel's Speculative Sentence," *Hegel-Studien* 10 (1975): 212–30; and Günter Wohlfahrt, *Der speculative Satz* (Berlin: de Gruyter, 1981). I will return to say more about Hegel's speculative proposition in Chapter 4.

24. Judith Butler, *Subjects of Desire: Hegelian Reflections in Twentieth-Century France* (New York: Columbia University Press, 1987), 20.

25. See Daniel Cook's commentary on this passage in *Language in the Philosophy of Hegel*, 64–65.

2. Live or Tell

1. Jean-Paul Sartre, *Nausea,* trans. Lloyd Alexander (New York: New Directions, 1964), 39.

2. Stephen Crites, "Pseudonymous Authorship as Art and as Act," in *Kierkegaard: A Collection of Critical Essays,* ed. Josiah Thompson (Garden City, N.Y.: Doubleday, 1972), 225. See also Raymond Anderson: "Objective truth is a quality of propositions; subjective truth, a quality of persons." "Kierkegaard's Theory of Communication," *Speech Monographs* 30 (March 1963): 4.

3. Jean-Paul Sartre, *The Words,* trans. Bernard Frechtman (New York: George Braziller, 1964), 40, 56, 59–60, 141–42, 51, 61.

4. The first three sections of the *Phenomenology* explore sensation, perception, and understanding as modes of knowledge of the external world.

5. Sigmund Freud, "On Narcissism," in *The Standard Edition of the Complete Psychological Works of Sigmund Freud,* 24 vols., ed. James Strachey (London: Hogarth 1953–74), 14:100. Henceforth *SE.*

6. For a fuller account of the nostalgic face of desire, see Daniel Berthold-Bond (now Berthold), "The Two Faces of Desire: Evolution and Nostalgia in Hegel's Phenomenology of Desire," *Clio* 19, no. 4 (1990): 367–88.

7. Martin Heidegger, *Being and Time,* trans. John Macquarrie and Edward Robinson (New York: Harper, 1962), 286.

8. Ibid., 281–83.

9. Ibid., 283–84.

10. Ibid., 280 (emphasis added).

11. Ibid., 263.

12. Ibid., 188.

13. Ibid., 126–28.

14. Ibid., 127.

15. See Emmanuel Levinas, "A propos de *Kierkegaard Vivant,*" trans. Jonathan Rée, included as "Two Notes" in *Kierkegaard: A Critical Reader*, ed. Jonathan Rée and Jane Chamberlain (Oxford: Blackwell, 1998), 33–38. See also Emmanuel Levinas, "The Trace of the Other," trans. Alphonso Lingis, in *Deconstruction in Context,* ed. Mark C. Taylor (Chicago: University of Chicago Press, 1986), 345–59.

16. Hegel's theology is notoriously multifaceted and ambiguous. What I attribute to him here is true at least of his account of the religious consciousness in the *Phenomenology.*

17. Cited by Josiah Thompson, "The Master of Irony," in *Kierkegaard: A Collection of Critical Essays*, 108.

18. Crites, "Pseudonymous Authorship as Art and as Act," 199.

19. Sartre, *Nausea,* 1.

20. Ibid., 39.

21. Ibid.

22. Ibid., 33.

23. Sartre, *Words,* 56.

24. Sartre, *Nausea,* 126–33.

25. Ibid., 129.

26. Ibid., 135.

27. Simone de Beauvoir, *Mémoires d'une jeune fille rangée* (Paris: Gallimard, 1958), 484.

28. Sartre, *Saint Genet: Actor and Martyr,* trans. Bernard Frechtman (New York: G. Braziller, 1963), 512, and see 364–65.

29. Sartre, interviewed by John Gerassi, *New York Times Magazine,* October 17, 1971.

30. Sartre, *Nausea,* 127.

31. Jean-Paul Sartre, *Being and Nothingness,* trans. Hazel Barnes (New York: Philosophical Library, 1965), 365, 366, 376.

32. Ibid., 366.

33. Ibid., 376.

34. Ibid., 364.

35. Ibid., 373–74.

36. Ibid., 370.

37. Ibid., 367.

38. Crites, "Pseudonymous Authorship as Art and as Act," 216.

39. Thompson, "Master of Irony," 109.

40. Ibid., 116.

41. Jonathan Rée, "Baffled Traveller," *London Review of Books,* November 30, 2000, 3.

3. Kierkegaard's Seductions

1. Friedrich Nietzsche, *Beyond Good and Evil*, trans. Walter Kaufmann, in *Basic Writings of Nietzsche*, ed. Walter Kaufmann (New York: Random House, 1968), §419.

2. See *FT* 91–129 for Johannes de Silentio's discussion of Abraham's silence ("Problem III: Was Abraham ethically defensible in keeping silent about his purpose . . . ?").

3. Louis Mackey, *Points of View: Readings of Kierkegaard* (Tallahassee: Florida State University Press, 1986), 134.

4. On language as the "destruction" of the other, see "A"'s account of language in his essay on the "Musical Erotic," *E/Or* 1:63–72.

5. Georges Cuvier (1769–1832) established the sciences of comparative anatomy and paleontology. Swenson informs us that Cuvier "affirmed that from a single bone a scientist could reconstruct the whole animal" (*E/Or* 1:456n9).

6. See, for example, Sylviane Agacinski, *Aparté: Conceptions et morts de Søren Kierkegaard* (Paris: Aubier-Flammarion, 1977); Wanda Warren Berry, "The Heterosexual Imagination and Aesthetic Existence in Kierkegaard's *Either/Or*, Part One," in *International Kierkegaard Commentary: Either Or, Part I*, ed. Robert L. Perkins (Macon, Ga.: Mercer University Press, 1995), 201–8; Leslie A. Howe, "Kierkegaard and the Feminine Self," in *Feminist Interpretations of Søren Kierkegaard*, ed. Céline Léon and Sylvia Walsh (University Park: Penn State University Press, 1997), 217–47; Céline Léon, "The No Woman's Land of Kierkegaardian Seduction," in *International Kierkegaard Commentary: Either/Or, Part I*, ed. Perkins, 229–50; Tamsin Lorraine, "Amatory Cures for Material Dis-ease: A Kristevian Reading of *The Sickness unto Death*," in *Kierkegaard in Post/Modernity*, ed. Martin Matutík and Merold Westphal (Bloomington: Indiana University Press, 1995), 98–109; Robert L. Perkins, "Woman-Bashing in Kierkegaard's 'In Vino Veritas': A Reinscription of Plato's *Symposium*," in *Feminist Interpretations of Søren Kierkegaard*, ed. Céline Léon and Sylvia Walsh (University Park: Penn State University Press, 1997), 83–102; Sylvia Walsh, "On 'Feminine' and 'Masculine' Forms of Despair," in *International Kierkegaard Commentary: The Sickness unto Death*, ed. Robert L. Perkins (Macon, Ga.: Mercer University Press, 1987), 121–34; and Julia Watkin, "The Logic of Kierkegaard's Misogyny, 1854–1855," *Kierkegaardiana* 15 (1991): 79–93.

7. Howe, "Kierkegaard and the Feminine Self," 227.

8. Jane Duran, "The Kierkegaardian Feminist," in *Feminist Interpretations of Søren Kierkegaard*, ed. Céline Léon and Sylvia Walsh (University Park: Penn State University Press, 1997), 251.

192 ‡ NOTES TO PAGES 73–82

9. Howe, "Kierkegaard and the Feminine Self," 231.

10. Stephen Crites, "Pseudonymous Authorship as Art and as Act," *Kierkegaard: A Collection of Critical Essays,* ed. Josiah Thompson (Garden City, N.Y.: Doubleday, 1972), 223.

11. Robert L. Perkins, "Woman-Bashing in Kierkegaard's 'In Vino Veritas,'" in *Feminist Interpretations of Søren Kierkegaard,* ed. Céline Léon and Sylvia Walsh (University Park: Penn State University Press, 1997), 97.

12. Nietzsche describes "woman" as a surface hiding a depth, as a mask, as disguise and veil, as a born deceiver, and as a beast of prey (see *Beyond Good and Evil,* preface and §§232, 239, and Friedrich Nietzsche, *The Gay Science,* trans. Walter Kaufmann [New York: Random House, 1974], preface, §4)—all traits he regularly ascribes to himself. For more on Nietzsche's and Kierkegaard's views on the feminine, see Chapter 6. For commentaries on the purportedly feminine nature of Nietzsche's writing, see the following articles in *Feminist Interpretations of Friedrich Nietzsche,* ed. Kelly Oliver and Marilyn Pearsall (University Park: Penn State University Press, 1998): Jacques Derrida, "The Question of Style," trans. Ruben Berezdivin, 50–65; Kathleen Marie Higgins, "Gender in *The Gay Science,*" 130–51; Sarah Kofman, "Baubô: Theological Perversion and Fetishism," trans. Tracy Strong, 21–49; Kelly Oliver, "Woman as Truth in Nietzsche's Writing," 66–80. See also Derrida, *Spurs: Nietzsche's Styles/ Éperons: Les styles de Nietzsche,* trans. Barbara Harlow (Chicago: University of Chicago Press, 1979), and Luce Irigaray, *Marine Lover of Friedrich Nietzsche,* trans. Gillian C. Gill (New York: Columbia University Press, 1991).

By indicating that there are problems with these readings of what Irigaray calls Nietzsche's "feminine style," I do not of course mean to imply that they are doomed to failure. All of the examples of this sort of reading I have just cited are, in fact, deeply provocative and meticulous readings of Nietzsche.

13. William is playing on the opening move of Hegel's *Logic* here, where the category of "being" is exposed as collapsing, or being annulled (*aufgehoben*) into the category of "nothing" (*EL* §§86–87).

14. Crites, "Pseudonymous Authorship as Art and as Act," 217.

15. Emmanuel Levinas, "The Trace of the Other," trans. Alphonso Lingis, in *Deconstruction in Context,* ed. Mark C. Taylor (Chicago: University of Chicago Press, 1986), 345–59; Emmanuel Levinas, "A propos de *Kierkegaard Vivant,*" trans. Jonathan Rée, included as "Two Notes" in *Kierkegaard: A Critical Reader,* ed. Jonathan Rée and Jane Chamberlain (Oxford: Blackwell, 1998), 33–38.

16. See *PV* 41: "Although ever so many parsons were to consider this method [of indirection and deception] unjustifiable, . . . I for my part tranquilly adhere to Socrates."

17. A good analysis of this exhibitionism is Joakim Garff's "The Eyes of Argus: *The Point of View* and Points of View on Kierkegaard's Work as an Author," trans. Jane Chamberlain and Belinda Ioni Rasmussen, in *Kierkegaard: A Critical Reader,* ed. Jonathan Rée and Jane Chamberlain (Oxford: Blackwell, 1998), 75–102.

4. Hegel's Seductions

1. Ludwig Feuerbach, *The Essence of Christianity,* trans. George Eliot (New York: Harper and Row, 1957), xxxiv–v.

2. Friedrich Engels, Appendix to *A Contribution to the Critique of Political Economy,* by Karl Marx, trans. Maurice Dobb (New York: International Publishers, 1972), 224.

3. Karl Marx, *Capital,* vol. 1, trans. Ben Fowkes (New York: Penguin, 1990), 103.

4. Martin Heidegger, *Nietzsche,* ed. David Farrell Krell (New York: Harper and Row, 1987), 4:148.

5. There is also a passage in the preface to his *Phenomenology* where Hegel uses this image. There, he seeks to expose the impression of philosophic thinking being a "walking on its head" as a prejudice of "the natural consciousness," which never seeks beneath the surface of things and can only suffer disorientation when it encounters a way of thinking that challenges its cherished certainties: "When natural consciousness entrusts itself straightaway to [philosophy], it makes an attempt . . . to walk on its head . . . just this once; the compulsion to assume this unwonted posture and to go about in it is a violence it is expected to do to itself, all unprepared. . . . Let [philosophical thinking] be in its own self what it may, relative to immediate self-consciousness it presents itself in an inverted posture" (*PS* 15).

6. Martin Heidegger, *Being and Time,* trans. John Macquarrie and Edward Robinson (New York: Harper, 1962), 128, 127, 43.

7. Albert Camus, "An Absurd Reasoning," in *The Myth of Sisyphus and Other Essays,* trans. Justin O'Brien (New York: Random House, 1955), 21.

8. For example, William Werkmeister says that "Hegel's basic orientation, his whole mode of thinking, is essentially religious." "Hegel's Phenomenology of Mind as a Development of Kant's Basic Ontology," in *Hegel and the Philosophy of Religion,* ed. Darrel E. Christensen (The Hague: Martinus Nijhoff, 1970), 102. See also the other essays in Christensen's anthology, as well as Emil Fackenheim, *The Religious Dimension in Hegel's Thought* (Chicago: University of Chicago Press, 1967); Quentin Lauer, *Essays in Hegelian Dialectic* (New York: Fordham University Press, 1977), 12; and J. Hutchison Sterling, *The*

Secret of Hegel (New York: Putnam's, 1898), xxii. The support for such readings is obvious, since Hegel speaks regularly of God and the divine. I am more persuaded, however, that Heinrich Heine had it right when he recounts how one evening while visiting Hegel he listened as "the maestro . . . composed [the music of atheism], though in very obscure and ornate signs so that not everyone could decipher them—I sometimes saw him anxiously looking over his shoulder, in fear that he had been understood." Heine, *Werke,* ed. Ernst Elster (Leipzig: Bibliographisches Institut, 1922), 4:148–49.

9. Camus, "An Absurd Reasoning," 28–29.

10. Judith Butler, *Subjects of Desire: Hegelian Reflections in Twentieth-Century France* (New York: Columbia University Press, 1987), 19, 20.

11. Dylan Evans, *An Introductory Dictionary of Lacanian Psychoanalysis* (New York: Routledge, 1996), 114.

12. Jacques Lacan, *Écrits,* trans. Bruce Fink (New York: Norton, 2006), 502.

13. Martin Heidegger, *Hegel's Phenomenology of Spirit,* trans. Parvis Emad and Kenneth Maly (Bloomington: Indiana University Press, 1994), 66.

14. Jean-Luc Nancy, *La rémarque speculative* (Paris: Editions Galilée, 1973), 113.

15. Heidegger, *Being and Time,* 165, 160.

16. Ibid., 60, 62.

17. Alexandre Kojève, *Introduction to the Reading of Hegel,* trans. James H. Nichols, ed. Allan Bloom. Ithaca, N.Y.: Cornell University Press, 1969), 176, 171.

18. Jean-Paul Sartre, "The Wall," trans. Lloyd Alexander, in *The Wall and Other Stories* (New York: New Directions, 1975), 5, 6.

19. Gary Shapiro, "Some Genres of Post-Hegelian Philosophy," *Metaphilosophy* 13, no. 3–4 (1982): 269.

20. Butler, *Subjects of Desire,* 22. The reference to Kierkegaard (actually Constantin Constantius) is to *Repetition,* 200.

21. See Antonio Zirión Quijano, "The Call 'Back to the Things Themselves' and the Notion of Phenomenology," *Husserl Studies* 22 (2006): 29–51.

22. Martin Heidegger, "Building Dwelling Thinking," in *Basic Writings,* ed. David Farrell Krell (New York: Harper, 1977), 327–29.

23. Michel Foucault, *The Archaeology of Knowledge,* trans. A. M. Sheridan Smith (New York: Pantheon, 1972), 235.

24. Kojève, *Introduction to the Reading of Hegel,* 168.

25. Roland Barthes, "Death of the Author," in *Image, Music, Text,* trans. Stephen Heath (New York: Hill and Wang, 1977), 148.

26. Sartre, *Being and Nothingness,* 259–61, 255.

27. Ibid., 288.

28. Jacques Derrida, *Gift of Death,* trans. David Wills (Chicago: University of Chicago Press, 1995), 63.

5. Talking Cures

1. Franz Anton Mesmer, *Précis historique des faits relatifs au Magnétisme-Animal jusques en Avril 1781* (London: n.p., 1781), 22–23.

2. See Daniel Berthold-Bond (now Berthold), *Hegel's Theory of Madness* (Albany: State University of New York Press, 1995), 202–6.

3. "As soon as the unconscious processes concerned [in a given symptom of neurosis] have become conscious, the symptom must disappear. Here you will at once perceive a means of approach to therapy." Sigmund Freud, *Introductory Lectures on Psychoanalysis,* in *The Standard Edition of the Complete Psychological Works of Sigmund Freud* (24 vols.), ed. James Strachey (London: Hogarth, 1953–74), 15:279. Hereafter *SE.*

4. Ibid., 15:17. See also Sigmund Freud, *The Question of Lay Analysis, SE* 20:187–88.

5. Sigmund Freud, "Preface to the Translation of Bernheim's Suggestion," *SE* 1:75.

6. James Phillips, "Madness of the Philosophers, Madness of the Clinic," *Philosophy, Psychiatry, and Psychology* 16, no. 4 (2009): 313–17.

7. Ibid., 316 (emphasis added).

8. See Berthold, *Hegel's Theory of Madness,* 180–89.

9. Ibid., chap. 2.

10. Sigmund Freud, "Psychoanalysis and Religious Origins," *SE* 17:94.

11. Sigmund Freud, *The Resistances to Psychoanalysis, SE* 19:217.

12. *Letters of Sigmund Freud,* ed. Ernst Freud, trans. Tania Stern and James Stern (New York: Basic Books, 1960), 232 (letter 110).

13. I do not mean to conflate language with the symbolic here, since Lacan also speaks of language's having an Imaginary (presymbolic) dimension. *The Seminar of Jacques Lacan,* book 2: *The Ego in Freud's Theory and in the Technique of Psychoanalysis, 1954–1955,* trans. Sylvana Tomaselli (Cambridge: Cambridge University Press, 1988), 306. But the symbolic dimension of language is that of what he calls "full" or "true speech," whereas the Imaginary dimension is that of "empty speech." Jacques Lacan, *Écrits,* trans. Bruce Fink (New York: Norton, 2006), 206–9. See also *The Seminar of Jacques Lacan,* book 1: *Freud's Papers on Technique, 1953–1954,* trans. John Forrester (Cambridge: Cambridge University Press, 1988), 107.

14. Lacan, *Écrits,* 435.

15. *The Seminar of Jacques Lacan,* book 11: *The Four Fundamental Concepts of Psychoanalysis,* trans. Alan Sheridan, ed. Jacques-Alain Miller (New York: Norton, 1981),11.

16. Lacan, *Écrits,* 835.

17. According to Nathan Fialko, "Hegel possessed all the medical knowledge available in his time, and in that he exceeded many of his contemporaries, physicians and [philosophical] writers [alike]." "Hegel's Views on Mental Derangement," *Journal of Abnormal and Social Psychology* 25, no. 2 (1930): 246.

18. See Hegel's correspondence to his sister (*Letters* 406–22). See also M. J. Petry's notes to his translation of *Hegel's Philosophy of Subjective Spirit* (part 3 of the *Encyclopedia*) (Dordrecht, Holland: D. Reidel, 1979), 2:561–63.

19. Sigmund Freud, "On Narcissism," *SE* 14:82.

20. For helpful accounts of Hegel's theory of the soul, see Murray Greene, *Hegel on the Soul: A Speculative Anthropology* (The Hague: Martinus Nijhoff, 1972), and Errol Harris, "Hegel's Theory of Feeling," in *New Studies in Hegel's Political Philosophy,* ed. Warren E. Steinkraus (Cambridge: Cambridge University Press, 1984), 114–36.

21. Freud, *Introductory Lectures on Psychoanalysis, SE* 16:368, 359.

22. Lacan, *Écrits,* 93–100.

23. Ibid., 95.

24. Ibid., 97.

25. See ibid., 121, 314, 432; Lacan, *Seminar* 1:223; Lacan, *Seminar* 11:219–21; and *The Seminar of Jacques Lacan,* book 17: *The Other Side of Psychoanalysis,* trans. Russell Grigg (New York: Norton, 2007), 173–75.

26. Lacan, *Écrits,* 165; Lacan, *Seminar* 1:167.

27. Lacan, *Seminar* 1:62.

28. Lacan, *Écrits,* 835.

29. Lacan, *Seminar* 2:188.

30. See Hegel, *PS* 109–10; and Lacan, *Seminar* 1:47; Lacan, *Écrits,* 181, 268.

31. As Diane Rabinovich puts it, for Lacan "There is no given natural subject; . . . we are first an object." "What Is a Lacanian Clinic?" in *The Cambridge Companion to Lacan,* ed. Jean-Michel Rabaté (Cambridge: Cambridge University Press, 2003), 212.

32. Lacan, *Écrits,* 251, 427, 835.

33. Ibid., 809–10.

34. See Judith Butler's discussion of Lacan's departure from Hegel's (supposedly) "romantic" theory of language and expression. *Subjects of Desire: Hegelian Reflections in Twentieth-Century France* (New York: Columbia University Press, 1987), 198.

35. Lacan, *Écrits,* 802.

36. Ibid., 293.

37. See my discussion of the nostalgic character of desire in Hegel's phenomenology: Daniel Berthold-Bond, "The Two Faces of Desire: Evolution

and Nostalgia in Hegel's *Phenomenology of Desire.*" *Clio* 19, no. 4 (1990): 367–88.

38. See Hegel's account of the "unhappy consciousness" (*PS* 126–38, 454–60, 476).

39. Lacan, *Écrits,* 804.

40. *The Seminar of Jacques Lacan,* book 20: *Encore, 1972–1973,* trans. Bruce Fink (New York: Norton, 1998), 76–77. Jouissance is the painful pleasure of transgressing the prohibitions imposed on the subject's enjoyment by the very structure of language that requires a renunciation of the subject's quest for unlimited enjoyment (see Lacan, *Écrits,* 319: "Jouissance is forbidden to him who speaks"). Jouissance is also conceived of as the quest for the Real—the unsayable, the ineffable, a sense of wholeness utterly beyond language and expression (*Seminar* 11:167), and ultimately, for God (*Seminar* 20:76–77). To complicate matters, it is specifically *feminine* jouissance (a "jouissance of the Other") that Lacan refers to as "the God face" of desire (*Seminar* 20:76–77).

41. On Kierkegaard's notion of his "borderline" madness, see John Llewelyn, "On the Borderline of Madness," in *The New Kierkegaard,* ed. Elsebet Jegstrup (Bloomington: Indiana University Press, 2004), 88–111.

42. Friedrich Nietzsche, *The Gay Science* trans. Walter Kaufmann (New York: Random House, 1974), §333 (emphasis added).

43. Lacan, *Écrits,* 835.

44. Lacan, *Seminar* 1:66, and see Lacan, *Écrits,* 388.

45. Bruce Fink, *The Lacanian Subject: Between Language and Jouissance* (Princeton: Princeton University Press, 1995), 25.

46. Lacan, *Écrits,* 319.

47. See Lacan, *Seminar* 1:66; Lacan, *Seminar* 20:53; Lacan, *Écrits,* 388.

48. Lacan, *Seminar* 11:162; Lacan, *Seminar* 1:67; Lacan, *Seminar* 3:321.

49. See discussions by Lee Edelman, *No Future: Queer Theory and the Death Drive* (Durham, N.C.: Duke University Press, 2004), 25; and Marie Hélène Brousse, "The Imaginary," in *Reading Seminars I and II: Lacan's Return to Freud,* ed. Richard Feldstein, Bruce Fink, and Maire Jaanus (Albany: State University of New York Press, 1996), 127.

50. Lacan, *Écrits,* 103. Compare Kierkegaard, who writes of his position as an author that "I am impersonal, or am personal in the second person, a *souffleur,*" or stage manager (*CUP* 551).

51. Lacan, *Écrits,* 586, 641, 351, 617, 641.

52. Lacan, *Seminar* 11:11.

53. Lacan, *Écrits,* 181.

54. Butler, *Subjects of Desire,* 198.

55. Lacan, *Seminar* 11:6, 11.

56. Lacan, *Écrits,* 265, 431, 427.

57. Louis Sass, "Madness and the Ineffable: Hegel, Kierkegaard, Lacan," *Philosophy, Psychiatry, and Psychology* 16, no. 4 (2009): 320.

58. Ibid., 322.

59. Ibid.

60. See the discussion in Chapter 6.

61. Sass, "Madness and the Ineffable," 322.

62. See Alan Olson, *Hegel and the Spirit* (Princeton: Princeton University Press, 1992); also Berthold, *Hegel's Theory of Madness,* 61–63.

6. A Penchant for Disguise: The Death (and Rebirth) of the Author in Kierkegaard and Nietzsche

1. Bruce Kirmmse, *Encounters with Kierkegaard: A Life as Seen by His Contemporaries* (Princeton: Princeton University Press, 1966), 103. The friend was Emil Boesen (Joakim Garff, *Søren Kierkegaard: A Biography,* trans. Bruce Kirmmse [Princeton: Princeton University Press, 2000], 793). Compare Kierkegaard's *Point of View,* where he has his "poet" say in his eulogy that "historically [Kierkegaard] died of a mortal disease, but poetically [he] died of longing for eternity" (*PV* 103).

2. Walter Kaufmann, *Nietzsche: Philosopher, Psychologist, Antichrist* (Princeton: Princeton University Press, 1977), 67; Rüdiger Safranski, *Nietzsche: A Philosophical Biography,* trans. Shelley Frisch (New York: Norton, 2003), 304–16.

3. Michel Foucault, "What Is an Author?" in *The Foucault Reader,* ed. Paul Rabinow (New York: Pantheon, 1984), 102–3.

4. Roland Barthes, "The Death of the Author," in *Image, Music, Text,* trans. Stephen Heath (New York: Hill and Wang, 1977), 142.

5. John Searle, *Speech Acts: An Essay in the Philosophy of Language* (Cambridge: Cambridge University Press, 1969), 43.

6. Lou Andreas-Salomé, as quoted in Karl Jaspers, *Nietzsche: An Introduction to the Understanding of His Philosophical Activity,* trans. Charles Wallraff and Frederick Schmitz (Chicago: Henry Regnery, 1965), 38.

7. Friedrich Nietzsche, *Thus Spoke Zarathustra,* in *The Portable Nietzsche,* trans. and ed. Walter Kaufmann (New York: Viking, 1966), 238.

8. Jaspers, *Nietzsche,* 95, 96.

9. See Roger Poole's comment on Kierkegaard's authorship: "The texts demonstrate to a nicety the Lacanian perception that all we are ever offered in a text is an endless succession of signifiers." *Kierkegaard: The Indirect Communication* (Charlottesville: University Press of Virginia, 1993), 9.

10. Barthes, "Death of the Author," 143.

11. Friedrich Nietzsche, *Beyond Good and Evil,* in *Basic Writings of Nietzsche,* trans. and ed. Walter Kaufmann (New York: Random House, 1968), §237.

12. Judith Butler, *Gender Trouble: Feminism and the Subversion of Identity* (New York: Routledge, 1999), 174–77.

13. Ibid., 33. Butler cites Friedrich Nietzsche, *The Genealogy of Morals,* trans. Walter Kaufmann (New York: Vintage, 1969), 45. The same quotation may be found in Friedrich Nietzsche, *The Genealogy of Morals,* in *Basic Writings of Nietzsche,* trans. and ed. Walter Kaufmann (New York: Random House, 1968), part 1, §13.

14. Butler, *Gender Trouble,* 33.

15. Ibid., 177.

16. Carl Pletsch, "The Self-Sufficient Text in Nietzsche and Kierkegaard," *Yale French Studies* 66 (1984): 179.

17. Foucault, "What Is an Author?" 102.

18. Arthur Rimbaud, "Lettre du Voyant," in *Rimbaud: Complete Works, Selected Letters,* trans. Wallace Fowlie, ed. Seth Whidden (Chicago: University of Chicago Press, 2005), 374.

19. Plato's second letter, in *Plato: Timaeus, Critias, Cleitophon, Menexenus, Epistles,* trans. R. G. Bury (Cambridge: Harvard University Press, 1999), Stephanus pagination, III.314c.

20. Catullus, poem 16, in *Innovations of Antiquity,* ed. R. Hexter and D. Selden (New York: Routledge, 1992), 477–78.

21. Cervantes, *The Ingenious Gentleman Don Quixote of La Mancha,* trans. Henry Edward Watts (London: Adam and Charles Black, 1895), throughout. See also Margaret Oliphant, *Cervantes* (London: Blackwood, 1881), 141.

22. Jonathan I. Israel, *Radical Enlightenment: Philosophy and the Making of Modernity, 1650–1750* (Oxford: Oxford University Press, 2002), 710.

23. See Ronald Taylor, *Berlin and Its Culture: A Historical Portrait* (New Haven: Yale University Press, 1997), 101. I am indebted to my colleague at Bard College, the poet Robert Kelly, and to my student Lilli Cartwright, for the references to Catullus, Cervantes, and E. T. A. Hoffmann.

24. Foucault, "What Is an Author?" 102.

25. Barthes, "Death of the Author," 147.

26. Josiah Thompson, "Master of Irony," in *Kierkegaard: A Collection of Critical Essays*, ed. Josiah Thompson (Garden City, N.Y.: Doubleday, 1972), 161.

27. Cited without reference in Walter Lowrie, *A Short Life of Kierkegaard* (Princeton: Princeton University Press, 1965), 39.

28. Jaspers, *Nietzsche,* 64.

29. *Selected Letters of Friedrich Nietzsche,* ed. and trans. Christopher Middleton (New York: Hackett, 1996), 206–7.

30. Friedrich Nietzsche, *Ecce Homo,* in *Basic Writings of Nietzsche,* trans. and ed. Walter Kaufmann (New York: Random House, 1968), 681.

31. Jaspers, *Nietzsche,* 37–38.

32. Nietzsche, *Genealogy of Morals,* §382.

33. Jaspers, *Nietzsche,* 56.

34. Lowrie, *A Short Life of Kierkegaard,* 223–24 (cited without reference).

35. See also the *Point of View:* "What reconciled me with my fate and with my suffering was that I, the so unhappy, so much tortured prisoner, had obtained [the] unlimited freedom of being able to deceive, so that I was allowed to be absolutely alone with my pain" (*PV* 78–79).

36. Lowrie, *A Short Life of Kierkegaard,* 107 (cited without reference).

37. Jaspers, *Nietzsche,* 86.

38. Friedrich Nietzsche, *The Gay Science,* trans. Walter Kaufmann (New York: Random House, 1974), §381; Nietzsche, *Beyond Good and Evil,* §§290, 278.

39. Nietzsche, *Beyond Good and Evil,* §40.

40. Plato, *Republic,* 3.414b–c.

41. Foucault, "What Is an Author?" 102.

42. Barthes, "Death of the Author," 143.

43. Nietzsche, *Gay Science,* §361.

44. Garff, *Søren Kierkegaard,* 100.

45. Nietzsche, *Ecce Homo,* 782.

46. Barthes, "Death of an Author," 143, and see 148.

47. Nietzsche, *Gay Science,* §§348, 213; Nietzsche, *Ecce Homo,* 259.

48. Nietzsche, *Thus Spoke Zarathustra,* 121, 296.

49. Nietzsche, *Gay Science,* §234.

50. Friedrich Nietzsche, *The Antichrist,* trans. Walter Kaufmann, in *Basic Writings of Nietzsche,* §38; Nietzsche, *Beyond Good and Evil,* §26.

51. Nietzsche, *Thus Spoke Zarathustra,* 190.

52. Nietzsche, *Beyond Good and Evil,* §259; Nietzsche, *Ecce Homo,* 782.

53. Nietzsche, *Beyond Good and Evil,* §40.

54. See Pletsch's "The Self-Sufficient Text in Nietzsche and Kierkegaard" for a discussion of some of the differences between Kierkegaard's and Nietzsche's "silences" (esp. 176–78).

55. Nietzsche, *Thus Spoke Zarathustra,* 186.

56. Ibid., 219.

57. Nietzsche, *Gay Science,* §374.

58. Nietzsche, *Beyond Good and Evil,* §278.

59. Jacques Derrida, *The Gift of Death,* trans. David Wills (Chicago: University of Chicago Press, 1995), 77–78, 286, 287.

60. *CUP* 286.

61. Nietzsche, *Beyond Good and Evil,* §42; Nietzsche, *Gay Science,* §200.

62. Jean-Paul Sartre, *Being and Nothingness*, trans. Hazel Barnes (New York: Philosophical Library, 1965), 365.

63. Nietzsche, *Thus Spoke Zarathustra,* 264.

64. Barthes, "Death of the Author," 148.

65. Friedrich Nietzsche, *Daybreak,* trans. R. J. Hollingdale (Cambridge: Cambridge University Press, 1982), §115.

66. Jacques Lacan, *Écrits,* trans. Bruce Fink (New York: Norton, 2006), 835.

67. Nietzsche, *Gay Science,* §354.

68. Derrida, *Gift of Death,* 60.

69. Nietzsche, quoted in Jaspers, *Nietzsche,* 50, 51. Jaspers quoted from *Nietzsches Briefwechsel mit Franz Overbeck* (Leipzig: Inselverlag, 1916). The letter is from Nietzsche to Overbeck, July 2, 1885.

70. Foucault, "What Is an Author?" 102.

71. Barthes, "Death of the Author," 145.

72. Jaspers, *Nietzsche,* 86.

73. Walter Kaufmann, Note on the Publication of *Ecce Homo,* in *Basic Writings of Nietzsche,* trans. and ed. Walter Kaufmann (New York: Random House, 1968), 669.

74. Cited in Joakim Garff, "The Eyes of Argus: *The Point of View* and Points of View on Kierkegaard's Work as an Author," trans. Jane Chamberlain and Belinda Ioni Rasmussen, in *Kierkegaard: A Critical Reader,* ed. Jonathan Rée and Jane Chamberlain (Oxford: Blackwell, 1998), 98. The *Papirer* reference is X 2 A 171.

75. Nietzsche, *Ecce Homo,* 673.

76. Henning Fenger, *Kierkegaard, The Myths and Their Origins,* trans. George C. Schoolfield (New Haven: Yale University Press, 1980), 26.

77. *P* X 2 A 171. Cited in Garff, *Søren Kierkegaard,* 559–60.

78. Louis Mackey, *Points of View: Readings of Kierkegaard* (Tallahassee: Florida State University Press, 1986), 249.

79. Jacques Derrida, "The Question of Style," translated by Ruben Berezdivin, in *Feminist Interpretations of Friedrich Nietzsche,* ed. Kelly Oliver and Marilyn Pearsall (University Park: Penn State University Press, 1998), 64.

80. Pletsch, "The Self-Sufficient Text in Nietzsche and Kierkegaard," 178.

81. Nietzsche, *Ecce Homo,* 259; and see Nietzsche, *Gay Science,* §213; Nietzsche, *Thus Spoke Zarathustra,* 283.

82. Nietzsche, *Gay Science,* §381.

83. Walter Lowrie says of Clemens Alexandrinus that "in his *Stromateis* he often says that he presents the Christian doctrine in a disguised form so that it might not be misunderstood and abused by the uninitiated, but he does not speak expressly of heretics" (*R* 142n89).

84. Nietzsche, *Ecce Homo*, 310. In an earlier letter to Overbeck (1884), Nietzsche was even more explicit about his wish for apostles: "I need disciples while I am still alive, and if the books that I have written so far are not effective as fishing hooks, then they have 'missed their calling'" (Jaspers, *Nietzsche*, 85).

85. Roland Barthes, "Writers, Intellectuals, Teachers," in *Image, Music, Text*, trans. Stephen Heath (New York: Hill and Wang, 1977), 195.

86. Sartre, *Being and Nothingness*, 373.

87. Nietzsche, *Gay Science*, §68.

88. Nietzsche, *Beyond Good and Evil*, §239.

89. Sara Kofman discusses Nietzsche's fear of the "self-sufficiency" of woman in "The Narcissistic Woman: Freud and Girard," *Diacritics* 10, no. 3 (1980): 36–45.

90. See, for example, Nietzsche, *Beyond Good and Evil*, §§232, 238, 239.

91. Lowrie, *A Short Life of Kierkegaard*, 146 (cited without reference).

92. Garff, *Søren Kierkegaard*, 801–2; Lowrie, *A Short Life of Kierkegaard*, 147.

93. Lowrie, *A Short Life of Kierkegaard*, 147 (cited without reference).

94. Jaspers, *Nietzsche*, 71–73.

95. Kaufmann, *Nietzsche*, 52.

96. Lowrie, *A Short Life of Kierkegaard*, 135–43; Garff, *Søren Kierkegaard*, 185–91.

97. Jaspers, *Nietzsche*, 72; Kaufmann, *Nietzsche*, 62.

98. Pletsch, "The Self-Sufficient Text in Nietzsche and Kierkegaard," 187–88.

99. Nietzsche, *Thus Spoke Zarathustra*, 296.

100. Derrida, *Gift of Death*, 60.

101. Nietzsche, *Ecce Homo*, 681.

102. Jaspers, *Nietzsche*, 85.

103. Plato, *Phaedo* 67e.

104. Nietzsche, *Ecce Homo*, 676.

105. Nietzsche, *Thus Spoke Zarathustra*, 190.

106. Barthes, "Death of the Author," 148.

107. See Laird McLeod Easton, *The Red Count: The Life and Times of Harry Kessler* (Berkeley: University of California Press, 2002), chap. 14, "A Monument for Nietzsche" (185–95).

108. See Lowrie, *A Short Life of Kierkegaard*, 254.

109. Kaufmann, *Nietzsche,* 68.

110. Nietzsche, *Ecce Homo,* 782.

111. As an epilogue to the story of Nietzsche's grave site, the German parliament is debating, as of this writing, whether to allow a mining company to dig up the cemetery where Nietzsche is buried, where they hope to find brown coal (lignite). The German press is having a wonderful time with the story, publishing such articles as "Übermensch Undermined" (*Der Spiegel International Newsletter Online,* March 25, 2008, http://www.spiegel.de/international/germany/0,1518,543222,00.html). If the mining company is successful, then a couplet from Nietzsche's poem "Ecce Homo" will have come true: "Kohle alles, was ich lasse/Flamme bin ich sicherlich!"—All I touch becomes light/ All I leave behind is coal! (*Gay Science,* Prelude in Rhymes, §62).

112. Garff, *Søren Kierkegaard,* 812; Lowrie, *A Short Life of Kierkegaard,* 256.

7. Passing Over: The Death of the Author in Hegel

1. Arthur Schopenhauer, *World as Will and Representation,* trans. E. F. J. Payne (New York: Dover, 1969), 1:429.

2. Arthur Schopenhauer, *Parerga and Paralipomena: Short Philosophical Essays,* trans. E. F. J. Payne (Oxford: Oxford University Press, 2000), 96, 168.

3. Otto Gruppe, *Die Winde, oder, Ganz absolute Konstruction der neuern Weltgeschichte durch Oberons Horn, gedichtet von Absolutus von Hegelingen* (1830) (Leipzig: Wilhelm Nauck, n.d.).

4. Otto Gruppe, *Antäus,* ed. Friedrich Mauthner (Munich: Georg Müller, 1914), 454. An excellent discussion of Gruppe may be found in Hermann Cloeren's *Language and Thought: German Approaches to Analytic Philosophy in the Eighteenth and Nineteenth Centuries* (Berlin: Walter de Gruyter, 1988), 78–109. The translation from *Antäus* is Cloeren's.

5. Dale Snow, "F. W. J. Schelling," in *The Columbia History of Western Philosophy,* ed. Richard H. Popkin (New York: Columbia University Press, 1999), 529.

6. Friedrich Engels, "Schelling on Hegel," in *Karl Marx, Frederick Engels: Collected Works,* 50 vols. (New York: International Publishers, 1975–2004), 2:181–88.

7. Friedrich Engels, *Ludwig Feuerbach and the End of Classical German Philosophy,* ed. C. P. Dutt (New York: International Publishers, 1978), 44: "The dialectic of Hegel was placed upon its head; or rather, turned off its head, on which it was standing, and placed upon its feet."

8. Cloeren, *Language and Thought,* 130.

9. Gilles Deleuze and Claire Parnet, *Dialogues,* trans. Hugh Tomlinson and Barbara Habberjam (New York: Columbia University Press, 1987), 112.

10. Georges Bataille and Raymond Queneau, "La critique des fondements de la dialectique hégélienne," *Deucalion* 5 (1955): 47.

11. Jean Hyppolite, *Genesis and Structure of Hegel's Phenomenology of Spirit,* trans. Samuel Cherniak and John Heckman (Evanston, Ill.: Northwestern University Press, 1974), 86n7.

12. Jacques Lacan, *Écrits,* trans. Bruce Fink (New York: Norton, 2006), 617, 641.

13. Judith Butler, *Subjects of Desire: Hegelian Reflections in Twentieth-Century France* (New York: Columbia University Press, 1987), 183.

14. William Desmond, *Art and the Absolute: A Study of Hegel's Aesthetics* (Albany: State University of New York Press, 1986), 90–91.

15. Georges Bataille, "Hegel, Death, and Sacrifice," trans. Jonathan Strauss, *Yale French Studies* 78 (1990): 9–28.

16. Alexandre Kojève, *Introduction to the Reading of Hegel,* trans. James H. Nichols, ed. Allan Bloom (Ithaca, N.Y.: Cornell University Press, 1969), 168.

17. Alexandre Kojève, *L'introduction à la lecture de Hegel* (Paris: Gallimard, 1947), 413.

18. Stanley Rosen, *G. W. F. Hegel: An Introduction to the Science of Wisdom* (New Haven: Yale University Press, 1974), 279.

19. Georges Bataille, *Inner Experience,* trans. Leslie Anne Boldt (Albany: State University of New York Press, 1988), 109. See also Bataille, "Hegel, Death, and Sacrifice," 12.

20. Roland Barthes, "The Death of the Author," in *Image, Music, Text,* trans. Stephen Heath (New York: Hill and Wang, 1977), 148.

21. Michel Foucault, "What Is an Author?" in *The Foucault Reader,* ed. Paul Rabinow (New York: Pantheon, 1984), 102–3.

22. Butler, *Subjects of Desire,* 19, 20.

23. Of course, to fully make the case that Hegel's critics misread the ostensibly authoritarian tone of his philosophic voice—moving too quickly to portray him as the self-appointed Wise Man and misreading the significance of his invocation of "absolute knowledge"—I would have to engage their arguments much more fully than I do here. My goal in this chapter is simply to provoke further debate by sketching out the case for Hegel's death as an author.

24. Martin Heidegger, "Letter on Humanism," in *Basic Writings,* ed. David Farrell Krell (New York: Harper, 1977), 238.

25. Martin Heidegger, "The Age of the World Picture," in *The Question concerning Technology and Other Essays,* trans. William Lovitt (New York: Harper and Row, 1977), 115–54. See also Martin Heidegger, *Nietzsche,* 4 vols., trans. David Farrell Krell (New York: Harper and Row, 1987), 2:96–138.

26. Martin Heidegger, "The Origin of the Work of Art," trans. Albert Hofstadter, in *Basic Writings,* ed. David Farrell Krell (New York: Harper, 1977), 152; Heidegger, "Question concerning Technology," 298; Heidegger, "Age of the World Picture," 129–30.

27. Heidegger, *Nietzsche* 4:178.

28. Ibid., 4:22.

29. Richard Rorty, *Consequences of Pragmatism* (Minneapolis: University of Minnesota Press, 1982), 187.

30. Lacan, *Écrits,* 303.

31. Dylan Evans, *An Introductory Dictionary of Lacanian Psychoanalysis* (New York: Routledge, 1996), 149.

32. See Immanuel Kant, *Logic,* trans. Robert Hartman and Wolfgang Schwartz (New York: Bobbs-Merrill, 1974), 56: "Truth, one says, consists in the agreement of cognition with the object. . . . Now I can, however, compare the object with my cognition only by cognizing it. . . . [But] since the object is outside me and the cognition in me, I can judge only whether my cognition of the object agrees with my cognition of the object. Such a circle of explanation was called by the ancients *diallelus.* . . . The charge was well founded indeed; but the solution of the task in question is completely impossible for anyone."

33. Immanuel Kant, *Critique of Pure Reason,* trans. Norman Kemp Smith (London: Macmillan, 1973), Bxx (see also A42, B298). References are to the standard Preussische Akademie pagination. "A" refers to the first edition (1781), "B" to the second (1787).

34. Friedrich Nietzsche, *Twilight of the Idols,* in *The Portable Nietzsche,* trans. and ed. Walter Kaufmann (New York: Viking, 1966), 486.

35. Jacques Derrida, *The Gift of Death,* trans. David Wills (Chicago: University of Chicago Press, 1995), 60.

36. Jean-Paul Sartre, *Being and Nothingness,* trans. Hazel Barnes (New York: Philosophical Library, 1965), 422, 423.

37. Kojève, *Introduction to the Reading of Hegel,* 4.

38. Georges Bataille, *On Nietzsche,* trans. Bruce Boone (New York: Paragon, 1992), 190.

39. Bataille, *Inner Experience,* 170.

40. Bruce Baugh, *French Hegel: From Surrealism to Postmodernism* (New York: Routledge, 2003), 76.

41. Quoted without reference in Walter Lowrie, *A Short Life of Kierkegaard* (Princeton: Princeton University Press, 1965), 70.

42. Barthes, "Death of the Author," 147.

43. Kojève, *L'introduction à la lecture de Hegel,* 537, 540. See also Jean Hyppolite, "The Concept of Existence in the Hegelian Phenomenology," in *Studies*

on Hegel and Marx, trans. John O'Neill (New York: Basic Books, 1969), 28; Bataille, "Hegel, Death, and Sacrifice," passim; and Jacques Derrida, *Speech and Phenomena,* trans. David B. Allison (Evanston, Ill.: Northwestern University Press, 1973), 102.

44. Eric Voegelin, "On Hegel—A Study in Sorcery," *Studium Generale* 24 (1971): 337, 349.

45. Kojève, *L'introduction à la lecture de Hegel,* 548.

46. Slavoj Žižek, *Tarrying with the Negative: Kant, Hegel, and the Critique of Ideology* (Durham, N.C.: Duke University Press, 1993).

47. Bataille, *Inner Experience,* 115; Georges Bataille, *Guilty,* trans. Bruce Boone (Venice, Calif.: Lapis Press, 1988), 128.

48. Jacques Derrida, *Glas,* trans. John Leavey and Richard Rand (Lincoln: University of Nebraska Press, 1986), 191.

49. Jean-François Lyotard, *The Post-modern Condition,* trans Régis Durand (Minneapolis: University of Minnesota Press, 1984), 81–82.

50. Michel Foucault, "Nietzsche, Genealogy, History," trans. Donald Bouchard and Sherry Simon, in *The Foucault Reader,* ed. Paul Rabinow (New York: Pantheon, 1984), 88.

51. Jean Hyppolite, *Figures de la pensée philosophique* (Paris: Presses Universitaires de France, 1991), 142; Hyppolite, *Genesis and Structure of Hegel's Phenomenology of Spirit,* 577.

52. Roland Barthes, *Roland Barthes by Roland Barthes,* trans. Richard Howard (New York: Hill and Wang, 1977), 172.

Clearly I am far from giving full voice to Hegel's critics here. We could not possibly determine the outcome of the contest between these critical readings and my own counterreading without an extended and sympathetic delving into the details and complexities of the various texts and contexts in which Hegel's critics develop their arguments. My hope is only that I have provided sufficient grounds for reengaging these critics in the light of a different perspective on the ethics of Hegel's authorship, which as I see it is an ethics of gift-giving through authorial death.

53. Jacques Derrida, *Dissemination,* trans. Barbara Johnson (Chicago: University of Chicago Press, 1980), 207–8; and see Baugh, *French Hegel,* 13435.

54. Barthes, "Death of the Author," 148.

55. Slavoj Žižek, *The Sublime Object of Ideology* (New York: Verso, 1989), 6.

56. Engels, *Ludwig Feuerbach and the End of Classical German Philosophy,* 11.

57. Mary O'Brien, "Hegel: Man, Physiology, and Fate," in *Feminist Interpretations of G. W. F. Hegel,* ed. Patricia Jagentowicz Mills (University Park: Penn State University Press, 1996), 178.

58. Robert Solomon, *In the Spirit of Hegel* (Oxford: Oxford University Press, 1983), 637.

59. I am indebted to Solomon for this nod to Gertrude Stein's famous phrase (alluding to Oakland, California) as a characterization of absolute knowledge (*In the Spirit of Hegel,* 17).

60. Bataille, *Guilty,* 128.

61. Derrida, *Dissemination,* 252–53, 351.

62. Quoted in Karl Jaspers, *Nietzsche: An Introduction to the Understanding of His Philosophical Activity,* trans. Charles Wallraff and Frederick Schmitz (Chicago: Henry Regnery, 1965), 86.

BIBLIOGRAPHY

Aelian. *Historical Miscellany* (*Varia Historia*). Edited and translated by N. G. Wilson. Cambridge: Harvard University Press, 1977.

Agacinski, Sylviane. *Aparté: Conceptions et morts de Søren Kierkegaard.* Paris: Aubier-Flammarion, 1977.

Anderson, Raymond. "Kierkegaard's Theory of Communication." *Speech Monographs* 30 (March 1963): 1–14.

Aristophanes. *The Clouds.* Translated by Alan H. Sommerstein. New York: Penguin, 1983.

Armstrong, Paul B. "Reading Kierkegaard—Disorientation and Reorientation." In *Kierkegaard's Truth: The Disclosure of the Self,* edited by Joseph H. Smith, 23–50. New Haven: Yale University Press, 1981.

Barthes, Roland. "The Death of the Author." In *Image, Music, Text,* translated by Stephen Heath, 142–48. New York: Hill and Wang, 1977.

———. *Roland Barthes by Roland Barthes.* Translated by Richard Howard. New York: Hill and Wang, 1977.

———. "Writers, Intellectuals, Teachers." In *Image, Music, Text,* translated by Stephen Heath. 190–215. New York: Hill and Wang, 1977.

Bataille, Georges. *Guilty.* Translated by Bruce Boone. Venice, Calif.: Lapis Press, 1988.

———. "Hegel, Death, and Sacrifice." Translated by Jonathan Strauss. *Yale French Studies* 78 (1990): 9–28.

———. *Inner Experience.* Translated by Leslie Anne Boldt. Albany: State University of New York Press, 1988.

———. *On Nietzsche.* Translated by Bruce Boone. New York: Paragon, 1992.

Bataille, Georges, and Raymond Queneau. "La critique des fondements de la dialectique hégélienne." *Deucalion* 5 (1955): 45–59.

Baugh, Bruce. *French Hegel: From Surrealism to Postmodernism.* New York: Routledge, 2003.

Beauvoir, Simone de. *Mémoires d'une jeune fille rangée.* Paris: Gallimard, 1958.

Berry, Wanda Warren. "The Heterosexual Imagination and Aesthetic Exis-
tence in Kierkegaard's *Either/Or,* Part One." In *International Kierkegaard
Commentary: Either Or, Part I,* edited by Robert L. Perkins, 201–8. Macon,
Ga.: Mercer University Press, 1995.

Berthold-Bond (now Berthold), Daniel. *Hegel's Theory of Madness.* Albany:
State University of New York Press, 1995.

———. "The Two Faces of Desire: Evolution and Nostalgia in Hegel's Phenomenology of Desire." *Clio* 19, no. 4 (1990): 367–88.

Bodammer, Theodor. *Hegel's Deutung der Sprache.* Hamburg: F. Meiner, 1969.

Bretall, Robert, ed. *A Kierkegaard Anthology.* New York: Random House, 1946.

Brousse, Marie Hélène. "The Imaginary." In *Reading Seminars I and II: Lacan's
Return to Freud,* edited by Richard Feldstein, Bruce Fink, and Maire Jaanus, 118–22. Albany: State University of New York Press, 1996.

Butler, Judith. *Gender Trouble: Feminism and the Subversion of Identity.* New
York: Routledge, 1999.

———. *Subjects of Desire: Hegelian Reflections in Twentieth-Century France.*
New York: Columbia University Press, 1987.

Cameron, W. S. K. "[Writing] about Writing about Kierkegaard." *Philosophy
Today* 39 (Spring 1995): 56–66.

Camus, Albert. "An Absurd Reasoning." In *The Myth of Sisyphus and Other
Essays,* translated by Justin O'Brien, 3–48. New York: Random House,
1955.

Catullus. "Poem 16." In *Innovations of Antiquity,* edited by R. Hexter and D.
Seiden. New York: Routledge, 1992.

Cervantes. *The Ingenious Gentleman Don Quixote of La Mancha.* Translated by
Henry Edward Watts. London: Adam and Charles Black, 1895.

Christensen, Darrel E., ed. *Hegel and the Philosophy of Religion.* The Hague:
Martinus Nijhoff, 1970.

Cloeren, Hermann. *Language and Thought: German Approaches to Analytic Philosophy in the Eighteenth and Nineteenth Centuries.* Berlin: Walter de
Gruyter, 1988.

Cook, Daniel. *Language in the Philosophy of Hegel.* The Hague: Mouton, 1973.

Crites, Stephen. *In the Twilight of Christendom: Hegel vs. Kierkegaard on Faith
and History.* Chambersburg, Penn.: American Academy of Religion, 1972.

———. "Pseudonymous Authorship as Art and as Act." In *Kierkegaard: A
Collection of Critical Essays,* edited by Josiah Thompson, 183–229. Garden
City, N.Y.: Doubleday, 1972.

Cruysberghs, Paul. "Hegel Has No Ethics: Climacus' Complaints against
Speculative Philosophy." *Kierkegaard Studies: Yearbook* (2005): 175–91.

Deleuze, Gilles, and Claire Parnet. *Dialogues.* Translated by Hugh Tomlinson
and Barbara Habberjam. New York: Columbia University Press, 1987.

Der Spiegel International Newsletter Online. "Übermensch Undermined."
March 25, 2008. http://www.spiegel.de/international/germany/
0,1518,543222,00.html.

Derrida, Jacques. *Dissemination.* Translated by Barbara Johnson. Chicago:
University of Chicago Press, 1980.

———. *The Gift of Death.* Translated by David Wills. Chicago: University of
Chicago Press, 1995.

———. *Glas.* Translated by John Leavey and Richard Rand. Lincoln: University of Nebraska Press, 1986.

———. "The Question of Style." Translated by Ruben Berezdivin. In *Feminist Interpretations of Friedrich Nietzsche,* edited by Kelly Oliver and Marilyn
Pearsall, 50–65. University Park: Penn State University Press, 1998.

———. *Speech and Phenomena.* Translated by David B. Allison. Evanston, Ill.:
Northwestern University Press, 1973.

———. *Spurs: Nietzsche's Styles/Éperons: Les styles de Nietzsche.* Translated by
Barbara Harlow. Chicago: University of Chicago Press, 1979.

Desmond, William. *Art and the Absolute: A Study of Hegel's Aesthetics.* Albany:
State University of New York Press, 1986.

Dunning, Stephen. *Kierkegaard's Dialectic of Inwardness: A Structural Analysis
of the Theory of Stages.* Princeton: Princeton University Press, 1985.

Duran, Jane. "The Kierkegaardian Feminist." In *Feminist Interpretations of
Søren Kierkegaard,* edited by Céline Léon and Sylvia Walsh, 249–65. University Park: Penn State University Press, 1997.

Easton, Laird McLeod. *The Red Count: The Life and Times of Harry Kessler.*
Berkeley: University of California Press, 2002.

Edelman, Lee. *No Future: Queer Theory and the Death Drive.* Durham, N.C.:
Duke University Press, 2004.

Eliot, T. S. "The Hollow Men." In *T. S. Eliot: The Complete Poems and Plays,*
56–59. New York: Harcourt, Brace, 1952.

Engels, Friedrich. Appendix to *A Contribution to the Critique of Political Economy,* by Karl Marx, translated by Maurice Dobb, 218–27. New York: International Publishers, 1972.

———. *Ludwig Feuerbach and the End of Classical German Philosophy.* Edited
by C. P. Dutt. New York: International Publishers, 1978.

———. "Schelling on Hegel." In *Karl Marx, Frederick Engels: Collected Works*
(50 vols.), 2:181–88. New York: International Publishers, 1975–2004.

Euripides. *Orestes.* Translated by William Arrowsmith. In *Euripides IV,* edited
by David Grene and Richmond Lattimore. Chicago: University of Chicago
Press, 1958.

Evans, Dylan. *An Introductory Dictionary of Lacanian Psychoanalysis.* New
York: Routledge, 1996.

Fackenheim, Emil. *The Religious Dimension in Hegel's Thought.* Chicago: University of Chicago Press, 1967.

Faulkner, William. Interview with Jean Stein vanden Heuvel. *The Paris Review Interviews* 12 (Spring 1956): 1–27.

Feldstein, Richard, Bruce Fink, and Maire Jaanus, eds. *Reading Seminars I and II: Lacan's Return to Freud.* Albany: State University of New York Press, 1996.

Fenger, Henning. *Kierkegaard, the Myths and Their Origins.* Translated by George C. Schoolfield. New Haven: Yale University Press, 1980.

Feuerbach, Ludwig. *The Essence of Christianity.* Translated by George Eliot. New York: Harper and Row, 1957.

Fialko, Nathan. "Hegel's Views on Mental Derangement." *Journal of Abnormal and Social Psychology* 25, no. 2 (1930): 241–67.

Fink, Bruce. *The Lacanian Subject: Between Language and Jouissance.* Princeton: Princeton University Press, 1995.

Flay, Joseph. "Hegel, Heidegger, Derrida: Retrieval as Reconstruction, Destruction, Deconstruction." In *Ethics and Danger: Essays on Heidegger and Continental Thought,* edited by Arleen Dallery and Charles Scott, 199–213. Albany: State University of New York Press, 1992.

———. *Hegel's Quest for Certainty.* Albany: State University of New York Press, 1984.

Foucault, Michel. *The Archaeology of Knowledge.* Translated by A. M. Sheridan Smith. New York: Pantheon, 1972.

———. "Nietzsche, Genealogy, History." Translated by Donald Bouchard and Sherry Simon. In *The Foucault Reader,* edited by Paul Rabinow, 76–100. New York: Pantheon, 1984.

———. "What Is an Author?" In *The Foucault Reader,* edited by Paul Rabinow, 101–20. New York: Pantheon, 1984.

Freud, Sigmund. *Introductory Lectures on Psychoanalysis.* In *The Standard Edition of the Complete Psychological Works of Sigmund Freud* (24 vols.), edited by James Strachey, 15, 16:9–463. London: Hogarth, 1953–74.

———. *Letters of Sigmund Freud.* Translated by Tania Stern and James Stern. Edited by Ernst Freud. New York: Basic Books, 1960.

———. "On Narcissism." *Standard Edition* 14:73–102.

———. "Preface to the Translation of Bernheim's Suggestion." *Standard Edition* 1:75–85.

———. "Psychical Treatment." *Standard Edition* 7:281–302.

———. "Psychoanalysis and Religious Origins." *Standard Edition* 17:259–63.

———. *The Question of Lay Analysis. Standard Edition* 20:183–258.

———. *The Resistances to Psychoanalysis. Standard Edition* 19:213–22.

Frost, Robert. *Mountain Interval.* New York: Henry Holt, 1926.

Garff, Joakim. "The Eyes of Argus: *The Point of View* and Points of View on Kierkegaard's Work as an Author." Translated by Jane Chamberlain and Belinda Ioni Rasmussen. In *Kierkegaard: A Critical Reader,* edited by Jonathan Rée and Jane Chamberlain, 75–102. Oxford: Blackwell, 1998.

———. *Søren Kierkegaard: A Biography.* Translated by Bruce Kirmmse. Princeton: Princeton University Press, 2000.

Greene, Murray. *Hegel on the Soul: A Speculative Anthropology.* The Hague: Martinus Nijhoff, 1972.

Gruppe, Otto. *Antäus.* Edited by Friedrich Mauthner. Munich: Georg Müller, 1914.

———. *Die Winde, oder, Ganz absolute Konstruction der neuern Weltgeschichte durch Oberons Horn, gedichtet von Absolutus von Hegelingen.* Leipzig: Wilhelm Nauck, n.d. (written in 1830).

Gutterer, Dietrich. "Der Spekulative Satz." *Kodikas/Code* 1 (1979): 235–47.

Harris, Errol. "Hegel's Theory of Feeling." In *New Studies in Hegel's Political Philosophy,* edited by Warren E. Steinkraus, 114–36. Cambridge: Cambridge University Press, 1984.

Hegel, G. W. F. *Aesthetics: Lectures on Fine Art.* 2 vols. Translated by T. M. Knox. Oxford: Clarendon Press, 1975.

———. *The Difference between Fichte's and Schelling's System of Philosophy.* Translated by H. S. Harris and Walter Cerf. Albany: State University of New York Press, 1977.

———. *Faith and Knowledge.* Translated by Walter Cerf and H. S. Harris. Albany: State University of New York Press, 1977.

———. *Hegel's Logic.* Part 1 of the *Encyclopedia of the Philosophical Sciences.* Translated by William Wallace. Oxford: Clarendon Press, 1975.

———. *Hegel's Philosophy of Subjective Spirit.* Part 3 of the *Encylopedia.* 3 vols. Translated by M. J. Petry. Dordrecht, Holland: D. Reidel, 1979.

———. *Hegels Werke.* 18 vols. Edited by P. Marheineke et al. Berlin: Duncker and Humblot, 1832–45.

———. *Jenaer Realphilosophie: Die Vorlesungen von 1803–4, 1805–6.* 2 vols. Edited by J. Hoffmeister. Hamburg: Felix Meiner Verlag, 1930.

———. *Lectures on the History of Philosophy.* 3 vols. Translated by E. S. Haldane and F. H. Simson. New York: Humanities Press, 1974.

———. *Lectures on the Philosophy of History.* Translated by J. Sibree. New York: Willey Book Co., 1900.

———. *The Letters.* Translated by Clark Butler and Christiane Seiler. Bloomington: Indiana University Press, 1984.

———. "Love." In *G. W. F. Hegel: Early Theological Writings,* edited by T. M. Knox, 302–8. Philadelphia: University of Pennsylvania Press, 1977.

————. *The Phenomenology of Spirit.* Translated by A. V. Miller. Oxford: Oxford University Press, 1979.

————. *The Philosophy of Mind.* Part 3 of the *Encyclopedia.* Translated by William Wallace, with translations of the *Zusätze* (additions) by A. V. Miller. Oxford: Clarendon Press, 1978.

————. *The Philosophy of Nature.* Part 2 of the *Encyclopedia.* Translated by A. V. Miller. Oxford: Clarendon Press, 1970.

————. *The Philosophy of Right.* Translated by T. M. Knox. London: Oxford University Press, 1976.

————. *The Science of Logic.* Translated by A. V. Miller. New York: Humanities Press, 1969.

————. *Werke.* 20 vols. Edited by Eva Moldenhauer and Karl Markus Michel. Frankfurt am Main: Suhrkamp Verlag, 1970–79.

Heidegger, Martin. "The Age of the World Picture." In *The Question concerning Technology and Other Essays,* translated by William Lovitt. 115–54. New York: Harper and Row, 1977.

————. *Being and Time.* Translated by John Macquarrie and Edward Robinson. New York: Harper, 1962.

————. "Building Dwelling Thinking." In *Basic Writings,* edited by David Farrell Krell, 347–63. New York: Harper, 1977.

————. *Hegel's Phenomenology of Spirit.* Translated by Parvis Emad and Kenneth Maly. Bloomington: Indiana University Press, 1994.

————. "Letter on Humanism." In *Basic Writings,* edited by David Farrell Krell, 189–242. New York: Harper, 1977.

————. *Nietzsche.* 4 vols. Translated by David Farrell Krell. New York: Harper and Row, 1987.

————. "The Origin of the Work of Art." Translated by Albert Hofstadter. In *Basic Writings,* edited by David Farrell Krell. 143–87. New York: Harper, 1977.

————. "The Question concerning Technology." In *Basic Writings,* edited by David Farrell Krell. 283–317. New York: Harper, 1977.

Heine, Heinrich. *Werke.* 7 vols. Edited by Ernst Elster. Leipzig: Bibliographisches Institut, 1922.

Higgins, Kathleen Marie. "Gender in *The Gay Science.*" In *Feminist Interpretations of Friedrich Nietzsche,* edited by Kelly Oliver and Marilyn Pearson, 130–51. University Park: Penn State University Press, 1998.

Howe, Leslie A. "Kierkegaard and the Feminine Self." In *Feminist Interpretations of Søren Kierkegaard,* edited by Céline Léon and Sylvia Walsh, 217–47. University Park: Penn State University Press, 1997.

Hyppolite, Jean. "The Concept of Existence in the Hegelian Phenomenology." In *Studies on Hegel and Marx,* translated by John O'Neill, 22–32. New York: Basic Books, 1969.

————. *Figures de la pensée philosophique*. Paris: Presses Universitaires de France, 1991.

————. *Genesis and Structure of Hegel's Phenomenology of Spirit*. Translated by Samuel Cherniak and John Heckman. Evanston, Ill.: Northwestern University Press, 1974.

Irigaray, Luce. *Marine Lover of Friedrich Nietzsche*. Translated by Gillian C. Gill. New York: Columbia University Press, 1991.

Israel, Jonathan. *Radical Enlightenment: Philosophy and the Making of Modernity, 1650–1750*. Oxford: Oxford University Press, 2002.

Jaspers, Karl. *Nietzsche: An Introduction to the Understanding of His Philosophical Activity*. Translated by Charles Wallraff and Frederick Schmitz. Chicago: Henry Regnery, 1965.

Jegstrup, Elsebet, ed. The New Kierkegaard. Bloomington: Indiana University Press, 2004.

Kafka, Franz. Quoted in "Poetry Critical: Online Poetry Workshop." http://poetrycritical.net/read/56256/.

Kant, Immanuel. *Critique of Pure Reason*. Translated by Norman Kemp Smith. London: Macmillan, 1973.

————. *Logic*. Translated by Robert Hartman and Wolfgang Schwartz. New York: Bobbs-Merrill, 1974.

Kaufmann, Walter. *Hegel: A Reinterpretation*. Notre Dame, Ind.: University of Notre Dame Press, 1978.

————. *Nietzsche: Philosopher, Psychologist, Antichrist*. Princeton: Princeton University Press, 1977.

————. Note on the Publication of *Ecce Homo*. In *Basic Writings of Nietzsche*, trans. and ed. Walter Kaufmann, 669. New York: Random House, 1968.

Kazin, Alfred. Quoted in *Think*. February 1963.

Kierkegaard, Søren. (Vigilius Haufniensis.) *The Concept of Dread*. Translated by Walter Lowrie. Princeton: Princeton University Press, 1957.

————. *The Concept of Irony*. Translated by Lee M. Capel. Bloomington: Indiana University Press, 1968.

————. (Johannes Climacus.) *Concluding Unscientific Postscript*. Translated by David F. Swenson and Walter Lowrie. Princeton: Princeton University Press, 1968.

————. *The Diary of Søren Kierkegaard*. Edited by Peter Rohde. New York: Philosophical Library, 1960.

————. *Edifying Discourses*. 4 vols. Edited by David Swenson and Lillian Swenson. Minneapolis: Augsburg, 1943.

————. (Victor Eremita.) *Either/Or*. 2 vols. Translated by David Swenson and Lillian Swenson. Princeton: Princeton University Press, 1971.

———. (Johannes de Silentio.) *Fear and Trembling.* Translated by Walter Lowrie. Princeton: Princeton University Press, 1974.

———. *Johannes Climacus, or De Omnibus Dubitandum Est.* Translated by T. H. Croxall. Stanford: Stanford University Press, 1967.

———. *The Journals of Søren Kierkegaard.* Edited and translated by Alexander Dru. London: Oxford University Press, 1938.

———. "The Lily in the Field and the Bird of the Air." In *The Essential Kierkegaard,* edited by Howard Hong and Edna Hong, 333–38. Princeton: Princeton University Press, 2000.

———. "My Activity as a Writer." Appended by Walter Lowrie to his edition of *The Point of View* (see below).

———. (Johannes Climacus.) *Philosophical Fragments.* Translated by Howard Hong and Edna Hong. Princeton: Princeton University Press, 1985.

———. *The Point of View for My Work as an Author: A Report to History.* Translated by Walter Lowrie. New York: Harper and Row, 1962.

———. *The Present Age.* Translated by Alexander Dru. New York: Harper and Row, 1962.

———. (Constantin Constantius.) *Repetition.* Translated by Walter Lowrie. New York Harper, 1964.

———. (Anti-Climacus). *The Sickness unto Death.* Translated by Walter Lowrie. Princeton: Princeton University Press, 1974.

———. *Søren Kierkegaard's Journals and Papers.* 6 vols. Edited and translated by Howard Hong and Edna Hong. Bloomington: Indiana University Press, 1967–1978.

———. *Søren Kierkegaards Papirer.* 20 vols. Edited by P. A. Heiberg, V. Kuhr, and E. Torsting. Copenhagen: Gyldendal, 1909–48.

———. (Hilarious Bookbinder.) *Stages on Life's Way.* Translated by Howard Hong and Edna Hong. Princeton: Princeton University Press, 1988.

———. (Anti-Climacus.) *Training in Christianity.* Translated by Walter Lowrie. Princeton: Princeton University Press, 1967.

———. *The Two Ages.* Translated by Howard Hong and Edna Hong. Princeton: Princeton University Press, 1978.

Kirmmse, Bruce. *Encounters with Kierkegaard: A Life as Seen by His Contemporaries.* Princeton: Princeton University Press, 1966.

Kofman, Sarah. "Baubô: Theological Perversion and Fetishism." Translated by Tracy Strong. In *Feminist Interpretations of Friedrich Nietzsche,* edited by Kelly Oliver and Marilyn Pearson, 21–49. University Park: Penn State University Press, 1998.

———. "The Narcissistic Woman: Freud and Girard." *Diacritics* 10, no. 3 (1980): 36–45.

Kojève, Alexandre. *L'introduction à la lecture de Hegel.* Paris: Gallimard, 1947.

————. *Introduction to the Reading of Hegel.* Translated by James H. Nichols. Edited by Allan Bloom. Ithaca, N.Y.: Cornell University Press, 1969.

Kroner, Richard. "Kierkegaard's Understanding of Hegel." *Union Seminary Quarterly Review* 21, no. 2, part 2 (1966): 233–44.

————. "Kierkegaard or Hegel?" *Revue Internationale de Philosophie* 19 (1952): 79–96.

Lacan, Jacques. *Écrits.* Translated by Bruce Fink. New York: Norton, 2006.

————. *The Seminar of Jacques Lacan,* book 1: *Freud's Papers on Technique, 1953–1954.* Translated by John Forrester. Cambridge: Cambridge University Press, 1988.

————. *The Seminar of Jacques Lacan,* book 2: *The Ego in Freud's Theory and in the Technique of Psychoanalysis, 1954–1955.* Translated by Sylvana Tomaselli. Cambridge: Cambridge University Press, 1988.

————. *The Seminar of Jacques Lacan,* book 11: *The Four Fundamental Concepts of Psychoanalysis.* Translated by Alan Sheridan. Edited by Jacques-Alain Miller. New York: Norton, 1981.

————. *The Seminar of Jacques Lacan,* book 17: *The Other Side of Psychoanalysis.* Translated by Russell Grigg. New York: Norton, 2007.

————. *The Seminar of Jacques Lacan,* book 20: *Encore, 1972–1973.* Translated by Bruce Fink. New York: Norton, 1998.

Lauer, Quentin. *Essays in Hegelian Dialectic.* New York: Fordham University Press, 1977.

Léon, Céline. "The No Woman's Land of Kierkegaardian Seduction." In *International Kierkegaard Commentary: Either Or, Part I,* edited by Robert L. Perkins, 229–50. Macon, Ga.: Mercer University Press, 1995.

Léon, Céline, and Sylvia Walsh, eds. *Feminist Interpretations of Søren Kierkegaard.* University Park: Penn State University Press, 1997.

Levinas, Emmanuel. "A propos de *Kierkegaard Vivant.*" Translated by Jonathan Rée. Included as "Two Notes" in *Kierkegaard: A Critical Reader,* edited by Jonathan Rée and Jane Chamberlain, 33–38. Oxford: Blackwell, 1998.

————. "The Trace of the Other." Translated by Alphonso Lingis. In *Deconstruction in Context,* edited by Mark C. Taylor, 345–59. Chicago: University of Chicago Press, 1986.

Llewelyn, John. "On the Borderline of Madness." In The New Kierkegaard, *edited by* Elsebet Jegstrup, 88–111. Bloomington: Indiana University Press, 2004.

Lorraine, Tamsin. "Amatory Cures for Material Dis-ease: A Kristevian Reading of *The Sickness unto Death.*" In *Kierkegaard in Post/Modernity,* edited by Martin Matuštík and Merold Westphal, 98–109. Bloomington: Indiana University Press, 1995.

Lowrie, Walter. *A Short Life of Kierkegaard.* Princeton: Princeton University Press, 1965.

Lyotard, Jean-François. *The Post-modern Condition.* Translated by Régis Durand. Minneapolis: University of Minnesota Press, 1984.

MacIntyre, Alasdair, ed. *Hegel: A Collection of Critical Essays.* Notre Dame, Ind.: University of Notre Dame Press, 1972.

Mackey, Louis. *Points of View: Readings of Kierkegaard.* Tallahassee: Florida State University Press, 1986.

Marx, Karl. *Capital.* Vol. 1. Translated by Ben Fowkes. New York: Penguin, 1990.

Matuštík, Martin, and Merold Westphal, eds. *Kierkegaard in Post/Modernity.* Bloomington: Indiana University Press, 1995.

Mesmer, Franz Anton. *Précis historique des faits relatifs au Magnétisme-Animal jusques en Avril 1781.* London: n.p., 1781.

Mills, Patricia Jagentowicz, ed. *Feminist Interpretations of G. W. F. Hegel.* University Park: Penn State University Press, 1996.

Nancy, Jean-Luc. *La rémarque speculative.* Paris: Editions Galilée, 1973.

Nietzsche, Friedrich. *The Antichrist.* In *Basic Writings of Nietzsche,* translated and edited by Walter Kaufmann. New York: Random House, 1968.

———. *Beyond Good and Evil.* In *Basic Writings of Nietzsche,* translated and edited by Walter Kaufmann. New York: Random House, 1968.

———. *The Birth of Tragedy.* In *Basic Writings of Nietzsche,* translated and edited by Walter Kaufmann. New York: Random House, 1968.

———. *Daybreak.* Translated by R. J. Hollingdale. Cambridge: Cambridge University Press, 1982.

———. *Ecce Homo.* In *Basic Writings of Nietzsche,* translated and edited by Walter Kaufmann. New York: Random House, 1968.

———. *The Gay Science.* Translated by Walter Kaufmann. New York: Random House, 1974.

———. *The Genealogy of Morals.* In *Basic Writings of Nietzsche,* translated and edited by Walter Kaufmann. New York: Random House, 1968.

———. *Selected Letters of Friedrich Nietzsche.* Edited and translated by Christopher Middleton. New York: Hackett, 1996.

———. *Thus Spoke Zarathustra.* In *The Portable Nietzsche,* translated and edited by Walter Kaufmann. New York: Viking, 1966.

———. *Twilight of the Idols.* In *The Portable Nietzsche,* translated and edited by Walter Kaufmann. New York: Viking, 1966.

O'Brien, Mary. "Hegel: Man, Physiology, and Fate." In *Feminist Interpretations of G. W. F. Hegel,* edited by Patricia Jagentowicz Mills, 177–208. University Park: Penn State University Press, 1996.

Oliphant, Margaret. *Cervantes.* London: Blackwood, 1881.

Oliver, Kelly. "Woman as Truth in Nietzsche's Writing." In *Feminist Interpretations of Friedrich Nietzsche,* edited by Kelly Oliver and Marilyn Pearsall, 66–80. University Park: Penn State University Press, 1998.

Oliver, Kelly, and Marilyn Pearsall, eds. *Feminist Interpretations of Friedrich Nietzsche.* University Park: Penn State University Press, 1998.

Olson, Alan. *Hegel and the Spirit.* Princeton: Princeton University Press, 1992.

Perkins, Robert L., ed. *International Kierkegaard Commentary: Either Or, Part I.* Macon, Ga.: Mercer University Press, 1995.

———, ed. *International Kierkegaard Commentary: The Sickness unto Death.* Macon, Ga.: Mercer University Press, 1987.

———. "Woman-Bashing in Kierkegaard's 'In Vino Veritas': A Reinscription of Plato's *Symposium.*" In *Feminist Interpretations of Søren Kierkegaard,* edited by Céline Léon and Sylvia Walsh, 83–102. University Park: Penn State University Press, 1997.

Phillips, James. "Madness of the Philosophers, Madness of the Clinic." *Philosophy, Psychiatry, and Psychology* 16, no. 4 (2009): 313–17.

Plato. *Complete Works.* Edited by John M. Cooper. Indianapolis: Hackett, 1977.

———. "Second Letter." *Plato: Timaeus, Critias, Cleitophon, Menexenus, Epistles.* Translated by R. G. Bury. Cambridge: Cambridge University Press, 1999.

Pletsch, Carl. "The Self-Sufficient Text in Nietzsche and Kierkegaard." *Yale French Studies* 66 (1984): 160–88.

Poole, Roger. *Kierkegaard: The Indirect Communication.* Charlottesville: University Press of Virginia, 1993.

Quijano, Antonio Zirión. "The Call 'Back to the Things Themselves' and the Notion of Phenomenology." *Husserl Studies* 22 (2006): 29–51.

Rabinovich, Diane. "What Is a Lacanian Clinic?" In *The Cambridge Companion to Lacan,* edited by Jean-Michel Rabaté, 208–20. Cambridge: Cambridge University Press, 2003.

Rée, Jonathan. "Baffled Traveller." *London Review of Books,* November 30, 2000, 3–7.

Rée, Jonathan, and Jane Chamberlain, eds. *Kierkegaard: A Critical Reader.* Oxford: Blackwell, 1998.

Ricoeur, Paul. "Two Encounters with Kierkegaard: Kierkegaard and Evil; Doing Philosophy after Kierkegaard." In *Kierkegaard's Truth: The Disclosure of the Self,* edited by Joseph H. Smith, 313–42. New Haven: Yale University Press, 1981.

Rimbaud, Arthur. "Lettre du Voyant." In *Rimbaud: Complete Works, Selected Letters,* translated by Wallace Fowlie, edited by Seth Whidden. Chicago: University of Chicago Press, 2005.

Rorty, Richard. *Consequences of Pragmatism.* Minneapolis: University of Minnesota Press, 1982.

Rosen, Stanley. *G. W. F. Hegel: An Introduction to the Science of Wisdom.* New Haven: Yale University Press, 1974.

Safranski, Rüdiger. *Nietzsche: A Philosophical Biography.* Translated by Shelley Frisch. New York: Norton, 2003.

Sartre, Jean-Paul. *Being and Nothingness.* Translated by Hazel Barnes. New York: Philosophical Library, 1965.

———. *L'être et le néant.* Paris: Éditions Gallimard, 1943.

———. Interview with John Gerassi. *New York Times Magazine,* October 17, 1971.

———. *Nausea.* Translated by Lloyd Alexander. New York: New Directions, 1964.

———. *Saint Genet: Actor and Martyr.* Translated by Bernard Frechtman. New York: G. Braziller, 1963.

———. "The Wall." Translated by Lloyd Alexander. In *The Wall and Other Stories.* New York: New Directions, 1975.

———. *The Words.* Translated by Bernard Frechtman. New York: George Braziller, 1964.

Sass, Louis A. "Madness and the Ineffable: Hegel, Kierkegaard, Lacan." *Philosophy, Psychiatry, and Psychology* 16, no. 4 (2009): 319–24.

Schopenhauer, Arthur. *Parerga and Paralipomena: Short Philosophical Essays.* Translated by E. F. J. Payne. Oxford: Oxford University Press, 2000.

———. *World as Will and Representation.* 2 vols. Translated by E. F. J. Payne. New York: Dover, 1969.

Searle, John. *Speech Acts: An Essay in the Philosophy of Language.* Cambridge: Cambridge University Press, 1969.

Seneca, Lucius Annaeus. "On Consolation." In *The Stoic Philosophy of Seneca: Essays and Letters of Seneca.* Translated by Moses Hadas. New York: Doubleday, 1958.

Shapiro, Gary. "Some Genres of Post-Hegelian Philosophy." *Metaphilosophy* 13, no. 3–4 (1982): 267–76.

Smith, Joseph H., ed. *Kierkegaard's Truth: The Disclosure of the Self.* New Haven: Yale University Press, 1981.

Snow, Dale. "F. W. J. Schelling." In *The Columbia History of Western Philosophy,* edited by Richard H. Popkin. New York: Columbia University Press, 1999.

Solomon, Robert. *In the Spirit of Hegel.* Oxford: Oxford University Press, 1983.

Sophocles. *The Women of Trachis.* Translated by Michael Jameson. *Sophocles II.* Edited by David Grene and Richmond Lattimore. New York: Washington Square Press, 1973.

Steinkraus, Warren E., ed. *New Studies in Hegel's Political Philosophy*. Cambridge: Cambridge University Press, 1984.

Sterling, J. Hutchison. *The Secret of Hegel*. New York: Putnam's, 1898.

Stewart, Jon. *Kierkegaard's Relations to Hegel Reconsidered*. Cambridge: Cambridge University Press, 2003.

Surber, Jere Paul. "Hegel's Speculative Sentence." *Hegel-Studien* 10 (1975): 212–30.

Taylor, Charles. "The Opening Arguments of the Phenomenology." In *Hegel: A Collection of Critical Essays,* edited by Alasdair MacIntyre, 151–87. Notre Dame, Ind.: University of Notre Dame Press, 1972.

Taylor, Mark C. "Aesthetic Therapy: Hegel and Kierkegaard." In *Kierkegaard's Truth: The Disclosure of the Self,* edited by Joseph H. Smith, 343–80. New Haven: Yale University Press, 1981.

———. *Journeys to Selfhood: Hegel and Kierkegaard*. Berkeley: University of California Press, 1980.

Taylor, Ronald. *Berlin and Its Culture: A Historical Portrait*. New Haven: Yale University Press, 1997.

Thompson, Josiah, ed. *Kierkegaard: A Collection of Critical Essays*. Garden City, N.Y.: Doubleday, 1972.

———. "The Master of Irony." In *Kierkegaard: A Collection of Critical Essays,* edited by Josiah Thompson, 103–63. Garden City, N.Y.: Doubleday, 1972.

Thulstrup, Niels. *Kierkegaard's Relation to Hegel*. Translated by George Stengren. Princeton: Princeton University Press, 1980.

Voegelin, Eric. "On Hegel—A Study in Sorcery." *Studium Generale* 24 (1971): 335–68.

Wahl, Jean. *Études Kierkegaardiennes*. Paris: Fernard Aubier, 1938.

Walsh, Sylvia. "On 'Feminine' and 'Masculine' Forms of Despair." In *International Kierkegaard Commentary: The Sickness unto Death,* edited by Robert L. Perkins, 121–34. Macon, Ga.: Mercer University Press, 1987.

Watkin, Julia. "The Logic of Kierkegaard's Misogyny, 1854–1855." *Kierkegaardiana* 15 (1991): 79–93.

Werkmeister, William. "Hegel's Phenomenology of Mind as a Development of Kant's Basic Ontology." In *Hegel and the Philosophy of Religion*, edited by Darrel E. Christensen. The Hague: Martinus Nijhoff, 1970.

Westphal, Merold. "Kierkegaard and Hegel." In The Cambridge Companion to *Kierkegaard, edited by Alastair* Hannay, 101–24. New York: Cambridge University Press, 1998.

Wohlfahrt, Gunter. *Der speculative Satz*. Berlin: de Gruyter, 1981.

Žižek, Slavoj. *The Sublime Object of Ideology*. New York: Verso, 1989.

———. *Tarrying with the Negative: Kant, Hegel, and the Critique of Ideology*. Durham, N.C.: Duke University Press, 1993.

NAME INDEX

SUBJECT INDEX

absolute knowledge, 12, 41, 96, 99, 160,
   161, 163, 172, 173, 175–78,
   204n23, 207n59
abstraction, 4, 20, 22, 23, 28, 30, 32, 37,
   39, 41–44, 49, 53, 55, 73, 85, 87,
   113, 122, 159, 168
the absurd, 67, 88, 89, 172
acknowledgment. *See* recognition,
   acknowledgment
action, 10, 39, 40, 42, 46–48, 52, 111,
   171, 173, 177
the aesthetic, 7, 67, 68, 70, 71, 78, 80,
   158. *See also* art, the artist
alienation, estrangement, 50, 104, 108,
   118, 120, 122, 173–76
aloneness, loneliness, 20, 48, 62, 83,
   116, 135–37, 153, 179. *See also*
   solitude
animals, 17, 20, 24, 57, 118
art, the artist, 7, 15, 69, 70, 79, 80; art
   for art's sake, 7, 51. *See also* the
   aesthetic
assertion, 4, 11, 31, 33–35, 93, 97, 99,
   111, 166
authority, 1, 9, 12, 30, 31, 35, 61, 62,
   65–67, 80, 96, 99, 132, 135, 138,
   139, 149, 151, 152, 155, 160–63,
   167, 168, 171, 176
authorship, the author, *passim.*
   death of the author, 9, 12, 99, 110,
   124, 129–36, 138, 139, 141–43,

145, 146, 149, 150, 152, 154, 156,
   157, 161–63, 166, 167, 169–72,
   176, 178, 179, 181
the ethics of authorship, xi, 3, 4,
   6–9, 18, 19, 25, 26, 32, 35, 38, 40,
   60, 74, 87, 119, 135, 138, 142, 151,
   155, 169, 176, 181
resurrection of the author, 131, 146,
   149, 151, 154

the beautiful soul, 20, 36, 37, 116, 125,
   178
the beyond, 41, 50, 89, 90
the body, 115, 156
the boring, 68–70

the child, the infant, 45, 46, 108, 135,
   174
Christ, 150
Christianity, 31, 34, 35, 113, 115
communication, 3, 4, 9–11, 16, 19, 25,
   26, 35, 37, 59, 62, 65, 66, 71, 81,
   113, 119, 120, 126, 129, 138–40,
   142, 144, 162, 166, 176
   direct, 4, 25, 26, 30, 31, 34, 57, 59, 60,
   72, 83, 84, 113, 137, 144
   indirect, 3, 10, 11, 16, 25–28, 30, 31,
   33–35, 37, 57–61, 66, 67, 71,
   74–79, 81, 82, 84, 113, 119, 126,
   129, 134